Pattie Boyd

WONDERFUL TODAY

Pattie Boyd

WONDERFUL
TODAY

The Autobiography

with Penny Junor

headline
review

First published in 2007 by HEADLINE REVIEW

An imprint of Headline Publishing Group

1

Cataloguing in Publication Data is available from the British Library

Hardback ISBN 978 0 7553 1642 7
Trade paperback ISBN 978 0 7553 1646 5

Typeset in Aldine by Avon DataSet Ltd,
Bidford on Avon, Warwickshire

Printed and bound in Great Britain by
Clays Ltd, St Ives plc

Headline's policy is to use papers that are natural, renewable and recyclable products and
made from wood grown in sustainable forests. The logging and manufacturing processes
are expected to conform to the environmental regulations of the country of origin.

HEADLINE PUBLISHING GROUP
An Hachette Livre UK Company
338 Euston Road
London NW1 3BH

www.reviewbooks.co.uk
www.hodderheadline.com

To my darling brothers and sisters with thanks
for all their love and support and to my dearest friends
who bring me nothing but happiness.

Very special thanks from us both to the wonderful Ivan Massow – a true friend – who introduced us to one another. Without him this book might never have been written – and we would have missed out on all that laughter. Moments may have been painful, but the partnership has been a joy.

Pattie Boyd and Penny Junor

Contents

Acknowledgements

I would like to say a very big thank you to all those loyal and lovely people who have been there for me over the years, to those who encouraged me to write this book and to all the friends and members of my family who subsequently helped jog my memory. Among them are Mummy, Colin, Jenny, Paula, David, Boo, and Jock Boyd; Lesley Aggar, Mary Bee, Bobby and Aline Bell, Cilla Black, Pat Booth, Jill Briggs, Peter Brown, Terry Doran, Francesca Findlater, Jose Fonseca, Roger Forrester, Bobbie Gaymer-Jones, Adi Hunter, Lulu Hutley, Chris O'Dell, Dick Polak, Guy Pullen, Melanie Rendall, Alan Rogan, Edina Ronay, Angie Rutherford, Linda Spinetti, Ringo Starr, Giles and Vanessa Swarbreck, Belinda Volpelière-Pierrot, Carolyn Waters, Rod Weston and Ronnie Wood.

A special thank you also to Eric Clapton for so generously giving me permission to reproduce the first verse of 'Wonderful Tonight', from the 1977 *Slowhand* album, and to quote from some of the beautiful letters he has written to me over the years. Thanks, too, to Christopher Simon Sykes, and to all the photographers, many of them friends, who have allowed me to reproduce their work, particularly Lesley Aggar.

I would also like to thank my publisher Val Hudson and the fabulous team at Headline who have been so supportive, creative and such fun to work with. Also Shaye Areheart and everyone at Random House US.

My thanks too to Caroline Michel, my agent, and all at William Morris UK, and Dorian Karchmar and all at William Morris US.

Also a big thank you to Ginny Manning for all her help and brilliance in sourcing and sorting the photographs.

And to Penny Junor for coaxing my life story out of me – no mean feat!

Preface

People have been trying to persuade me to write a book for years. And for years I have resisted. I have had the most extraordinary life, and ultimately the most rewarding and enriching life, and I wouldn't change a day of it. I was part of the sixties revolution, I have known the most beautiful, talented people, and I have been married to two exceptionally creative musicians. My resistance has not been for want of something to say. It was partly because I have always been an intensely private person and have never spoken easily about my feelings, and partly because I have lived through a lot of pain and didn't want to write my story until I felt strong enough to talk about it from a healthy perspective.

Now I feel that time has come. And for the sake of everyone who has shared similar experiences in their lives but not yet come through to that position of strength, I feel it is important to have my say. My experiences of childhood, of divorced parents and a step-father, of marriages that went wrong, of unfaithful husbands, addictive personalities and childlessness are not unique. All that is unique is that it happened to me in a very high-profile, crazy rock 'n' roll world. And as I discovered at Al Anon, realising that other people are going through exactly what you are is incredibly comforting and therapeutic. Secrets are not healthy.

So I am finally letting go of mine.

But it is important to say that this is the story as I remember it. I behaved throughout my life and reacted to situations as I did because of the way I had been brought up. We all do; it's human nature. So I attach no blame to any of the characters in my story. They did the best they could with the tools they had. We are all the product of our upbringing. I hope and pray that none of the people I love so dearly will feel I am letting them down in any way.

This is *my* truth, which may not necessarily be as others remember it. But if my story is to have any validity I have to tell the truth as I see it.

CHAPTER ONE

Childhood in Kenya

My earliest memory is of sitting in a high chair spitting out spinach – strange for someone who turned into such a passionate foodie. In my late teens I became determined to improve the experience, even enjoy it, and today spinach is one of my favourite vegetables – but it has to be right: steamed, chopped and mixed with double cream, white pepper and nutmeg. Delicious. Raw in a salad, it's even better. But at the age of two I couldn't get the repellent dark green mess out of my mouth fast enough.

I was living in Scotland, at a house in West Lothian my grandparents had bought when I was a year old in 1945. We lived with them at that time, and my mother remembers the move from Somerset: taking me on a train – in an ordinary carriage, as she puts it – with all our belongings, and the embarrassment of having to feed me during the journey amid a group of soldiers. I was her first child, of six, and she was a young, nervous mother. Shortly after we arrived in Scotland my brother, Colin, was born. He is almost exactly two years younger than I am and I remember examining him when he was a baby and noticing that there was a small difference between us. He was a huge baby, and as soon as he could walk he followed me everywhere.

Another early memory is of holding a stick in my hand and telling Colin to pick up a wasp I could see stuck in the crack between some paving stones and delighting in the howls that followed. I am told I also tried to feed him with a petrol capsule – the sort used to fill lighters. It looked like a miniature baby's bottle so I pushed it into his mouth and the poor little thing had burns all over his lips. I don't remember that episode but I do remember trying to kill him by burying him in the sandpit in the garden. Luckily my mother noticed in the nick of time and rescued him.

My parents were living at Howleigh House, near Taunton in Somerset, when I was born. My mother and her twin brother, John, had spent most of their childhood there. They had been born in India but sent to boarding-school in England at the age of eight, and in the holidays they stayed with an aunt at Howleigh House. Their father, Lieutenant Colonel Alexander E. Drysdale DSO MC, was in the Indian Army and Vivian, his wife, a rather exotic figure with a penchant for pink gin, visited England and the twins about twice a year. So sad, but Vivian had also been born in India and shipped home to be educated in England so history was repeating itself.

My great-grandfather sounds splendid. His name was Alexander Stuart-Martin and he was born near Lucknow, in India, in 1870. His father had fought in the Indian Mutiny and the British government rewarded him for his bravery with indigo and sugar plantations, which made the family wealthy. Alexander, too, was educated in England, as most colonials were, then became an engineer and built many of the bridges and railways in India. It was on a trip to England that he met and married the beautiful Elizabeth Sabin who, unusually for those times, was a divorcee, having managed to escape from a terrifyingly brutal husband. They returned to India together where she had two daughters, Vivian, my grandmother, and Frances, but there were complications with the second delivery and Elizabeth died soon after she had given birth. Alexander lived on – in some style. He drove around in a magnificent Bentley that he had had shipped out from England. For years it behaved beautifully in the heat and dust, but finally gave up the ghost. Undaunted, my great-grandfather hitched it up to a couple of oxen and continued to travel in the style to which he was accustomed.

The two daughters, Vivian and Frances, were sent to school in England, where they were looked after by relatives, returning to India once a year to visit their father. You could only travel by sea in those days and the journey took two weeks. On one of the voyages the young Vivian met Alexander Drysdale, my grandfather, on his way to join his regiment. Many years later they met again, at a tennis party in Lucknow, fell in love, married and Vivian gave birth to twins: Diana Frances, my mother, and John, my uncle, who never married and has spent most of his life abroad.

The twins were well looked after at Howleigh, and there was no shortage of money. A cook, a scullery-maid and a pantry-maid ran the domestic side of life, but the aunt was Scottish born and bred, and life was simple. She didn't entertain much or lay on anything for the children, so Diana and John seldom saw other children during their stays. I can't imagine how bereft they must have felt with their parents thousands of miles away, or how a mother could bear to see her children no more than two or three times a year, but I suppose in those days she would have had no choice. And, having suffered the same fate as a child, she probably thought there was nothing unusual about it.

I was born, weighing seven pounds, on St Patrick's Day, 17 March 1944; hence my name. My mother had been convinced she was having a boy and had thought of me as Michael for nine months, so as she had put no thought into girls' names, I was called Patricia Anne. I don't know whether it was the shock of discovering that I

5

was not a Michael, or the inordinate length of time I took to be born, but she had a sort of breakdown afterwards – I suppose you would call it post-natal depression today – and to begin with I was looked after by the now aged aunt, May, who had cared for Mummy, and by my grandmother, who was back from India. My grandfather had retired from the army, leaving India for good, and they planned to settle in Britain. They stayed initially in Somerset with Aunt May, but when she sold Howleigh House they bought a house in Scotland and the whole family moved there.

Brigg House was beautiful, with extensive grounds and a walled vegetable garden, but the cold, damp West Lothian winters proved detrimental to my grandfather's health so in 1947 he sold it and moved to Kenya with my grandmother, leaving my parents, Colin and me to fend for ourselves. We moved south and rented a house near Guildford, in Surrey, where my sister Jenny was born in November 1947, when I was three and a half. She wasn't actually christened Jenny: my mother named her Helen Mary, to please a couple of aunts, but I had a favourite teddy at the time called Jenny and I insisted my new sister be called by the same name.

My parents married when they were young and inexperienced and, like hundreds of other couples who married during the war, they knew next to nothing about each other when they walked up the aisle. My mother was seventeen when she met Jock Boyd at a dance in Somerset. He was twenty-three and, of course, dashing in his RAF uniform, with smart brass buttons and gold wings on the left shoulder. Also, he danced like a dream. He was tall and handsome with blond curly hair and cornflower-blue eyes; she was petite and beautiful, with luxuriant chestnut hair. They danced all night, and after just two more brief meetings Jock wrote to Diana and asked her to marry him. Her mother, my grandmother, who was a controlling sort of woman, encouraged her to say yes. I think she wanted to get my mother off her hands, and Jock, she had established, came from a good family. He had money, too, or so she had been told by his mother. All in all, he was the perfect catch. But once they were married it turned out that he had no money, and my mother, having been used to quite a grand lifestyle, found it difficult to manage.

Jock's real name was Colin Ian Langdon Boyd. His parents had a farm in the Fowey valley in Cornwall. His mother was a strange woman. By the time I knew her she and Jock's father had separated and she was living with lots of dachshunds. According to my mother, she had never really liked children so Jock, his younger brother and sister were brought up by aunts living in Bideford. Poor Jock had a miserable childhood but he spent a lot of it hunting and shooting, and horses were his passion. He was sent to Kelly College, a small public school in Tavistock, then went on to Sandhurst and into the Cheshire Regiment. But he never fought as a soldier. A car crash prevented him going out to the front with his regiment and he was seconded to the RAF, first flying Lysanders and later, when he joined Bomber Command, Wellingtons. When he met my mother his squadron was stationed at Weston Zoyland in Somerset and he and his friends went regularly to the Castle in Taunton for a drink or two in the evenings.

Soon after they were engaged, just weeks after that first meeting in early 1942, Jock was sent to Malta, where he had the most terrible accident. There was a strip of runway, with bombers taking off and landing from opposite directions, controlled by traffic-lights. He was taking off in a plane fully laden with bombs and fuel with the green light in his favour, but there was a fault: the light at the other end of the runway was also green and the two planes collided head on and burst into flames. My father jumped clear before the plane exploded but his face and right hand were very badly burned. He was lucky to be alive. Several of his crew and men from the other aircraft were killed – including two who got out of one plane but lost their bearings in the smoke and were decapitated by the propeller.

Jock was flown home and taken straight to East Grinstead, in Sussex, to the burns unit at Queen Victoria Hospital run by the famous pioneering plastic surgeon, Archibald McIndoe, where he became one of McIndoe's Guinea-pigs – so called because of the experimental reconstructive work McIndoe was doing on burn victims. Before him, people with burns as severe as my father's would probably not have survived. My mother went to see him in hospital, fearing that she wouldn't recognise him – the ward was full of heavily bandaged men with missing noses and ears. Jock's head was covered with bandages but she could see two very blue eyes and knew at once it was him. I have the same colour eyes and so does Colin – and it was the Boyd eyes, years later, that made me certain that someone who thought she might be my half-sister, who lived in America, really was.

As soon as my mother sat down beside Jock's hospital bed he said, 'I've got something for you.' He opened a drawer and out came a matchbox with lots of cotton wool, inside which was a ruby and diamond engagement ring. It had belonged to his mother, but because she was such a horrible woman, my mother disliked the ring from the start.

It was not a good omen. Apart from the ring, though, Mummy was uncertain about the marriage. The accident seemed to have changed Jock. She went to see him in hospital several times and they would sit together not saying a word. She was very shy and didn't know what to talk about, and he would sit staring vacantly ahead.

Physically, they patched him up as well as they could. He was left with a badly burned forehead and the tendons in his right hand had been irreparably damaged so he never flew again. Emotionally, I don't think he ever recovered. From that day on he was locked into himself. He would never talk about the accident; in fact, he would scarcely talk about anything. My mother had fallen in love with this handsome, spirited, brave young pilot, who had swept her off her feet on the dance-floor, and he had gone, the spark had died. But having said she would marry Jock, and with the terrible thing that had happened to him, she didn't have the heart or the courage to call it off.

Six months after the accident, on 14 September 1942, they married. It was a big wedding for the time, with two hundred guests and a reception at Howleigh House, but my mother says that even as she was walking out of the church she knew she'd made a big mistake. She didn't feel comfortable with Jock: there seemed to be a barrier between them. They went on honeymoon to Scotland and, as my mother puts it, muddled along. Jock now says he felt the same way and that, anyway, they were far too young when they married.

My father went back repeatedly to East Grinstead for treatment over the following months and spent time in various other rehabilitation places to try to get his fingers moving but without success. His right hand remained claw-like and both were discoloured; as children, we found his injuries fascinating. Unable to fly, he ended up in the War Office, which was enough, according to him, to drive anyone mad, so when my grandparents suggested that he and Mummy join them in Kenya, he leapt at the idea.

When I was four, we moved to Africa, to the large, sprawling house that my grandfather had built in Langata, near Karen, about half an hour from Nairobi. I remember that flight – it took hours: there were no direct flights from England to Africa in those days because the planes needed to refuel at regular intervals. Flying BOAC from London, we stopped at Cairo, Khartoum, Addis Ababa and finally Nairobi. I was horribly sick throughout the trip, into the sturdy brown bags that were routinely tucked into the back pockets of the seats in front.

My grandparents' house stood at the bottom of a long, winding gravel drive – on which, some years later, I learnt to ride a bicycle – with glorious views in every direction across the game reserve that surrounded it. It was a single-storey house with a veranda that ran almost all the way round it. My grandparents had brought paintings, china and cutlery from the house in Scotland but they had had the furniture made in Nairobi of *mooli*, the most beautiful honey-coloured local wood. There was a huge garden, with lawns, standard roses, peach trees and nasturtiums, that ran straight into the wilderness. It was quite common for giraffe, lion or other wild animals to wander in and, because of the bushes, it wasn't always easy to see them. The dogs, though, would bark incessantly until the interlopers left.

One night my grandfather was sleeping in a small bedroom leading on to the veranda. It was a hot, still night, the doors ajar, and in slunk a leopard, which leapt on to sleeping Grandpa. He woke immediately but as he reached for the pistol under his pillow the big cat jumped on to the floor. It had smelt dog, and took the Alsatian, which was asleep under the bed. Grandpa shot wildly as the protest-ing dog was dragged out on to the veranda. Next morning there was no sign of either animal. My grandfather was distressed at having lost his favourite Alsatian, but it could so easily have been him.

He was quite a pukka, conservative character, my grandfather, very much the retired army colonel home from India, who seemed to spend all his time playing golf. He and my father, who did nothing on arrival in Kenya but sit and stare, didn't see eye to eye. As a military man he couldn't understand Jock's condition and had no patience with his inactivity. My grandmother felt much the same, and she was furious that she had been misled into thinking he had money.

Although Granny was quite fierce, I found her loving and easy to be with. I remember making fudge with her – she dyed it green – and standing on a wooden chair to reach the stove. She wore coloured stockings long before anyone else. She wasn't very tall and probably fatter than she should have been, but she loved life, glamorous clothes and laughed a lot. I am probably much more like her than my mother. My grandparents spent a lot of time on Cunard liners, sailing to South Africa, East Africa and India, and had wonderful trunks with drawers and space inside to hang their clothes.

I had a bedroom to myself at Granny's house and I remember her coming in to kiss me goodnight and smelling sweetly of juniper from the pink gin she always drank. She took me on holiday to the coast at Mombasa once, where she had rented a house for the week. There were vast white sandy beaches and I couldn't believe how delicious the sea was. I pretended I had already learnt to swim, knowing she wouldn't let me into the water otherwise. I remember her giving me a teddy bear, which went everywhere with me – I still have it – and becoming hysterical when she hid it once because I had been naughty. She was much more accessible to me than my mother was; she had more time for me and a far greater influence over me.

I have practically no memory of my mother during my childhood, apart from the smell of her Dior perfume and her singing voice, which was beautiful. In retrospect, I think life must have been difficult for her, suddenly transported to Africa with three young children, a man she didn't love and with whom she couldn't communicate, no friends and no money. She must have been deeply unhappy, but I was too young to appreciate that.

My grandparents were wealthy so there were several servants and nannies to look after us. And although I saw a lot of Granny, it was the nannies who brought us up. At night they bathed us and put us to bed while the grown-ups went off to their favourite watering-holes – the Karen Club nearby (named after Karen Blixen of *White Mischief* fame – we arrived in Kenya just after that era) or the Muthaiga Club in Nairobi. At about this time I started having flying dreams, and when the grown-ups were out of the house, I would make Colin and Jenny stand on a table and try to teach them to fly.

The servants were Kikuyu, the most common tribe in Kenya, and they and their families lived in rondavels, traditional circular mud huts with thatched roofs, in a little community at the top of the drive. They adored my grandparents and when, some years later, during the Mau Mau uprising which began in 1952, they were threatened with death if they carried on working for white people, they came to my grandparents and said how sorry they were that they had to leave. It was a scary time in Kenya and a lot of white people slept with guns under their pillows for fear that their servants would try to murder them during the night. Many white farmers were killed.

One would call the Mau Mau freedom fighters today, I suppose, but I saw them as terrorists who were trying to incite and enrage the Africans I knew and loved. They wanted to overthrow British rule and evict the white settlers who had taken their land. Their tactics worked: there was an exodus of Europeans during the fifties. However, when my grandparents came back to England it was not because of the Mau Mau: it was my grandfather's health.

I used to spend a lot of time with the Kikuyu who worked for my grandparents; they were my friends. They made the most delicious food, mostly Indian-based – lentils, spicy vegetables, curries – which they cooked outside on open fires and wrapped in chapattis. My father had a couple of horses and I remember riding bareback out into the bush one day with one of the Kikuyu stable-boys. We came across a watering-hole in a thicket and as the horses were drinking I suddenly realised we were not alone. I turned and saw a group of tribespeople with painted faces staring at me. It was the first time I'd seen anyone like them but the boy talked to them and told me not to be frightened. I wasn't: I was used to so much being strange in Africa. I was fascinated by them and the jewellery they wore, earrings, bracelets and necklaces.

I loved Kenya. I loved the huge skies, the vast landscapes, the incredible feeling of space, and the sky at night, full of bright, bright stars, so close you felt you could almost reach up and touch them. At night I would lie in bed and listen to the noises: the cicadas, tribespeople chattering, the rhythmic beating of drums in the distance, the howl of hyenas and jackals, and the unmistakable roar of lions. But what encapsulates Africa for me is the smell: the smell of pepper trees and wild herbs combined with heat and dust. It's an unforgettable mix and every time I go back to Kenya, which I have done several times as an adult, that smell takes me straight back to my childhood.

It was quite a wild life, but wonderful for a child – there were few rules. I don't remember any toys or presents – except the teddy bear my grandmother gave me. I don't remember birthdays or Christmases either, although I do remember writing a letter to Father Christmas one year and the letter being gone the next day. We played outside; we rode bicycles, or went into the wood to explore. I remember bouncing on my bed one night, watching a huge snake inch its way under the door and screaming for help. The house-boys rushed in, grabbed it and killed it.

By that time my charmed existence was crumbling at the edges. After nearly a year, my grandparents had had enough of Jock doing nothing but ride his horses and told him he had to get a job to support his wife and family. He and my mother effectively split up for about six months, at the end of which he had started work with the Jockey Club in Nairobi and we had a series of far less opulent houses. Eventually we moved to one that you reached via a long dirt drive, a series of thatched rondavels linked by corridors. My mother hated it but I thought it was wonderful. She had been used to considerable comfort with her parents, and must have found it a shock to adapt to such straitened circumstances, particularly with the arrival of a fourth child. In March 1951, my sister Paula was born in Nakuru hospital. I remember someone, probably Granny, taking Colin, Jenny and me to see her, and spotting her and Mummy through the window as we walked round the outside of the building.

I had now started school – the first of many. Loretta Convent was in Nairobi and smelt of powdered paint. My mother took me on my first day and I was excited – until I arrived. The school was enormous, or so it seemed to me, and I had never seen so many people. Suddenly all of the children were running around, which frightened me, and then my mother said she was going. I panicked and held on to her skirt, begging her not to leave me, but of course she did. A nun took me aside and introduced me to painting, which I enjoyed. And that's all I remember doing at Loretta, lots of painting and playing with the other children.

A year later, at the age of eight, I was uprooted from everything I knew and sent to boarding-school in Nakuru. I had never felt so miserable. I didn't know what I had done wrong, why I was being punished. I didn't understand why my mother didn't want me at home with her. I felt completely and utterly bereft – unloved, unwanted, unimportant. With hindsight, I think I sensed something bad was going on at home but I was too young to know what it was – and that made my insecurity even worse. Every time I had to go back to school I would cry and my mother would smile and say goodbye. I couldn't work out what message she was delivering and it left me feeling confused. I had the same sensation when I saw my first Laurel and Hardy movie. The two characters were being chased by someone in a car up a hill and at the top there was a sheer cliff – it was clear to me that they were going to die. I was weeping, yet everyone else was laughing. I couldn't understand why they thought it was so funny.

Despite the tears and the trauma of being ejected from the nest, my memories of Nakuru School are good. It was a big school, surrounded by acres of brown playing-fields – the predominant colour of Africa – and with a long flight of steps leading up to the main entrance. I was terribly short-sighted, although I didn't know it until many years later, and at the end of one term my grandmother was coming to collect me. I didn't want anyone to think she was my mother because she was much older and not nearly as beautiful as Mummy, so I kept an eye open for her car so I could leap into it before she had a chance to get out and everyone saw her. At last her car drew up and I sped down the steps, jumped into the front passenger seat and, to my astonishment, a man, a complete stranger, said, 'Hello, little girl. And who are you?' Crimson, I fled.

We slept in big dormitories on black iron bedsteads with thin, lumpy mattresses and every morning we had to tie up the mosquito nets that hung over us from the ceiling. I had long hair, which I wore in plaits, and one night after I had washed it, two girls decided they would dry it for me. They each took a towel and rubbed either side of my head until my hair was so knotted it had to be chopped off. Misdemeanours were punished with a whack on the calf with a ruler. I was never very rebellious so I am still not sure what I did wrong but I seemed always to have stinging legs and I was often made to sit in front of the class. It was an English school for expatriates, and I remember some Australian girls but I don't imagine there were any black children, although I didn't notice the difference. It was only when I arrived in England some years later and wondered where all the black people were that I appreciated there was a pecking order. I do remember being out for a walk at school once and coming across a line of African convicts digging beside a road, chained to each other. That horrified me.

The post was my lifeline at school, parcels my only joy, in which came jars of damson or medlar jam, peanut butter or Marmite, which I loved. One day an envelope arrived from Granny; when I opened it I was dismayed to discover she had forgotten to put the letter inside. Every Sunday we had to write to our parents and one week I wrote mine in milk, saying, 'If you really want to read this you'll have to light a fire.' Someone had told me that it was secret writing and if you held it up to heat, the words would reveal themselves. I went home at half-term but there were no other exeats or weekends out, and I have no memory of either parent visiting me.

On one half-term holiday, I was taken to a new house in Nairobi. Inexplicably my mother had moved. There, she dropped a bombshell. She introduced me to a tall, dark stranger and said, 'Darling, this is your new father.'

I was stunned. What had been going on while I was away? What had happened to our home? Where was Daddy? I shall never forgive myself for not asking that last question. I meekly said, 'Hello,' and shook his hand. The next thing, I was back at school.

Apparently, my father had been spending a suspicious amount of time with a woman who was as mad about horses as he was. She would come to breakfast, according to my mother, then she and Jock would go riding together. I think my mother seized on this as proof that he was having an affair, and one night while I was at school, she woke my brother and sisters, bundled them into the car and left him. She must have done some kind of secretarial course in preparation, because she had found herself a clerical job, which came with a house of sorts. She had told Jock she wanted a divorce. He seems to have been either powerless or unwilling to dissuade her, and their marriage, with our family unit, had been dissolved. But we children knew none of this. Neither my mother nor my father had said a word to us. All I know about their divorce is that the riding partner was not cited as co-respondent; my father put forward some other woman's name.

My mother had met Bobbie Gaymer-Jones, the man who became my 'new father', at a dinner party. There was not enough cutlery so she said she would go and get some from her house and he went with her. She was thirty-one and still very beautiful but utterly impoverished, living in what Bobbie described as a shack, with Porkie, as he called Paula, and a collection of cats and dogs. Paula was the only one of us my mother had with her: when she left Jock, she had deposited Colin and Jenny in some kind of boarding nursery school. They can remember nothing about it, except there being lots of Dinky toys. I don't know why my mother didn't go back to live with her parents while she had such young children. She must have been miserable on her own in Nairobi and can't have had many

16

friends; at that time divorce was taboo among her social circle and divorcees were frequently ostracised. Bobbie's attentions must have been irresistible.

Bobbie was twenty-eight and very good-looking. He had been a captain in the Life Guards during the war and ADC to General Gayle, General Operations Commander, Middle East and Mediterranean. After the war he had joined the Dunlop Rubber Company and been sent out to Tanganyika (now Tanzania) for two years to develop the rubber market in that part of Africa. There were no roads or tourists in Tanganyika at that time – there was only one stretch of Tarmac in Kenya – and few Europeans lived in Dar Es Salaam. There was also a dearth of single women. He was in need of company as much as she was and, in no time at all, Bobbie and my mother were married.

Bobbie didn't tell his parents about Diana until they were married and it was too late for any argument. He knew they would disapprove: a divorced woman three years older than him with four children in tow was not what they would have wished for their son and, predictably, they were very upset. I didn't go to the wedding; I must have been at school. It took place in a register office in Dar Es Salaam in February 1953. Colin and Jenny remember it.

The three of us spent the next school holidays at my father's house. I don't know why we went there and not to my mother's. I can only imagine that she and Bobbie had baby Paula and didn't want us hanging around. They were the perfect nuclear family – and could even, perhaps, pass off Paula as Bobbie's. We didn't look anything like him. But in my childhood nothing was ever explained; everything was a mystery. We still don't really know the truth. And I couldn't ask my father what was going on: he was a figure behind a newspaper. He wasn't approachable in any way: he was awkward, humourless, distant and silent. Mealtimes were the worst. We were not allowed to speak, but I discovered that if I wiggled my ears I could make Colin and Jenny dissolve into fits of suppressed giggles and, without a word, we could escape to a little world of our own. None of us knew our father. In later years when my mother was cross with me, she would say, 'You're so like your father!' I didn't know what she meant but it wasn't a compliment.

While we were with my father we were looked after by a nanny called Salome. My grandmother must have paid her – she paid my school fees, too, and probably for a lot more besides. Salome was Ankole, from northern Uganda, and I remember her baking a cake with purple icing to celebrate the Queen's coronation in 1953, which we sat and ate in the usual excruciating silence. I felt sick afterwards, and it turned out that I had mumps. I was taken to hospital and the only consolation was that my mother came to visit me.

At night Salome would tie up my hair and Jenny's in long white rags, and in the morning she would pull them out, leaving us with ringlets. Salome was fun but she could also be scary. She would tell me the most horrific bedtime stories and said that if I was naughty the Mau Mau would come and get me. I used to have terrible nightmares.

Mummy came to see us just once while we were staying with Daddy. Colin, Jenny and I were in the bath, splashing around and playing with Salome when our mother burst in and announced that she was going to wash us. Salome told her to leave; she said that she would bath us and a huge row erupted. In the end Salome was thrust out of the door and Mummy rolled up her sleeves. We were mystified. We had no idea what was going on and it was a relief to be out of the bath and into bed. And that was it: Mummy vanished as mysteriously as she had arrived.

Soon afterwards she vanished for good. At least, that was how it felt. She, Bobbie and Paula set sail for England leaving Colin, Jenny and me behind. I felt as though my world had ended; and I don't understand to this day why she did it. Was it too expensive to take us all on the ship? Or maybe Bobbie didn't want us to travel with them.

What twenty-eight-year-old in his right mind would want three pesky children aged nine, seven and six competing for his wife's attention? They had only been married for three months when they left. I was desolate. I longed to be a bird so that I could fly after her to England. I started sleep-walking and waking up night after night by the locked front door trying to escape.

I don't know how long it was that we three stayed on in Kenya after my mother had left. It might have been six months; it might have been a year. I have no memory either of saying goodbye to my father, and certainly no fear, when I boarded the aeroplane alone at Nairobi airport, that I might never see him again. All I know is that, for whatever reason, Colin, Jenny and I, young as we were, travelled separately.

And suddenly, in December 1953, I was in England in a fairytale world of artificial light. At night Kenya was pitch black, the only light from the moon and the stars. I had never seen street lighting, and here I was in London at Christmas, with fairy-lights on the buildings, flashing Belisha beacons on zebra crossings, neon-lit advertising and the whole city bathed in a fabulous phosphorescent glow. I could barely contain my excitement.

CHAPTER TWO

A New Father

No sooner had I arrived in London and been joyously reunited with my mother and siblings than Mummy gave birth to David, the first of our half-brothers, and Colin and I were dispatched to Northamptonshire to stay with some great-aunts. It was snowing and neither of us had ever been so cold. The only thing that kept our circulation going was an electric fire in our bedroom, which we were allowed to turn on. Neither of us knew anything about electric fires, of course, and one morning I put my icy-cold clothes over it to warm, then began to play with Colin. When I turned round my underwear was ablaze. We beat out the flames and hid the evidence.

For a brief period before David was born, home was a small flat in East Putney, south-west London, and I was fleetingly enrolled in Hazeldean School nearby. All I remember of the experience was that we had sausages and baked beans for lunch on Wednesdays. The luxury of a day school was short-lived, however. My parents – my step-father, Bobbie, insisted on being called 'Daddy' – moved to Wimbledon, and I was sent to boarding-school in East Grinstead. Westcroft, in Victoria Drive, was a 1930s house that Bobbie's father, an eminent surgeon, had bought for us. I can only assume that the arrival of a grandchild had brought about a change of heart in the doctor and his wife, and Bobbie certainly needed the gesture: he and my mother had very little money. Having been paid extremely well by Dunlop to work overseas, he came back to his regular salary and, with five children and a wife to support, it wasn't enough.

My new school was St Agnes and St Michael, another convent. I was driven there at the beginning of the first term, crying all the way, and for the first few nights I was so disturbed I wet the bed. I felt so humiliated and ashamed. At ten or eleven I knew I was much too old to do such a thing. Desperate that no one should know, I covered the damp patch with a towel each night in the hope that the sheets would be dry by morning; and if anyone did find out they never told me so.

The dormitories were divided into cubicles with a curtain round each bed, like in a hospital ward. We slept on thin mattresses, and beside each bed there was a chair for our clothes at night and a little chest of drawers. My only comfort was Teddy, my beloved bear, who lived on the bed and listened patiently to my secrets every night. The uniform was navy blue; pinafore dresses with wide pleats worn over white shirts and ties – all neatly marked P. Boyd on the white Cash's nametapes that my mother had painstakingly sewn into every last sock. My tie was only ever tied at the beginning of each term. At night I loosened the knot and slipped it off over my head. We had a bath three times a week, according to a rota, and I have a feeling we changed our knickers three times a week too.

At that school I felt like a fish out of water. I had nothing in common with the other girls. I hadn't read many books in Kenya and television was still a revelation to me – I had only watched it for a couple of months. I couldn't even discuss my family: no one else

22

had divorced parents. All I knew was Africa – I could talk about lions, zebra and elephant, and snakes coming into my bedroom, which didn't go down at all well. They would say to each other, 'Don't talk to Pattie Boyd. She's mad.'

The convent was an old building with no central heating, just a few big radiators, which we used to sit on in an effort to keep warm – we were told not to because that would give us piles and chilblains. I was always cold, particularly in winter. Sometimes I would feign illness to get a couple of days in bed where I would be warm. I would go to the matron who would take my temperature. While her back was turned I would whip the thermometer out of my mouth and run it under hot water for a couple of seconds. It worked a treat every time and I would be packed off to bed. The only compensation for winter was the daily dose of Radio Malt with cod-liver oil, the most delicious, sweet, sticky gloop that apparently kept colds away. Every day we would go to the dispensary and line up for a spoonful. Most people hated it; I thought it was nectar.

I couldn't wait for the holidays when I went home to Colin and Jenny. In the absence of my mother, emotionally, they had become all important to my sense of security and I to theirs. We developed a strong bond, and when I look back at photographs of us as children, we always seem to be leaning on each other. That was how it felt at the time: it was 'us' in the family and 'them'. They were the grown-ups and represented everything that was unsafe and untrustworthy.

Jenny had been the first to leave Kenya and at six, shy and on her own with no older siblings to support her, she was compliant. When I arrived I think my step-father could see trouble ahead and decided to nip it in the bud. He called Jenny to his study one night after she had gone to bed and wouldn't let me in. He told Jenny that she was the good girl in the family and Pattie was the naughty girl and that she shouldn't listen to me because I was a bad influence on her. Jenny remembers going back upstairs and realising, even though she was so young, that he was trying to divide and rule us, and that she had a choice: she could either be on their side or mine and Colin's. As far as she was concerned, there was no contest. She had felt so unloved by our mother in Kenya, even before she left us there, that she had stopped looking to Mummy as a source of comfort and transferred that expectation to us. We were her family, not the adults; we were her safety net.

I remember the incident vividly: sitting upstairs in my bedroom, furious that I had been excluded, unable to hear what was being said behind the closed study door, and desperate to know why Jenny had been called down without me. And then finally, after what seemed like an age, she came into my bedroom, closed the door tight, climbed into bed with me and told me exactly what our new father had said.

My step-father was a frightening character, and we were all scared of him, including, I think, my mother although she would never have said so. I thought he was a bully. He had loved his time in the army and treated us as though we were his own personal foot-soldiers, wanting his boots polished, his food on the table, the children silent and everything just so in the house. He was always telling us to stand or sit up straight, always finding fault. Mealtimes were excruciating. I have no memory as a child of ever hearing or being a part of cheerful family banter around a dining-table. No one had spoken in my real father's house, and now we were not allowed to speak in my step-father's. We ate in the dining room, which felt very stiff and formal, with hard, heavy chairs. And if any of us did anything at the table that displeased him we would be sent to the corner of the room to stand with our hands on our head. We had to stay like that for a long time and after a while it was agonising. I remember Jenny once being sent into the corner for stirring her Instant Whip too vigorously. One minute she was harmlessly stirring her pudding and suddenly, 'Go to the corner with your hands on your head!' Of course, there were some happy times as well.

Christmas was always fun and Bobbie would play Santa Claus – I know because one year I saw him.

One day he was cross with all of us, Paula included, and said he'd had enough. He lined us up and took a photograph of us, which he said he was going to send to our father in Kenya and ask if he would take us back. For weeks and weeks I waited anxiously for my father's response, terrified that I would be sent away. On another occasion he lined us up in the garden, holding hands, and told me to put my hand on a part of the car engine. A shock surged through me and, via our linked hands, though Colin, Jenny and Paula. It might have been his idea of a joke, but it seemed odd to me. I also found it rather odd when he set fire to the ends of my hair, saying it was very good for hair to be singed.

We were occasionally beaten for small misdemeanours. He would tell us to bend over, and we would say we were sorry, knowing what the sting felt like. Paula remembers him delaying the beating. He had clipped the edges of the lawn round the flower-beds and asked her to pick up the clippings. She decided it would be simpler to bury them, which she did. Bobbie was furious and told her he would beat her in three hours' time. Three hours later he sent Jenny to find a stick, but he said the stick wasn't thin enough and the whole thing turned into a sick game. Paula begged him not to hit her. She promised she would give him all of her pocket money for the rest of her life if he didn't, but her pleading fell on deaf ears.

One day he asked Jenny to close the drawing-room door. She didn't hear him, and continued whatever she was doing, so he repeated himself, and again she didn't hear him. Interestingly, he was partially deaf: he had lost much of his hearing during the war, so he tended to shout. Finally he ran out of patience. 'If I have to ask you to close that door one more time,' he threatened, 'I'm going to beat you.' Poor little Jenny still didn't hear and ended up being beaten. He said, 'It's not like you, Jenny, to be so rebellious. What is the matter with you?' The matter with her was that she had been camping the night before and had stuffed cotton wool into her ears to stop earwigs climbing in and forgotten to take it out. It was only when she developed a temperature and earache the next day that a doctor was called and the problem discovered.

My mother never intervened in my step-father's punishments. I think she was too frightened; and if you ask her about it today she denies it happened. She will say what a kind and generous man Bobbie was. I think she was eternally grateful to him for rescuing her after Jock, and was always eager to please him. She was also a product of her age, the last, perhaps, of the generations of wives who vowed to love, honour and obey their husbands and meant it, without question. So there was no point in going to her for protection. We had to look after ourselves, and we developed our own strategies for coping. As the eldest I felt a great sense of responsibility for my siblings. And now, with the wisdom of age, I realise Bobbie was simply a product of his own upbringing. His father beat and bullied him, so he repeated the pattern and feels no shame about it. He now says that corporal punishment would sort out the young of today.

Colin was probably beaten more than the rest of us and, as a boy at boarding-school at that time, he was used to it. But even he finally snapped. He had wanted to play a game with David in the garden one day and Bobbie said he couldn't: he was teaching David to read. Colin must have said something or made a face to provoke him. Next thing Bobbie took out a golf club and whacked Colin a couple of times. Colin grabbed the stick, which snapped in Bobbie's hand and, as they wrestled, cut a jagged line into our step-father's flesh, so deep he had to go to hospital for stitches. Later Bobbie told Colin that if he had still had a Luger in the house, which he had until a recent post-war amnesty, he would have shot him.

Bobbie had no idea how to handle us. The real problem was that he couldn't relate to children, didn't understand them and probably didn't like them very much – at least, not the rebellious, ready-made family he had acquired. He seemed to have a knack for bringing out the worst in us. If we didn't behave, the only way he knew of bringing us into line was by force. It didn't occur to him that showing us a little kindness might have earned him some respect, and we might have done willingly what he asked. His childhood must have been very Victorian. His parents were austere, and children, in their eyes, were to be seen and not heard. Colin and I went to stay with them once and it was ghastly. They didn't like us, and their idea of a fun day at the seaside was to drive to Eastbourne, where we had to sit primly in the back of the car, which might have been a Daimler, with a flask of tea and a chocolate cornflake cake. We were only allowed on to the beach for half an hour. Bobbie's sister became a nun, and later committed suicide.

Eventually Bobbie became sales director with Dunlop Tyres. He was proud of the company and I remember whenever we were out in the car we played a game spotting Dunlop signs.

Wherever we lived, Lilie came with us. She had been in service since the age of thirteen and used to tell us proudly that she had had half of her stomach removed. She wore a nylon housecoat with a pinny over the top and was seldom far from a cigarette. She had been with Bobbie's parents for years and had no family of her own. She was wonderful: everyone else in the house was uptight, but you could talk to Lilie. The food she cooked was deeply dull and disgusting but we loved eating in the kitchen with her on the rare occasions we could escape from the dining room when our parents entertained. Lilie's joys in life were her weekly copies of *Woman* and *Woman's Own* and her cigarettes. I used to go into her room, lie on her bed and look at her magazines – all the more exciting because my step-father forbade me to read the love stories.

Colin never let me down. Each holiday he would bring home from his boarding-school some new boyish torture that he practised on me. I remember Chinese burns being a special favourite. But my hours spent drying the cutlery after supper were not unproductive:

I was a master at flicking a damp tea-towel and regularly caught him on the back of the legs.

I was not allowed to wear jeans (too revolutionary), experiment with makeup or go out with boys. I remember joining a tennis club once so I would meet some. There were two I fancied, Andrew Miller and Anthony Milner, and when one invited me to the cinema, Bobbie wouldn't let me go unless Colin and Jenny came too – I was sixteen! He even censored what I watched on television. I was allowed to see the news and *I Love Lucy*. And he absolutely forbade me to see *Jail House Rock*, Elvis Presley's first film. It caused such a stir. Audiences went crazy, getting up and dancing in the aisles. I loved Elvis but my step-father thought I shouldn't be exposed to him and that was that. My mother wouldn't allow us children to go to the cinema on our own – to this day I never have been inside one alone. She also said we were never to sit next to little old ladies in case they were to stick hypodermic needles into us and spirit us away into the white-slave trade – where she got this idea from I shall never know. But she had double standards: when she put me on the train to go back to boarding-school she would say, 'Let's find a little old lady to look after you.' One minute they were potential abductresses and the next they were guardians.

I was only ever driven to school at the start of the first term. After that I took the train. I don't think it made me feel unloved – I could see that my mother was too busy to drive me to East Grinstead. She now had another child to look after. Less than two years after David was born, she'd had Robert (known as Boo). Occasionally they would come down on a Sunday to take Colin and me out to lunch and we would go to the Felbridge Hotel in East Grinstead, where everyone else went with their parents. It was agony to watch all the other parents and children chatting over their roast beef while we sat in the usual silence.

I was hopeless at English, hopeless at maths, loved history, geography and art – but that was due to the teacher, Miss Hill, who decided she would pay me some attention. She was the only teacher who was not a nun. My piano teacher was a nightmare. Every time I made a mistake she would hit my hand with a ruler. Religion, inevitably, played a large part in my education. We had to go to church on Friday evenings and twice on Sundays. I have no idea why I was sent to Roman Catholic convents: we were Church of England. My mother was quite religious and we went to church every Sunday. Yet at school I had a very different experience with priests, nuns and lots of incense, which I loved. However, I had difficulty accepting much of what I was taught. How on earth could Jesus have been born from a virgin? How could he have risen from the dead? None of the nuns was prepared to explain anything: we had to take it all at face value. None of it was inspirational because the nuns weren't – except one, Sister Mary, who, I decided, had probably had a tragic childhood or a crisis in her late teens. She had a passion for poetry and the written word. She helped me understand and learn to love them too.

In 1958, when I was fourteen, we moved house again. My step-father had bought a rather grand eight-bedroom Edwardian house called Gosmore, in Hadley Wood, Hertfordshire. And I moved school again. Later I discovered that my sudden departure from St Agnes and St Michael had led to rumours that I had been expelled. Nothing so glamorous: I wasn't nearly naughty enough for that. So my mother had to go through the usual last-minute panic of sewing nametapes on to the new uniform and I had the trauma of that first day at a new school, getting to know a new building, a new routine and having to make new friends.

St Martha's Convent was in Hadley Wood too, but I was sent there as a full boarder – and I remember, yet again, saying goodbye to my mother and fighting back tears as I watched her car disappear down the drive. I stood awkwardly with my trunk, not knowing a soul and watching the other girls shrieking with excitement at the sight of their friends, then regaling one another with their exploits during the holidays.

My dormitory had twelve narrow beds each screened from the next by a curtain, with a wash-basin at one end and a noticeboard with a list of Dos and Don'ts pinned to it. Lights out was at nine, and no talking. That first night there *was* no talking – just muffled weeping as the less robust of us got into the ghastly routine.

Every morning we were woken by a small nun wielding a large loud bell, which she rang up and down the corridors and in the dormitories. Ten minutes later she appeared again, chanting prayers. That was our cue to scramble into our gymslips, strip our beds and race off to breakfast. There was compulsory chapel on Friday evenings and twice on Sunday, as there had been at my previous school. Different priests would take the services each week, muttering incantations, swinging an incense burner. I found the heavy scent and smoke quite intoxicating.

I never got over the dread of going back to school – and the ubiquitous smell of floor polish, ink and pencil sharpenings, and the melancholy sound of someone in a far-away room practising scales on the piano – but I enjoyed my time at St Martha's. I made some good friends; I joined the Girl Guides, which I loved – I had been a Brownie at St Agnes and St Michael. I played netball and tennis, and was in the school teams. The best bit about matches was the orange quarters they gave us at half-time, and the tea we had at the end, when we entertained a visiting team. Cucumber sandwiches and all sorts of cake. Delicious.

One weekend at school I was bored and found myself licking the honeycomb out of a Crunchie Bar. I licked until I had created a wonderful hollow inside the chocolate shell, and kept on until there was virtually no honeycomb left. Then I had a brilliant idea. I wrote to Fry's, who made Crunchies, and explained that I was lonely and unhappy at boarding-school and my only pleasure was a weekly Crunchie Bar. This week, I continued, I had taken a bite and discovered that my weekly treat was hollow. I finished off my letter, 'Yours weeping, Pattie Boyd', put it into the post and thought no more about it. Three weeks later a huge parcel arrived, with 'Fry's' stamped all over it. It contained one of every chocolate bar they made, and a letter saying how sorry they were that I had had a faulty Crunchie; they hoped this collection would help to restore my faith and make amends. My feelings of guilt lasted about thirty seconds – and I was suddenly very popular with my friends.

Towards the end of term we would stockpile our tuck for a midnight feast. One person would be deputed to go round the dormitory waking everyone up and we would make our way in dressing-gowns and slippers, whispering and giggling, to the appointed secret destination. How we were never caught remains a mystery. I suspect the nuns recognised it as a bit of harmless end-of-term fun and turned a blind eye. Sadly, they viewed my having a copy of *Lady Chatterley's Lover* hidden under my pillow as a much more serious offence. I was made to report to the reverend mother, who was furious. She threatened either to expel me or to tell my step-father. I couldn't decide which would be worse. It was the first sexy book I had read and I found it riveting.

I knew nothing about sex. My mother didn't talk about it and at that time there was no sex education in schools – and certainly not in a convent. When I had my first period I thought I was going to die. I was about thirteen and woke up one morning to find the sheets covered with blood. Luckily I was at home and ran to my mother in a state of great alarm. She didn't explain anything, just changed the sheets and gave me sanitary towels. At about that time I remember messing around with Colin when he knocked into me. My chest hurt, which it never had before, and Mummy said, rather ominously, 'You can't play with your brother any more. He might hurt you.' All our information came from friends at school and it wasn't entirely accurate. Jenny remembers me telling her the facts of life when she was very young. I went through what the man did and, with great authority, explained that afterwards the woman bled for ever and ever.

According to Bobbie, the reason we moved away from Victoria Drive was that property prices had gone up in Wimbledon and the geographical area he was responsible for at Dunlop had increased, so in moving to a cheaper house at Hadley Wood, he could make money. Bobbie's only interest in life, it seemed, was money. I never appreciated, as a child, how tight things were for him or how difficult it was to make ends meet. I think he may have thought that when my grandparents died my mother would inherit a lot of money.

They left Kenya about two years after we did, at the height of the Mau Mau rebellion, and a lot of their wealth stayed behind, tied up in the house. It was difficult to sell and worth next to nothing in that climate of fear, and there would have been no point in shipping the furniture home as they didn't have a house to move into. So the millions never materialised.

At first they lived in a furnished flat in Regent's Park then moved to another in Putney, but Grandpa was not well. He had had a series of strokes, and when he and my grandmother were staying in a hotel at the end of our road in Hadley Wood, he collapsed over pre-dinner drinks. I was sharing a room with Jenny, and I remember Lilie running in to wake us in the morning, saying, 'Come on, get up, your grandfather's dead.'

Afterwards my grandmother took herself off to live, very comfortably, in a grand hotel on the seafront in Brighton where Colin and I went to visit her. Poor Colin. It was painfully obvious that she preferred me. She had always had favourites and made no attempt to disguise it. My mother grew up knowing that she was second best, that her twin brother John was their mother's favourite. It had done nothing for her confidence and did nothing for Colin's either.

My beloved grandmother died when I was thirteen, about six

months after Grandpa. She was only fifty-eight but she suffered from a thyroid-related complaint. I remember going to the funeral, turning round in the church, looking at my mother and thinking, God she's so beautiful, and then that I shouldn't be thinking such things about my mother at her mother's funeral. By the time Granny died she had spent most of her money. She left a hundred pounds to each of us, not that Jenny or I ever saw ours; and I imagine rather more went to my mother, but nothing like the fortune Bobbie might have hoped for. When the money came through my mother spent it on a set of fine porcelain, which infuriated him.

As children we were convinced that the reason we had moved away from Wimbledon was because Bobbie had fallen in love with a neighbour. She was German, called Ingrid, and had moved into a house two doors away from ours shortly after we had arrived in Victoria Drive. Ingrid was beautiful, glamorous, sophisticated, tall, dark and vivacious, married to a short, stocky, rather solid German businessman called Wolf. He ran a company selling potash and often had to entertain customers in expensive restaurants and clubs in London and frequently invited my mother and Bobbie along too. He was quite nice but she was the gregarious one and he seemed to adore her. They had two young daughters and she was the perfect housewife – she was a fantastic cook, she made the most delicious chocolate biscuits, and her children were perfectly behaved and dressed. The two families became good friends and we children played together. But we could tell that something was not quite right in the way Ingrid and Bobbie behaved with each other. I noticed that he would often make an excuse to go over to her house, and Ingrid would wear very low-cut dresses. I remember sitting in the car once, waiting to go somewhere with Bobbie, and Ingrid leaning provocatively through the car window to chat to him.

I have no idea when they started their affair, but Bobbie bought Mummy a Triumph Herald – which I learnt to drive on the lawn at

Gosmore. I was conscious of an atmosphere in the house of silent fury and slammed doors. I climbed into the car one day and noticed a deep scratch on the windscreen. 'Look,' I said, pointing it out to my mother. She said a neighbour's wife had scratched it, but offered no further explanation. In fact, she knew that Ingrid had left it as a calling card for Bobbie: she must have scratched it with her diamond ring after some romantic encounter. But my mother chose not to challenge what was happening under her nose; she denied it, as she did everything else that was unpalatable. Ingrid remained her friend, and she, Wolf and their children were frequent visitors. I felt angry on Mummy's behalf, but in some ways I was as frightened of her as I was of Bobbie. She didn't confide in me, so I was in no position to help or even say anything to her.

Sometimes in the school holidays I would go to stay with Jane Blackiston, a friend from St Martha's. Her parents lived in a pretty Northamptonshire village and her mother bought milk in churns from the farm to make her own butter and cream – she also made the most delicious cherry pies I've ever eaten. But Jane would make me get on to her horrible pony and hit it over the rump so that it would race off and jump over huge branches that had fallen on the village green, secretly hoping, I have no doubt, that I would fall off. By some miracle, I never obliged.

During the long summer holidays Colin and I were often sent to Cornwall to stay with our grandfather on his farm near Liskeard. Grandpa Boyd was an extraordinary man, quite exotic. He rode a big Triumph motorbike and we didn't see him much because he was always rushing off. We would take the train from Paddington and meet our grandmother, his estranged wife, at Truro. I didn't like her, and I'm not sure why we met her there – maybe we had to change trains and she came to make sure we didn't get lost. She went everywhere with her dachshunds, and was very austere. We would say an awkward hello, then get back on the train and continue our journey.

We had wonderful summers on the farm. We learnt to milk the cows and helped take the churns on the tractor down to the end of the lane, where they were collected. We rode horses, fed the chickens, collected eggs and were chased by pigs. There was no electricity on the farm, so we ate supper by the light of a paraffin lamp and took candles up to bed with us; it was very romantic. Grandpa had a Cornish couple living in the house to look after him. Mrs Wills cooked everything with saffron, so we had yellow bread, yellow cakes and yellow buns; strange but delicious. After supper Grandpa would hop on to his motorbike and roar off to the pub for a pint. Some years later, when he felt he'd had enough of life, he drove to Bodmin Moor, parked his bike and walked until he could walk no further.

After about three years in Hadley Wood we were on the move again, to a huge six-bedroom flat in Hurlingham Court, a mansion block overlooking the Thames in Putney. I didn't know what my step-father's motivation was and assumed he wanted to be closer to Ingrid, who was still in Victoria Drive but whom we saw as often as ever. But apparently the reason for the move was financial. Bobbie was short of money again and the house in Hadley Wood had nearly doubled in value, so he sold it and rented the flat.

He bought himself a boat and we spent a lot of time on the river. I even swam in it. Bobbie once bet me two shillings I couldn't swim to a certain boat, so I jumped in, thought, Of course I'm going to do it, came back thrilled, happy, and couldn't understand why everyone was staring at me with horror. I had cut my knee on a piece of glass getting out of the water and blood was gushing down my leg. I had to be carted off to hospital and stitched up.

Bobbie's boat was a motor-cruiser called *Blue Boy*, which was moored quite close to the flat and had a little dinghy to ferry us to and from it. We used to go on trips upriver to places like Hampton Court and have picnics on the way. One evening Bobbie wanted to take the boat out for a late-night jaunt so we all piled in. He was steering and my mother was in the galley making supper when Bobbie shouted at Colin, 'What's that ahead?' Like all the Boyds, Colin was short-sighted and said he couldn't see anything. The next minute there was the most sickening, ear-splitting crash as we ploughed into a metal weir and the boat was impaled on a two-foot length of metal. Thank God it was stuck – otherwise it would have sunk like a stone and we would have drowned. My mother was scalded by a pan of boiling water but miraculously no one else was harmed, just terrified. Bobbie yelled at us to get out of the boat and stand on the weir while he blew the boat's horn until the weir-keeper arrived to rescue us. We were made to swear on our graves that we would never mention what had happened to Grandpa Gaymer-Jones.

In March 1961 I turned seventeen, and at the end of the summer term, with a sigh of relief, said farewell to St Martha's. My parents had never been particularly interested in my education, university was never mentioned, so with three O levels and no idea about what I might do before I married, which is all I had been prepared for, I left school. I had thought it might be fun to be an air hostess but I was told you needed to be very pretty and speak three languages. I didn't regard myself as pretty and, apart from English, I could only speak a little bit of French so that was out of the question. The other obvious option was a secretarial course but I didn't want to sit in an office all day. My only ambition was to get out of Hurlingham Court and away from the dysfunctional family we had become.

My mother knew someone who was quite senior at Elizabeth Arden and she pulled a few strings to get me and my friend Jane Blackiston a job each as apprentices at their beauty salon in Bond Street. In October Jane and I moved into a house in Clareville Mews, just off Queen's Gate in South Kensington, which we shared with two other girls. The sense of freedom was intoxicating: no nuns, no Bobbie, no tension. If I hadn't felt so guilty about abandoning my brothers and sisters, life would have been perfect.

CHAPTER THREE

Modelling

In June 1961 my mother and Bobbie, Wolf and Ingrid went on a two-week touring holiday in Germany and Italy. Five days into the trip, as they were preparing for dinner one night, Bobbie turned her world upside-down. He told my mother he thought they should get a divorce. Her diary entry from that night is heartbreaking, but typical:

> June 27th. A terrific thunderstorm last night. Shutters hitting against the windows kept us awake. After breakfast (in an almost deserted dining room) we all went shopping in funny little Ballagio. Bobbie bought me a blouse and scarf, and a pair of shoes for himself. Whatever else Bobbie might be he is certainly generous over money. Another thunderstorm. While we were changing for dinner Bobbie shocked me by saying he thought as we were always arguing we should get divorced. I am shattered. I prayed to God to help me. I feel numb.

Conversation at dinner impossible. Wolf suspicious and angry with Ingrid. A neglected husband and I a neglected wife!

Poor Mummy: she had carried on as though she and Ingrid were the best of friends and Bobbie's behaviour no more than boyish flirtation. She had probably thought the affair would eventually disintegrate. Now that the facts were staring her in the face, now that Bobbie had told her he was in love with Ingrid and wanted out, she swallowed her pride and continued as though it were a minor inconvenience. She didn't scream and shout; she didn't pack her bags and take the first train home. Bobbie's announcement didn't even interrupt the holiday. Wolf and he weren't talking for a while, and Wolf and Ingrid weren't either, but no one stormed out. The next morning they left Ballagio at nine thirty, arrived at their hotel in Sirmione at two o'clock, went for a walk in the gardens, swam, took a motorboat to the other side of the lake and sat down to dinner together on the terrace.

There were ructions when they got back: the affair was out in the open and it was an unsettling time. My mother and Bobbie continued to live at Hurlingham Court together, and in some respects life carried on as normal. His moods were worse. I remember that one night he didn't like something my mother had cooked for supper so he picked up his plate and threw it at her. Sometimes he would leave the flat and, moments later, Wolf would arrive, pie-eyed and wanting to talk.

It was a year before Bobbie finally left. He went to live with Ingrid in a house he'd bought in Wimbledon and two months later had the cheek to ring Hurlingham Court to invite Jenny to go over to see it. He walked out, leaving my mother with five children still to support and little money to do it with. Colin was fifteen and at boarding-school in Norfolk; he was immediately taken out of it and sent to Holland Park School in London, where he was one of two thousand pupils. Jenny was thirteen and at St Martha's. She, too, was sent to Holland Park. Aged eleven, Paula found the transition from private to state school less traumatic than the others, but it was a shock for them all. David and Boo were eight and six and both at boarding-schools in Sussex.

I was safely out of the equation in South Kensington, exploring the world of boys and bistros. But I had a new burden of guilt, which I discovered, years later, I was not alone in carrying; Colin and Jenny had felt the same, even though we knew that Bobbie had left Mummy because he had fallen in love with Ingrid. I couldn't help thinking that in some way it was my fault, that I had driven him away by being horrid to him. I thought maybe he had gone because he knew how much I disliked him. Years later I discovered that my mother felt I had let her down, that I should have been more supportive, but since she had never confided in me I don't know what more I could have done. She was just this angry person slamming doors and saying nothing. I think she found me quite hard to cope with at that time: I was young, nubile and had everything in front of me, while she was penniless with five children, no husband and bitterly unhappy. I remember her once slapping me across the face, probably giving herself as much of a fright as she did me. I suspect she was venting her pent-up rage. The slap might have been better directed at either Bobbie or Ingrid.

The job at Elizabeth Arden was deadly boring. I was training to be a beautician but my heart wasn't in it and I'm not sure I would have made the grade. Elizabeth Arden herself came in one day and berated me for my makeup. She didn't like the black pencil under my eyes; it was not the Elizabeth Arden look, she informed me. But if the way she was made up was anything to go by, I wasn't sure it was a look I wanted. But what I did enjoy in the salon were the glossy fashion magazines that were lying around for the clients. I had never seen one before because my mother didn't take magazines. Lilie's *Woman* and *Woman's Own* were the extent of my experience, and there was nothing high-fashion about either. Here, I saw wonderful titles like *Vogue, Vanity Fair, Tatler* and *Queen*, with photographs of fabulous models like Jean Shrimpton and Celia Hammond. They looked so different from the models of the fifties, who were stiff and sophisticated. These girls were young, fresh and different. I wanted to be like them.

Imagine my excitement when a client came into the salon one day and asked if I had ever thought of being a model. I said, 'No, but I certainly could.' Sadly, I can't remember her name but she worked for a fashion magazine called *Honey*, and invited me to come to her office in Farringdon Road, just round the corner from Fleet Street, the following Monday. When I arrived she had arranged for her in-house photographer, Anthony Norris, to take test shots of me. He had set up some lights in a little studio and she gave me a couple of outfits to wear – I remember a beret, and having to look sultry smoking a Gitanes. They were black-and-white, moody shots, with a bit of a Parisian feel.

Once she had seen the results, my fairy godmother phoned Cherry Marshall, who then ran one of the top model agencies, and said she was sending me to her. Anthony Norris went with me and told Cherry he thought she should take me on. Cherry was delightful and said I didn't need training to walk like a model – I already did. Posture was something my grandmother had been hot on: she would always put a hand behind my back and tell me to sit up straight. Who knows? Maybe all those years of my step-father's discipline had paid off too.

I was thrilled. I raced home and told Jane, and she was furious. Years later she said resentfully, 'You were the short fat one at Elizabeth Arden.' That wasn't entirely true: at five feet seven and a half inches I was half an inch shorter than her. In my early teens I had had puppy fat, which had mostly gone by the time I was seventeen. I had always had a big bust and long, skinny legs – at one time I had wanted to chop a bit off them – and in my netball shorts at school I looked gangly. I always felt top-heavy. But one day at school we were lying around reading and a girl called Paula said, 'Your eyes are the colour of cornflowers.' I thought, How lovely. What a nice thing to say.

Finding an agency was easy; finding a job was the hard part. Every day I would go out with a list of photographers' names and addresses and trudge round with my portfolio, hoping they would like what they saw in it and use me on a job. And if one did, I would try very hard to get him to give me some prints at a low rate so that I could add them to my portfolio. I must have travelled on every bus and tube in London, and when I was out of money I walked. My diary for those days is full of IOUs for the odd fiver I borrowed from Colin or friends to tide me over.

One day I went to see the great Norman Parkinson. He looked at my book, then looked at me and said, 'Come back when you've learnt how to do your hair and makeup properly.' I felt so humiliated. Six months later I got a job with *Vogue* and Parkinson was the photographer – he didn't recognise me.

I was lucky. The trekking round worked, and soon my diary was full of jobs. Modelling was fun. I loved trying on clothes and fiddling with my hair and makeup. We had to do it ourselves – there were no hair-stylists or makeup artists and certainly no chauffeur-driven cars to ferry us around. We were not celebrities in the way that today's top models are. For advertising jobs we even had to bring our own accessories. I have my old appointments diaries and they are full of instructions about what I had to take to a shoot. Usually it was light and dark court shoes, flatties, gloves, costume jewellery, hats or caps, and boots, plus makeup, wigs and hairpieces. You could spot a model a mile off from the heavy bags she was carrying.

I made lots of friends among the other models, and when one of the girls in the mews house left to get married, I moved into a flat in Stanhope Gardens with four other models. It was girly and disorganised. There were people coming and going at all hours, boys turning up to take us out – and leaving broken hearts – everyone borrowing everyone else's clothes, so nothing was ever where you thought it was, and no system for cleaning or shopping. You never knew whether or not there would be any food. One minute the fridge was bursting, the next it was empty. I was earning three pounds an hour but often the money didn't come through for weeks, and with rent to pay I didn't have a lot to spare – particularly if I'd treated myself to a nice pair of shoes, my weakness. I economised on food and most of the time lived on Bird's Eye frozen chicken pies. An invitation to dinner was a real treat.

One night I was asked out by a boy called Peter, who had an identical twin. I shall never forget him because he introduced me to avocado pears. I had seen them but never tasted one and, as a starter with vinaigrette, I loved it. They must have been very new in Britain because I remember introducing them to George Harrison and he introduced them to Cilla Black. The next week Peter and I had another date and I thought it odd that he should have forgotten everything I'd told him the week before – only to discover it wasn't Peter I'd been cosying up to but his twin brother. Not funny.

One of my best friends was a model called Marie-Lise Volpelière-Pierrot. Her brother, the gorgeous Jean-Claude, had introduced us. I had met him in the King's Road where I had been doing a modelling job with a girl called Sonia Dean. When we had finished she said, 'Let's go to the Kardomah coffee bar,' which was a great meeting-place, near Peter Jones – everyone hung out there. Off we went, and I still had all my makeup on, including false eyelashes. It was so smoky in there that my eyes watered. I couldn't bear it, I wanted to leave, but she was waiting for some guy because there was a party that night she wanted to go to. So we stayed and, suddenly, just as I felt something sliding down my face, a beautiful young man was standing over me, grinning. Jean-Claude introduced himself – while I tried to rescue the eyelash that had made a break for freedom – and asked if I'd like to go to a party. I said, 'Of course.' But I had no idea that he was the chap Sonia had been waiting for, and I think she was miffed that he'd come straight to me.

It was a terrible party and someone stole my handbag, which I'd left on the stairs with the coats, as everyone did in those days, but Jean-Claude and I became friends. And for a little while I fondly imagined he was my boyfriend. He took some wonderful photographs of me and introduced me to all sorts of people, including his sister, Marie-Lise, and his little brother, Danny. They were from Mauritius and had a father in London, but their mother was dead.

One night we were supposed to be going to a party at De Vere Gardens and I waited for Jean-Claude to collect me. He didn't come and didn't phone, and the hours went by. Finally I decided to go on my own. I arrived and found Jean-Claude already there, dancing with another girl, and I knew that that was it. I thought, She's so pretty, no wonder he's dancing with her. I was very upset, but I don't think he ever realised I'd felt as I did about him. The girl was called Belinda Watson, and not long afterwards Jean-Claude brought her to tea at Hurlingham Court. Eventually they married and had two children – and Belinda's mother married Jean-Claude's father.

Soon after that disappointment I started going out with another photographer, Eric Swayne, who was quite a bit older than I was. We all drove to Spain together, Jean-Claude, Marie-Lise, Danny, Eric and I. Danny played bongo drums all the way there, and I remember pulling up at traffic-lights next to a car laden with boxes of apricots and the driver giving us a box. We would stop by the road in little wooded picnic areas and have lunch – the joy of perfectly ripe Camembert with fresh baguettes and delicious red wine. We stayed in little *pensions* and I was shocked to find that every loo in France was a hole in the ground with a little place for your feet at either side. I was reminded of Africa and the rondavel house we had lived in where the loo was a hole in the garden. We children used to throw each other's things into it. But that trip through France was a gastronomic awakening for me. We would eat in tiny restaurants that were very cheap but the food was wonderful, and in Spain – we went as far as Cambrils in the north-east – I tasted *paella* for the first time. We stayed in a very cheap flat with cockroaches, and at lunchtime a local family would come to the beach, light a stove and make it for us. Danny couldn't swim and it was our priority to teach him.

I was a virgin when I met Eric Swayne. I was still sharing a flat with Jane Blackiston, who kept quizzing me about whether I had slept with anyone yet and I kept saying, 'No.' I was nervous of doing it because I knew she'd get out the moral whip. Part of me wanted to stay a virgin until I got married – the convent indoctrination rubbing off on me – but another part was decidedly wobbly about the whole business of marriage. Having witnessed my mother's experience, not once but twice, and seen how unhappy it had made her, I wasn't sure marriage was such a good thing.

Eric was not good-looking but quite cool – he had long dark hair and a straight, fine nose – and good company: he made everyone laugh. He lived in a flat in Chelsea Studios, a fifties building next to Chelsea football ground, with the photographer David Hurn next door. Grace Coddington, another model, who later became a legendary figure at *Vogue*, had the flat above. Eric was thirty and came from the East End of London. He looked up to David Bailey, who was from the same area. Bailey photographed Jean Shrimpton and they were emerging as fashion's golden couple. I think Eric wanted to do for me what Bailey had done for Jean: he wanted to be my style guru. He wanted to show me how to do my hair and makeup and to help me with my modelling. In the end he became too controlling, and I think he was quite dark in some ways, but he introduced me to lots of photographers and it was through him that I met Bailey and Jean Shrimpton. I was such a fan that I was dumbstruck when I met her. She was stunningly beautiful and he was so funny; they were a wonderful couple. She was much taller than him and came from Berkshire – her background was similar to mine.

Bailey had lots of girlfriends. One night Eric and I had dinner with him, Penelope Tree, another model, and the actor Yul Brynner, who, I think, Bailey had been photographing. We walked to a little restaurant in the King's Road – it was so weird being with Yul Brynner, who had just made *The King and I* and, with his shaven head, was instantly recognisable. Some smart aleck we passed in the street said, 'Oh, look, he thinks he's Yul Brynner.'

Eric and I didn't sleep together for quite a while. He kept asking and I kept refusing. Eventually I felt pressured and knew I'd have to give in, so although I didn't really want to, I agreed. He was kind and sweet, but it wasn't the big deal I had imagined. In fact, it was pretty painful and I regretted it. We didn't use any contraception – I didn't think about the possibility of becoming pregnant until later, when I panicked a bit. Mostly I felt I had let myself down.

Eric didn't have much money so we would go to restaurants like the Stockpot, which had several branches in central London, where the food was cheap and filling. One night we were at the one in the King's Road, with a friend called Peter Kernott, when Eric noticed Rudolf Nureyev, the Russian ballet dancer, sitting at a table on his own. I said, 'Let's invite him over,' so Eric did and he had coffee with us. I couldn't believe it – this beautiful boy. He didn't speak much English but after we had paid the bill he invited us back to his flat in Ennismore Gardens. He gave us a drink, then began to dance, leaping into the air, arms and legs outstretched, spinning, bounding, then sinking gracefully to the floor. It was a night of pure magic.

London was like that in the 1960s. You spoke to strangers and invited them back to your flat without thinking twice. The King's Road was like an exclusive school playground. Everyone went to the same parties, the same shops, the same coffee bars, bistros and pubs. And on Saturdays, if you weren't parading up and down the King's Road, you would migrate to Portobello Road, in Notting Hill, to meander up and down looking at the market stalls and people strutting their stuff. You could find some real bargains: bits of silver, antique jewellery and knick-knacks, wonderful old clothes and pieces of lace and velvet. Everyone looked glorious and was so relaxed and friendly.

We went to clubs like the Arethusa, ate in restaurants like the Picasso and the Casserole, all in the King's Road. You would go for lunch and find yourself still sitting chatting to your friends at dinner time and no one would hassle you to leave. Then there was Mr Chow's restaurant in Knightsbridge; he was going out with Grace Coddington and later married Tina Chow, whom everyone fell in love with. We went to quirky little boutiques, like Granny Takes A Trip, owned by Nigel Waymouth, who was a painter, and John Pearce. They sold paintings, posters and clothes – crushed velvet trousers and fitted jackets with thin arms in wonderful greens and burgundies. Everything was very tight and men wore boots, jackets and shirts with big collars – Regency, almost. There was an amazing number of new shops for men, who were refusing to be like their fathers. I loved Hung On You, and the shirt-makers Deborah and Claire in Beauchamp Place, Knightsbridge, Foale and Tuffin for dresses and Anello and Davide for boots. And Mary Quant, and Ossie Clark, and then there was Biba, Barbara Hulanicki's brainchild, first in Abingdon Road, then Kensington Church Street.

We went to the Chelsea Antiques Market. On the first floor there were second-hand clothes, delicious silks and chiffons. Jenny Kee, an Australian-Chinese girl, had a stall there, as did Australian Jenny and wonderful Swedish Ulla Larson. There was another great market in Kensington High Street and a shop in Langton Street where we used to buy Afghan coats. And patchouli oil – that was the smell of the sixties for me. We wore it all the time – probably to take away the terrible smell of those Afghan coats!

London belonged to the young. All the old class structures of our parents' generation were breaking down. All the old social mores were swept away. No one cared where you came from or what school you'd gone to, what accent you spoke with or how much money you had. All that mattered was what you could do, what you could create. Bohemian baronets smoked grass openly, dukes' daughters went out with hairdressers and everyone put two fingers up to the conventions of their youth and the expectations of their families. The capital was abuzz with creativity, bristling with energy. Everything was possible – and money was not the key to every door.

Painters, poets, writers, designers, ad men, media figures and, of course, musicians expressed themselves with fearlessness, freshness and freedom. They wore fabulous frocks and flowery shirts and grew their hair long. They weren't going to knuckle down and wear the uniform of their class. The rule book had been thrown away. A new age and a new value system had been born. People wanted to experiment and have fun. And, to use the old cliché, make love not war. As long as you were young, beautiful and creative, the world was your oyster. It was a golden age, an exciting time to be alive. As a model, working for the most successful photographers in London, I was in the thick of it.

One of the seminal books of the sixties was the coffee-table *Birds of Britain*, a collection of photographs of the girls whom photographer John D. Green thought epitomised the decade. I was on the front cover and most of my friends were in it. The introduction was written by Anthony Haden-Guest, who, I thought, had painted a perfect picture to set the scene:

Consider them [English girls] now. Resplendent! Sauntering, strolling, sitting, driving around the chosen streets and squares of Central London . . . warm vortices of flesh, supercool in sunglasses and flaming in a rag-bag kaleidoscope of stuffs and styles. Swathed in tulle and velvet and lace, sheathed in plastic and poly-vinyl, silk and satin, throwaway paper shirts and everlasting metal-alloy dresses. Like Venus in furs, or Hell's Angels in leather, they shimmer past, in Courrèges, in Vietnam combat-kit, in Gary Cooper denims, in antique Hussar Regimentals . . . Grandmother's formals swoop to the ground in a scarlet Niagara, or the hem disappears into a swirl of miniskirt, beneath which limbs flicker like jack-knives and glimmer like trout.

Limbs hadn't been seen before, except on the beach. Miniskirts were revolutionary. Women had been covered up in sensible tweeds and twin sets. Suddenly they were flaunting themselves, wearing luxurious fabrics, bright colours, huge hats, beads, big belts, buckles and thigh-length boots. You could wear what you wanted, do what you wanted, express yourself in any way that felt right – and in the 'in' parts of London, such as Chelsea and Notting Hill, no one turned a hair. Although homosexuality was still illegal until 1967, gay and bisexual men no longer felt the need to hide. Pregnant women were no longer ashamed to show their expanding tummies. Young mothers ditched old-fashioned prams and carried their babies in papooses on their backs. They breast-fed in public, too.

Extraordinary, exciting people were around – David Hockney, Celia Birtwell and Hockney's boyfriend Peter Schlesinger, Anita Pallenberg, Marianne Faithfull and the Rolling Stones. There were comedy clubs – the Establishment, the Round House, the Living Theatre – and comedians like the outrageous Lenny Bruce. There was nudity on the stage, exhilarating, extravagant musicals like *Oh! Calcutta!* and *Hair*, which shocked the establishment and had the young dancing in the aisles. On television *That Was The Week That Was* took an irreverent look at politics, while the Australian journalist Richard Neville caused regular outrage with *Oz* magazine. Richard Ingrams, Willie Rushton and Peter Cook poked fun at it all in the new satirical magazine *Private Eye*.

We were breaking new ground in every area, embracing everything that presented itself and, I suppose, living without a care for tomorrow. People were travelling to places like India and Afghanistan – the beginnings of the hippie trail – and bringing back exotic clothes, jewellery and drugs. We had no role models: we had no idea that drugs were potentially dangerous or that our friends might end up addicts or kill themselves with an overdose. We had not yet seen anyone spiralling out of control.

Most of the people I hung out with were photographers, rock 'n' rollers without the music. I worked with some, people like Michael Boys, Brian Duffy, Terry Donovan, Barry Lategan, John French, David Bailey and Maurice Engles, and others I knew as friends. They were mostly men but there was one woman photographer, Sarah Moon. Some made us look better than we actually did – Barry Lategan was brilliant at that. He had come from South Africa to work as Michael Boys's assistant.

I was doing a lot of work for Michael at the time and remember going to Portugal with him for a shoot. It was January and he thought it would be warmer by the sea in Portugal than it was in England. It was freezing. They had to revive me with brandy and by the end of the day I was feeling no pain. Then Barry took photos of me. All the models loved working for him because of his knack with lighting.

I didn't have overweening self-confidence, and I don't think any model did. I was flattered when people said or wrote nice things about me, but I saw beautiful girls every day and, compared with people like Jean Shrimpton, I felt I was way down the pecking order. That was the negative side of modelling. You had to look really good to get the jobs so you put yourself into a situation that fed your insecurities. If you didn't get a job, you'd think it was because you were not pretty enough. It allowed you – in fact, it forced you – to concentrate on your flaws and that was destructive. A girl who doesn't have to rely on her looks for her living is far more confident, and confidence is attractive – her looks are not integral to her self-esteem. Ours were.

A good photographer made the world of difference. I didn't get on with Patrick Lichfield because he couldn't communicate with his models in the way that others did. It was so frustrating: he would say,

'Do something – go,' which is impossible. An actress is given a role to play and comes up with a great performance for the camera. A model needs to be given a role to play, otherwise she has to rely on the clothes she is wearing, which may be uninspiring. You need to be told what to do and how to look, and the good photographers would encourage us, egg us on, telling us how beautiful we were, how sexy, that the pose was perfect.

Bailey was a sexy photographer, and it was easy to appear sexy with him because we reacted to what was coming from him. There might be other people in the studio but modelling is a one-on-one relationship, between you and the photographer, and you need to feel that he and the camera are one.

In those early years I worked long hours. Sometimes I had three or four different jobs in a day and frequently wouldn't finish until seven thirty or eight in the evening. It was mixture of advertising and fashion, working directly for magazines like *Honey*, *Vanity Fair* and *Vogue* or newspapers. I did a lot of fashion spreads for the *Daily Telegraph*, also *The Times*, the *Mirror* and the *Express*. In addition there would be the occasional catalogue shoot, which was always rather dull: the clothes were usually unexciting, but we would shoot over several days so the money was good. Soon I had an agent in Paris too, called Paris Planning, and I remember going to see them for the first time and being told how *mignon*, or cute, I was. I stayed in a small hotel in the 6th *arrondissement* and did the round of photographers with my portfolio, struggling with taxis and schoolgirl French but, again, it paid off. A single job for *Elle* magazine paid four hundred francs. But it was more fun to have company, and on subsequent visits other models came too – I remember doing a job with Sandra Paul, who married the politician Michael Howard, and Pauline Stone, who married Laurence Harvey.

The only time I ever did catwalk modelling was for Ossie Clark. We all modelled for him because we adored him and he made the most beautiful clothes. He was a thin, effete, stylish man, not very tall but with fine bones – and big workman's hands. He could sew magnificently and he was the finest fabric cutter in London. He cut on the bias beautifully. It was a real treat to watch. I remember being in the shop one day and at the back there was a long table where his cutters worked. He and I were going out when someone said something to him and he said, 'No, that's not the way to do it.' He took the scissors and, in a flash, had cut perfectly across the material.

He designed with his wife Celia Birtwell, who made all the prints and was also incredibly talented. She was a great friend of David Hockney. Hockney had a coterie of creative friends who hung out at his flat in Powis Square, Notting Hill. Ossie used to tell a wonderful story about when he and Hockney were on holiday together. Early one evening they caught the Trans-Siberian Express, had a bit of supper and went to bed. Next morning they were hungry and looking forward to breakfast. Unable to speak Russian, David used a paper napkin to explain what he wanted. He drew a boiled egg and gave it to the waiter, who came back with a ball of ice-cream. Little did the bemused Russian know that he had an original Hockney in his hand.

Ossie was magical. When he was up, he was the best person in the world to be with, but when he was down – and he really plumbed the depths – he could be vicious. He didn't like mixing with other designers and you were wise not to mention their names; he preferred to socialise with rock stars, painters and models. He felt, and it was true, that he had introduced the trouser suit way before Yves St Laurent, yet the latter always got the credit. With Celia, he also did printed chiffons long before anyone else. He was a real innovator.

I loved going out with Ossie. Usually I met him at Hockney's flat – I remember going there once, after a show or something, and he said, 'Come on, we're going out tonight.' I said I couldn't, I had nothing to wear, so he took me to his own flat in Linden Gardens, where there were lots of dresses. He threw one at me and said, 'Try this on.' As I was changing I saw Celia and their two babies – typical mother at home, nappies everywhere – and said, 'What about Celia?' And he said, 'No, no, no, she can't come out,' and off we went. I felt a bit guilty to leave her behind but that was how it was. He would go out all the time and her role was to stay at home.

Nothing was ever planned when we went out. He would say, 'Let's go to a recording studio,' or a show or someone's house. We would jump into his huge American car and he would drive down one-way streets the wrong way and into roads with no-entry signs. He was great fun to be with – unless it was after a collection. While he was working he would be up, up, up, and when it was over, he would go into a terrible depression and want to go on holiday when he should have been following up on orders and selling the clothes. His shows were spectacular with fabulous music that made you want to dance. They were real events, and he would sit up all night beforehand putting the finishing touches to the clothes – those great hands doing the most delicate sewing – and getting the sound just right. He didn't pay us any money, but the clothes were so amazing that most of us would have paid him to model them – and he always let us keep one outfit.

I can't remember how I met Ossie. It might have been at a party or perhaps one day I wandered into Quorum. It was in Radnor Walk off the King's Road. Alice Pollock, another designer, shared it. All sorts of people used to hang out there – the building was a mecca for the young and beautiful – and if he liked the look of you he would give you things. I don't know how he ever made any money. He was enormously talented but a hopeless businessman. David Gilmour, the great guitarist and song writer with Pink Floyd, was a friend and worked for Ossie as a driver; when he wasn't driving, he would be sitting in the cutting room putting buttons on leather jackets. Brian Jones, who played with the Rolling Stones, lived in a flat above the shop, and above that was a model agency called English Boy, run by Jose Fonseca and owned by Mark Palmer. When he eventually sold it, Jose started her own agency, Models One. English Boy had many famous names on its books, not just boys, including a number of my friends.

People say I was Ossie's muse. He liked to make clothes for women who looked like women, with busts and waists, narrow hips and long legs – and I had all of those. He used to say I had 'glass ankles' and some of the designs were called 'Pattie'. When I was modelling I was very thin and I worked at keeping myself that way. I would hardly eat, and then I discovered these diet biscuits that you could buy from the chemist. They were so filling I hardly had to eat anything else. I was a size eight – 34B/24/34. I have a narrow back and at that time I had a tiny ribcage. Recently I found some of my clothes from the sixties and I can't begin to get into them. They look as though they were made for a child.

In March 1963, I moved from the chaos of Stanhope Gardens to a flat in Hereford Square, where there were even more girls and even greater chaos. After three months, I was short of money and went to live at home for six months. With Bobbie gone, my mother had had to give up Hurlingham Court and move into the house that Bobbie and Ingrid had lived in, in Strathmore Road. I thought it very shabby and I was angry on her behalf. I couldn't understand why she had not stood up for herself and insisted on staying in Putney, instead of moving to his poky love nest in Wimbledon. Also, she should have ensured that she got a decent amount of maintenance. After his invitation to Jenny the year before, I had heard nothing from Bobbie. Since then, the only occasions on which I have seen him were David and Boo's weddings and occasional family parties – and when I was writing this book.

The silence from my real father was equally deafening. After we left Kenya at the end of 1953, apart from the occasional Christmas card and gift, we heard nothing.

CHAPTER FOUR

George

Who would have guessed that the humble potato would play such an important part in my life? In November 1963 I was in a rather charming television commercial for Smith's crisps. The director was Dick Lester, a good-looking, soft-spoken American who, at the age of twenty-six, had already made a name for himself with a short comedy classic called *The Running, Jumping & Standing Still Film*, with Spike Milligan and Peter Sellers. In this film, I had to pick crisps out of a packet and put them into my mouth, lisping about how much I loved Smith's crisps. It was the first television I had ever done and the first time I had had a speaking part. For someone who was as cripplingly shy as me, it was quite an ordeal, and in the end they used someone else's voice – which I felt decidedly miffed about – but the commercial was a great success and projected me to a new level of recognition.

A few weeks later I heard that a girl called Mary Bee was looking for someone to share a flat. She was originally a friend of Belinda

Watson – who had ensnared the lovely Jean-Claude – but when Belinda introduced us we realised we had already met. She had been at the Convent of the Sacred Heart while I was at St Martha's and we had played in school tennis matches and guzzled orange quarters together. And there were other connections. I had been at school with someone called Paula Derham, whose brother John had been my first boyfriend and the first boy I ever kissed. Mary Bee knew Paula because John Derham had been at school with Mary's brother John. Jean-Claude had also been there – it was a Roman Catholic school – and the three were friends. So, in December Mary and I moved into a gorgeous but tiny flat in Oakley Street, Chelsea with one little bedroom that we shared.

I was working flat out, not getting back until late and needing an alarm call to get me out of bed in the mornings – the phone number was Flaxman 4088. Mary was working for Mary Quant, one of the first designers to have a boutique in the King's Road. It was called Bazaar and, with her husband Alexander Plunkett Greene, she went on to build up a chain, then brought out a range of makeup and was very influential in the way people looked and dressed.

For me, as a model, no two days were the same and my eating pattern went haywire. Some days I would eat, other days not, and I never had more than a cup of tea for breakfast. I was still pre-occupied with keeping my weight down and I had found a doctor in Harley Street who gave me some pills that speeded up my metabolism so I was thirsty but not hungry. I'm sure it was very bad for me but that didn't cross my mind because we all did it. I wasn't much of a cook then either – sometimes Mary and I would give dinner parties, and had to ring our mothers for instructions. My mother was good for the basic things; Mary's was the one to ring when we attempted more exotic dishes.

I was still going out with Eric Swayne and doing a lot of work for him, but I wasn't in love. He could be severe, and the longer I was with him the more domineering he became. He was a bit like my step-father, I suppose, and he didn't bring out the best in me. He was almost obsessive about me and all that he would do for my career, and most of my friends found him a bit creepy.

Mary had a more adventurous social life than I did and was seeing a well-known married man. She wore the prettiest black lacy underwear and Guerlain Shalimar perfume when she went out to dinner with him and seemed so sophisticated. Married men were out of bounds, as far as I was concerned; having seen what Ingrid's affair with my step-father had done to my mother, I had no desire to break up a marriage. Neither, I am sure, did Mary. Leaving the morality issue aside, though, I didn't find older men attractive. I felt safer with people of my own age, boys who, like my brothers, would be friends and playmates – and photographers were usually pretty playful.

I was busy working with a photographer called Dudley Harris one morning in March 1964 when Cherry Marshall rang to tell me she had made an appointment for me at a casting session. It would take place at one o'clock in the Hilton Hotel, Park Lane, and the contact was Walter Shenson. I assumed it was an advertising-agency job. I was used to those interviews. They were ghastly, like a cattle market.

When I got there the usual models were clutching their portfolios, but when my turn came, I was surprised to see Dick Lester among the men in suits. I automatically assumed it was another commercial and asked him what product he was doing this time. He wouldn't say, which surprised me, but all became clear when I arrived home.

Cherry Marshall was soon on the phone to say that they wanted me. It was top secret and I wasn't supposed to tell a soul, but I had been offered a part in a Beatles film.

I panicked. 'No, I don't want to do it! I can't do it!' I wasn't an actress and had no aspirations in that direction. The idea of having to act and speak in front of a camera terrified me.

Cherry insisted I could do it; there was nothing to worry about. They knew I wasn't an actress, they wouldn't expect me to do anything I couldn't do. I had to play a schoolgirl, dressed in uniform. There were no lines and it was only two days' work. She wouldn't let me turn it down.

At that time Britain was in the early stages of Beatlemania. After years of hard slog in dingy Hamburg nightclubs, and at the Cavern in Liverpool, the Beatles had made it. In less than a year they had gone from being a talented group with a strong following in the north to major recording artists with millions of fans worldwide, fame, acclaim and the stardom that every rock star dreams of. The four boys with their floppy haircuts – John Lennon, Paul McCartney, George Harrison and Ringo Starr – had conquered Sweden, France, Spain and Italy; and before they started shooting this film, they took America by storm – a notoriously difficult task for British artists.

It had been a slow start in America. Three records they had released there had done nothing until the American news magazines *Time* and *Newsweek* had published articles about Beatlemania in Europe. Suddenly America was interested. 'I Want To Hold Your Hand' went straight to number one, and in February 1964 they were invited to appear on *The Ed Sullivan Show* in New York, the most prestigious chat-show in America. That night seventy-three million people watched – and afterwards George said proudly that he had been told no crime was reported while they were on.

Britain was equally transfixed. In September 1963 the Beatles' songs were number one in every bestseller chart there was. *Please Please Me* was the top-selling LP, 'Twist And Shout' was the number one EP and 'She Loves You' had outsold every other single. Before 'She Loves You' even had a title, thousands of copies had been ordered, and the day before it went on sale there were unprecedented advance orders of 500,000. They were all over the newspapers, even the serious broadsheets, they were mobbed everywhere they went, and at their concerts thousands of hysterical teenagers cried, swooned, charged the stage and screamed so loudly that no one could hear the music.

I was the exception. I didn't have any of the Beatles' records and hadn't paid much attention to them or their music. But, of course, the idea of meeting such famous people was exciting. I broke my vow of silence and confided in David Bailey, who insisted that I buy a copy of their album before I did the filming. Mary and I played *Please Please Me* in the flat on our Dansette record-player, and I really enjoyed it. My parents' music had never inspired me but I do remember thinking how exciting when the first free copy of *New Musical Express* fell out of their *Daily Express* one morning: news about music – what a good idea.

We had always had a radiogram at home, in a large mahogany cabinet in the drawing room. When you opened the doors a dim light fell on our record collection – about five LPs. Four were ghastly but the fifth was Glenn Miller and his orchestra, and in the absence of anything else, we played that as I grew up. As a teenager I liked Cliff Richard, Elvis, Ricky Nelson, Buddy Holly, Roy Orbison and the Everly Brothers.

The instructions for my first day's filming on *A Hard Day's Night* were to go to Paddington station and meet three other models, who had also been cast as schoolgirls, under the clock at eight a.m., then join a train half-way down platform one. About ten minutes out of London it ground to an unexpected halt at a tiny station, deserted but for four familiar figures, who leapt on board and bounced into our compartment to say hello. They introduced themselves fleetingly, one made a crack and we all laughed, then they bounced out. They were enchanting and we cursed our luck to be meeting them in gymslips.

The film crew had taken over the train and most of the action happened on the move. It was supposedly about two days in the life of the Beatles and the train scene began with the four racing into a station, chased by hundreds of screaming fans, then jumping into a train that pulled away leaving the fans forlornly on the platform. They had done that bit at Marylebone station before they met up with us. We were involved in the action once they had supposedly jumped into the carriage.

The train took us to Cornwall and back, not that I remember much of the scenery. I spent most of the day watching the action, chatting to everyone during the breaks and waiting to do my bit. The Beatles were so funny together, so quick-witted, and their laughter was infectious. I couldn't understand half of what they said because of the thick Liverpudlian accent – a revelation to me: I'd never heard anything like it. It was impossible to be in their company and not be helpless with laughter.

On first impressions, John seemed more cynical and brash than the others, Ringo the most endearing, Paul was cute, and George, with velvet brown eyes and dark chestnut hair, was the best-looking man I'd ever seen. At the break for lunch I found myself sitting next to him, whether by accident or design I have never been sure. We were both shy and spoke hardly a word to each other, but being close to him was electrifying.

As the train neared London and the filming was winding down I felt sad that such a magical day was ending. It had been pure joy and I wanted to capture it for ever. As if George had known what I was thinking, he said, 'Will you marry me?' I laughed, as I had at all the Beatles' jokes. I scarcely allowed myself to wonder why he had said it or whether he might feel as I did. Then he said, 'Well, if you won't marry me, will you have dinner with me tonight?'

I was thrown. Was he serious or just playing around? I felt awkward and said I couldn't, I had a boyfriend, but I was sure my boyfriend would love to meet him – maybe we could all go out. George didn't think so, so we said our farewells at the station and disappeared into the night.

I went home and told Mary Bee I thought I'd made a huge

mistake. She thought I was insane – 'And what's more,' she said, concluding the tirade, 'you don't even like Eric!'

The next day I was at a very unglamorous catalogue shoot with a model called Pat Booth in a dingy basement studio in Wardour Street. We'd been working together the day I heard I'd got the film job (and had indiscreetly told her, too), and she was dying to know how it had gone and what the Beatles were like. I told her that George Harrison had asked me out and I'd turned him down. We were sitting in a corner trying to put on our makeup. 'Are you crazy?' she said. 'You must be out of your mind.' I explained that the person I was going out with wouldn't like it. 'Of course he wouldn't,' said Pat, 'but he'll get over it. And if he doesn't, so what? You don't turn down the chance of going out with George Harrison. It would be such an adventure. You've got to go.'

Pat became a close friend, and if ever I don't know what to do about a situation I ask her. She's always so decisive and I'm the opposite. She's convinced it's because she's a Taurus, the bull, and I'm a Pisces, the fish that swims in both directions.

The second day's filming was about ten days later. I wasn't confident that George would ask me out again but I wanted him to, which made me realise I had to do something about Eric. We'd been going out together for about nine months and I didn't love him. He was very kind and sweet and gave me a lot of work, but that wasn't enough, and as long as he was my boyfriend I couldn't go out with anyone else. Until now, that hadn't been a problem: I hadn't fancied anyone else. But George was different. I had to tell Eric it was over and I dreaded it. I thought I'd feel trapped if I told him in his flat, so I arranged to meet him in the West End and we went to a restaurant near Oxford Street. He might have sensed what was coming. When I'd told David Bailey about the film job, he had predicted I would fall in love with Paul McCartney and had told Eric he'd be left on his own. Eric was so upset: he cried and said he'd throw himself under a bus. I felt cruel, and I was worried about him but I couldn't change the way I felt. In the end I had to get up and walk away.

I saw George again on 12 March, a few days before my twentieth birthday. He had turned twenty-one the month before. There was a press photocall at Twickenham Studios and each of us schoolgirls had to stand behind a Beatle and pretend to do their hair. I made a bee-line for George. He seemed pleased to see me and asked how my boyfriend was. I told him I'd dumped him. He grinned and asked me to have dinner with him.

We went to the Garrick Club in Covent Garden with the charismatic Brian Epstein, the Beatles' manager. He was slightly older, better educated and more worldly-wise than John, Paul, George and Ringo were. He was also much more to them than a manager: he had discovered them in Liverpool, shaped them and harnessed their talent but he had also become a father figure to them and kept a close eye on everything they did. They loved him, trusted him and did nothing without his say-so. I didn't resent his presence on our first date – he was good company and seemed to know everything about wine, food and London restaurants. And perhaps if George and I, two very young, very shy people, had been on our own in such a grown-up restaurant, it would have been too intense. As it was, we had a lovely evening and sat side by side on a banquette listening to Brian, hardly daring to touch each other's hand. I couldn't wait to get home and tell Mary all about it.

And that was it. We started going out together and on my twentieth birthday, on 17 March, I took him home to Strathmore Road to meet my family. We arrived in George's beautiful silver E-type Jaguar and everyone was excited. David and Boo were away at boarding-school but the others were at home and they were all Beatles fans. George sat down and told one funny story after another. He was so easy and friendly with everyone, and it was the same every time we went home. My mother adored him, and so did my brothers and sisters. Jenny used to wear horrible pink National

Health glasses, which she hated, and George suggested she should wear contact lenses. He said John Lennon had just started using them, and they had made a huge difference to his life – so she followed suit. He also taught her the chords to some Buddy Holly songs she was trying to play on the guitar.

At Easter George and I went to Ireland for the weekend with John and Cynthia Lennon. We flew from Heathrow to Shannon airport in a six-seater propeller plane – my ears were in agony all the way and I have never been so relieved to feel an aeroplane touch down. We were going to the Dromoland Castle Hotel, in County Clare, where President John F. Kennedy had stayed – miles from anywhere with beautiful gardens and landscaping – where Brian had booked us a magnificent suite. The trip had been kept secret from the press, but John and George were in disguise and Cynthia and I walked well behind them at the airports – I was nursing an ugly, painful stye on my eyelid.

As we swept up the Dromoland Castle drive there was neither a camera nor a journalist to be seen, but that evening the manager rang to warn us that reporters from the *Daily Mirror* had found us and booked into the hotel.

The next morning more were hanging around outside our windows. It was the first time I had experienced anything like it, and I found it quite intriguing. Whenever we tried to go anywhere they followed us, clicking away with their cameras and shouting to us for a comment. There were no mobile phones at that time, so the reporters used the hotel phones to send their stories to their offices and the hotel manager tapped the lines and let us listen. They were saying the most stupid things about us. We had to get away – but how, without being hounded? Then the enterprising manager came up with an idea. Cynthia and I were bundled out of the hotel's service entrance inside wicker laundry baskets. Neither the most dignified departure from a five-star hotel nor the most elegant arrival in a departure lounge but, under the circumstances, certainly the most effective.

Cynthia and John had met at art college in Liverpool – he was the first of the group to have a steady girlfriend – and when she became pregnant unexpectedly in 1962 they married. However, Brian was worried about the effect John's marriage might have on the band's popularity, so Cynthia and baby Julian were kept secret. It must have been hard on her: she had always enjoyed watching them at the Cavern but suddenly she wasn't allowed anywhere near a live performance. When John was away, which he was a lot in the early years, she wasn't allowed to travel with him. And she had a grim time at home. John had been brought up from the age of three by his mother's sister, Mimi, and in the early days when John and Cynthia had little money, they had lived with her. She was a bit of a snob and I gather she didn't think Cynthia good enough for her surrogate son.

I liked Cynthia, but of all the Beatle wives and girlfriends I found her the most difficult to make friends with. She and I came from such different backgrounds; she had no career, she was a young mother, and we had no point of reference apart from our attachment to a Beatle. She wasn't like my friends, who enjoyed a giggle and some fun: she was rather serious, and often, I thought, behaved more like John's mother than his wife. I tended to leave her to her own devices but invited her to join me for shopping. I think she felt a bit out of her depth in the smart, sophisticated circles in which the Beatles were now moving in London. And I don't think it helped that John thought I looked like Brigitte Bardot, or that I got on so well with him. There was a rumour – I don't know where it came from – that John and I had an affair, and I suppose Cynthia may have believed there was something in it. It was completely untrue: we never had an affair. I wouldn't have dreamt of it and neither, I am sure, would John.

Ringo's girlfriend, Maureen Cox, was also from Liverpool. She was a fan whose dream had come true. She had started out as one of the hundreds of teenage girls who queued day after day at the

Cavern to get close to the front of the stage for the best possible view of the Beatles and in the hope that they might catch the eye of one. Every fan had a favourite, and Ringo was hers. She wouldn't have called herself a fanatic – she would only queue, she said, for two or three hours while some girls were there all day – but she did run after Ringo in the street one day to get his autograph when she spotted him getting out of his car. She was seventeen, had just left school and was learning to be a hairdresser. Then, one day, it happened for her. Again, she and I had little in common but she was jolly and friendly, more relaxed than Cynthia. We got on but I felt there was definitely a north–south divide among the wives and girlfriends. And I had the definite impression that the girls from the north felt they had a prior claim to 'the boys'.

Jane Asher was the girlfriend with whom I felt most at home, but because we both had heavy work commitments she was also the one I saw least. She came from a professional family, had grown up in London and, like me, had been privately educated. The family lived in Wimpole Street; her father was a psychiatrist and her mother a music teacher – her brother Peter became half of the pop duo Peter and Gordon. She was three years younger than me but we got on well and I've always been pleased to see her whenever we've met. She had been an actress since the age of five and had met Paul when she was seventeen, shortly before I met George. She had gone to interview him, as a celebrity writer, for the *Radio Times*, and they fell in love at first sight. Soon afterwards Paul moved into a room at the Ashers' house.

In May Brian arranged a holiday for us all. He split us up into fours, and that was usually the way we holidayed from then on. Paul and Jane, Ringo and Maureen went off to the Virgin Islands, while John and Cynthia, George and I went to Tahiti, where we planned to spend four weeks island-hopping on a boat. It was a good way to split the group. John and Paul were the closest in some ways and immensely creative together, but they clashed if they were in each other's pockets for too long. We were travelling under pseudonyms – as we always did, although the names changed. On this occasion Paul was Mr Manning, Jane Miss Ashcroft, Ringo was Mr Stone and Maureen Miss Cockcroft. John and Cynthia were Mr and Mrs Leslie, George was Mr Hargreaves and I was Miss Bond. To complete the disguise, Cynthia and I wore wigs and dark glasses – and, to my intense irritation, I had another stye. John called it my 'holiday eye'.

We took a private plane to Amsterdam, and from there flew to Honolulu via Vancouver, where we had to refuel. We spent just twenty minutes on the ground, but by the time we reached Honolulu our cover was blown. For the two days we had to wait before we caught the connection to Tahiti we escaped to a secluded beach in the north of the island where no one knew us – or so we thought. It was incredibly hot so George asked me to cut his hair. When I'd done it I chucked the trimmings into the waste-paper basket. I heard later that the cleaners had found them and were the proud owners of George's locks. There and then I learnt to think like a spy, leaving no trace.

When we arrived in Tahiti, a wall of heat hit us as we stepped off the plane. The little airport looked as though it had been carved out of the jungle, and some prettily dressed local girls were waiting to greet us with rum punch in coconuts and garlands of frangipani flowers that they draped round our necks. It was terribly exotic and exciting. But it was followed by a long wait in the hot, steamy lounge, for the person who would take us to Papeete where we were due to meet the boat. Because Brian had organised everything, none of us knew the details. We never did: we set off like small children, trusting that the grown-ups would have everything under control. At that moment, though, it was as if Nanny had vanished. We were helpless. Finally someone led us to a vehicle and we were on our way.

The boat wasn't quite what we'd expected. It was very basic, a rather elderly wooden fishing-boat with no stabilisers. The locals were so excited to be taking us on the long trip around the islands that they had given the generator a coat of paint. The boat was crewed by six burly Tahitians with few teeth and no English, so communication was minimal but we climbed aboard, made ourselves comfortable in our cabins and, in the late afternoon, set sail. It was absolutely glorious until we were out of the harbour heading for one of the islands.

Suddenly the wind got up, the sea grew rough, the heavens opened and we found ourselves in the middle of a tropical storm. The boat rolled from side to side and rode up and down on huge waves that drenched us as they crashed over the hull. Great bolts of forked lightning lit the sky, followed by ear-splitting cracks of thunder. We went down into the cabin to get out of the rain, which was coming down in stair-rods, but the stink of new paint on the generator mixed with diesel fumes from the engine made me feel so sick that I had to go back on deck. George and Cynthia stayed below but John couldn't stomach it either and we lay on the deck, holding on for dear life, watching the crew wrestle with the sails. After more than an hour the storm eased, and as darkness fell the sea calmed and the wind dropped. We felt so exhausted and so ill that we went straight to our bunks and slept.

The next morning we looked out of the porthole to find we were in Paradise. We had dropped anchor in the lee of a beautiful coral island in a tranquil turquoise lagoon, and the crew was swimming in it, spearing fish for lunch. I wanted to stay there for ever. The water was aquamarine and so crystal clear that the seabed appeared no more than four inches from the surface and the shoals of multi-coloured fish were as visible as if they had been in a tank. Clean white sandy beaches and coconut palms beckoned. We swam and snorkelled, sailed from island to island and sunbathed; we read books and the boys played their guitars. At night, after the sun had gone down in a crimson sky, we ate and drank under the stars, then lay in our bunks listening to the soothing sound of wood creaking and the rigging tapping the mast. Days slid by as we sailed from one island to the next. Each time we lifted the anchor to leave, dolphins leapt into the air to escort us to a break in a coral reef, playing beside the boat until we were in open sea when they would leap again as, if waving farewell.

We had so much fun – it felt as though we did nothing but laugh. On one of the islands, John and George borrowed our black wigs, dressed up in some oilskin macs they had bought in Papeete and made a funny little 8-mm film about a missionary – John – who comes out of the ocean to convert the natives.

After four weeks we took a flying-boat back to Tahiti, then picked up a Pan Am 707 on its way from New Zealand to Los Angeles. Incredibly, we were the only passengers and slept lying flat on the floor; there were no flat-bed seats in those days, not even in first class.

When we arrived at Heathrow the press were waiting for us, and I was amazed to see in the next day's newspaper photos how healthy we looked. Days later I was booked by *Vogue* to be photographed by David Bailey wearing skimpy clothes showing long brown limbs. They were some of the best he ever took of me.

George and I spent as much time as we could together. I hated having to go off on location for photo shoots as much as I hated him going away on tour. I loved being with him. He was so beautiful and so funny. We would go out with Mary Bee and her boyfriend to clubs like the Ad Lib, which was full of musicians, or Annabel's, which George liked because it was members only and he could eat Steak Diane and drink fine wines, or we would go to see Jean-Claude and Belinda, or Tony and Mafalda Hall – Tony was a DJ, working for the BBC, and Mafalda was his French wife. Their home was in Green Street, which was where George was living when I first met him and they had been neighbours. Tony played great American music on his programme and at home.

Mary Bee had a friend called Ronan O'Reilly, who was embarking on something exciting: we were told to turn our radio on to a certain wavelength at a certain time in the morning. Radio Caroline, the first pirate radio station, was broadcasting from a ship ten miles offshore.

Other friends we saw were Dick Polak, a photographer, and Edina Ronay, the actress daughter of Egon, the restaurant guru. Dick and Edina lived on the top floor of a house in Redcliffe Square with no lift and no remote door release. When you rang the bell, they would look out of the window to find out who it was, and if they liked the look of you they would throw down the keys.

I almost forgot that George was a famous pop star. As far as I was concerned he was just my boyfriend. I saw the Beatles performing for the first time on *Ready Steady Go*. It was *the* pop show on television, presented by Cathy McGowan, and everyone watched it. There was George, doing what he did. I couldn't believe he looked so different, almost as if he was in uniform. Until then I'd had no experience of people who adopted a stage persona that was entirely different from the private one.

I had never met anyone like George before, or experienced anything like the glamorous world he inhabited. One weekend we went to Paris with Mary Bee and her boyfriend and stayed at the George V. Mary and I arrived ahead of the boys and were shown to a massive suite with sumptuous furnishings and huge beds. We skipped from room to room, saying, 'There's a room, and there's another room, and another room, and another – and all of them for us.' Then we ordered tea and had hysterics when it arrived on a silver salver, everything so grand and grown-up.

It was very different from life in Oakley Street.

I remember taking George there for the first time. Mary's and my little bedroom with twin beds was directly off a tiny square hall. When we came in, Mary was sitting up in bed reading a book and wearing a hat. She didn't normally wear hats in bed; she didn't normally wear hats full stop. The poor girl had had no idea I was bringing George home, and when we popped our heads round the bedroom door, I'm not sure which of them got more of a fright. He wasn't impressed by our choice of music. We played him 'My Boy Lollipop' by the Jamaican artist Millie Small, which we both thought was great. He couldn't believe we liked such an awful song.

Whether it was our choice of music or the cramped conditions, George didn't like coming to the flat and he told me to look for somewhere bigger for Mary and me to share, which he would rent. I found an adorable house in Ovington Mews, a cul-de-sac just off the Brompton Road. You drove into the mews through a huge archway and the house was near the end. It had a small drawing room and kitchen downstairs, two bedrooms and a bathroom above; tiny, but perfect for Mary and me, and we were happy there. This was where Mary and I learnt to cook in earnest, and if George was coming we would make a surprise dinner, which meant endless phone calls to Mary's mother.

The house was very close to George's own flat in William Mews, Knightsbridge, which Brian Epstein had bought for him and Ringo to share. Paul had a flat in the same building, while John and Cynthia were in Emperors Gate, not far from the Cromwell Road. One day I was in George's flat on my own and someone rang the bell. I opened the door and a weird-looking man tried to force his way in. I didn't know whether he was a salesman or a Jehovah's Witness, but he was most insistent. I said, 'This is outrageous,' and he burst out laughing. It was Paul in disguise.

The Beatles were away on tour for much of 1964 so our time together was intermittent. Soon after we had got back from Tahiti, they flew to Denmark, then Hong Kong, Australia and New Zealand. And the day we moved into Ovington Mews, in August, they set off for two months in America – the longest, most ambitious and most exhausting tour they ever did. They went to twenty-four cities in the States and Canada, played thirty-one concerts – and each one was sold out. Everywhere they went they had to be escorted by police and motorcycle outriders. Screaming fans were everywhere, invading the stage, invading their hotels, invading their lives, and no one could hear the music, either on or off stage. As their US agent remarked at the time, 'The Beatles and Elvis are in showbusiness. After that, any comparison is just a joke. No one, before or since, has had the crowds the Beatles had.'

George hated it. Even when he got away from the fans, he said, there were screaming policemen and lord mayors, their wives, hotel managers and their entourage. The only place he got any peace was locked into the bathroom in his hotel suite. I think the Beatles were quite frightened of their fans, who always wanted to touch them. They might easily have been crushed under such a weight of humanity.

I was frightened of the fans, too. I used to get hateful letters, particularly from American girls. Each one claimed she was George's rightful girlfriend and if I didn't leave him alone she would put a curse on me or kill me. One night Belinda, Mary Bee and I – I think Cynthia too – went to see the Beatles play at the Hammersmith Odeon. Terry Doran, who was an old Liverpool friend of John and worked as his assistant, had parked John's Mini at the front of the building and we left at the beginning of the last number to avoid getting caught up in the crowds at the end. As we went out through one of the side exits, about five girls followed us. I was wearing a disguise but they must have known who I was because as soon as we got into the alleyway that ran down the side of the building they set upon me and started to kick me. I called Terry, who grabbed one of them and wrenched her off me, but she fought like a wildcat and pulled out a chunk of his hair.

The fans might not have liked my relationship with George but the media were delighted by it and I was more in demand than ever. So, although I was always sad when George left to go on tour, I was busy with modelling jobs. I worked for *Vogue* with Ronald Traeger,

Tatler with Jeanloup Sieff, *Vanity Fair* with Peter Rand, and the American magazine *16*. I made TV commercials for Dop shampoo, in which I drove through a car wash in an open-topped car, and another for Smith's crisps – plus masses for the fashion pages of newspapers.

I was also busy with the vital task of finding a cleaner. To Mary's and my amazement, the only person who replied to our advert was a male ballet dancer. He wasn't quite Nureyev but he was terrific with a duster.

I counted the days until George was due back, just as I had counted the days until the end of term at boarding-school. Once he got back very early in the morning and jumped into bed to wake me, smelling of BOAC and exotic long-haul flights.

On the last leg of their marathon American tour, the Beatles had met Bob Dylan in New York. They had been thrilled – Dylan was their hero and mine – and George couldn't wait to tell us about him and how he had turned them on to marijuana. A mutual friend, Al Aronowitz, who worked for the *Saturday Evening Post*, had brought Dylan to their hotel. He had apparently misheard a line in their song 'I Want To Hold Your Hand': where they sang, 'I can't hide', he had heard, 'I get high', and had assumed they were seasoned drug-users. 'Right guys,' he said, as he walked into their suite. 'I've got some really good grass.' So Dylan had rolled a joint, they had opened a few bottles of wine and had a very jolly party. George was full of it: they had laughed all night.

Somehow George had managed to get hold of some marijuana while he was away and had brought it back for us to try. Mary and I were complete beginners so George rolled a joint and told us we had to inhale deeply. We passed it round and round, the three of us, each taking drags. It was quite dark in the room, we were listening to music, chatting away, until all of a sudden we were roaring with laughter and realised we were stoned. Then we decided it would be a good idea to go and visit someone – I can't remember who or why.

Outside one of us bumped into a dustbin and we were laughing again – we just couldn't stop. Everything seemed hilarious.

Between tours there were always holidays, and one of my happiest was spent with Brian Epstein in his favourite place in the South of France, the Hôtel Cap Estrelle near Eze. I think he used to go there with his parents when he was a little boy, and George and I went with him several times. It was a beautiful hotel right on the edge of the water. My mother still has the postcard I sent her during our first trip: 'Dear Mummy, Colin, Jenny, Paula, David and Boo. Our hotel is on the right with the spot on it. It is fabulous and at one time was privately owned as a house. Where I have drawn the line is the road. The weather is so hot and the food is great,' beside which George wrote '(For those who like French food)' and then I take over again: 'George has a bad tummy at the moment.'

We had the most amazing time. Brian took us to fabulous restaurants and to the casino in Monte Carlo, which in those days was terribly glamorous. Everyone dressed up – the women in cocktail dresses with little bits of fur, and men in dinner jackets – and a huge amount of money changed hands. Brian was a rather debonair gambler, successful too. No matter which table he played at he won; very James Bond – and he looked the part. He made everything possible for us; everything glorious . . .

CHAPTER FIVE

Mrs Harrison

The fans were making life intolerable for us, and not only when the Beatles were performing. None of them could go into or out of their flats without being grabbed, mauled and begged for autographs at any time of day or night. Brian decided they needed to move and asked the band's accountant, Dr Walter Strach, to find suitable houses. Walter's home was in Weybridge, Surrey, thirty miles south-west of London, so it was to that area that they migrated.

John and Ringo bought grand houses in St George's Hill, an exclusive estate that housed the rich and famous in safety and seclusion. George didn't like that idea and chose instead a modern four-bedroom bungalow in Esher, called Kinfauns, about fifteen or twenty minutes' drive from the others. Paul couldn't bring himself to move so far out of London and bought a house in St John's Wood, convenient for the EMI recording studios in Abbey Road.

Kinfauns had been built in the early 1960s in what had previously been the walled vegetable garden of Claremont Girls School, which had once belonged to Clive of India. With the addition of a fourteen-feet-high gate, it was very private. The gate was operated manually, though, and it wasn't long before the marauding fans discovered where George lived. Hordes of girls used to hang about outside, waiting for me to go out. If the gate was ever left open, they would come into the grounds. They also discovered that if they put stones into the sliding mechanism it wouldn't shut properly and they could squeeze through. Since we never locked any doors, the occasional one got into the house. I kept finding clothes missing and once George gave me a beautiful Piaget watch that disappeared. I presume some fan took it. Once when my brothers David and Boo were staying they woke up to find two girls in the drawing room. David was delighted.

The house was surrounded by three-quarters of an acre of garden, which Maurice, the gardener, looked after. Neither George nor I knew anything about gardening and had no particular interest in it. The only thing I remember planting was a climbing rose in the area by the swimming-pool where there were white wooden slats to screen it off. I was so thrilled when it grew big and beautiful that I took a photo one summer's day of the two of us standing in front of it. I went to great pains to set up a tripod but George got bored waiting for the shutter to close and it caught him looking away.

I was living in Ovington Mews when George bought Kinfauns but I helped him furnish it. We went off and bought big black leather sofas and other furniture from Habitat, which Terence Conran had recently opened in the Fulham Road. It was one of the first shops to specialise in good modern design and had everything from beds to butter knives. We bought a teak dining-table and chairs, and a pine table for the kitchen, which was where we ate most of the time. When the lease on Ovington Mews came up for renewal, Mary Bee moved to Cornwall. She had had a disastrous affair and found herself a job as an au pair by way of distraction. Meanwhile I moved into a little flat that George rented for me in South Audley Street.

He was still doing a lot of touring – during the first three years that I knew him the Beatles averaged three long tours in each, one British, one American and one that took in several other countries. When they weren't touring they were recording. The Beatles were producing about three singles a year, and one album, which represented many hours of studio time. They were often in the studio from eleven in the morning until eleven at night, if not midnight.

Eventually I abandoned the flat in London, where I was lonely on my own, and moved in with George. London was only forty-five minutes away – a quick whiz down the A3 – easy to get to for work or play. The latter meant parties, clubs, discos and dinners, theatre sometimes and films. Cubby Broccoli, the James Bond producer, owned a small private viewing theatre and we were invited to whatever new film was showing. We sat there with Scotch and Coke and the finest smoked-salmon sandwiches. Also we liked to go to Parkes, a restaurant in Beauchamp Place, where the Irish chef Tom cooked fantastic food and decorated it with flowers. He would get tulips and turn them inside out – whence the line in one of John Lennon's songs about 'bent-back tulips'. We usually went out as a group, with other Beatles and friends, and often my sister Jenny was with us and her boyfriend, Mick Fleetwood.

About a year after I'd moved in we converted the garage at Kinfauns into a big sitting room with a little one off it as a projection room so that we could show films. I was the chief projectionist but I think the only movie we ever saw was *The Producers*. We watched it all the time – George could recite nearly every line. On television, we loved *Rowan and Martin's Laugh-In*, the American comedy series that made Goldie Hawn famous. Later *Monty Python's Flying Circus* was a favourite – Eric Idle was one of George's heroes and often came to Friar Park. And we listened to Motown and other new artists from America – Marvin Gaye, Martha and the Vandellas, the Ronettes, the Byrds and Dylan.

The focal point of our new sitting room was a huge circular brick fireplace inspired by Salvador Dalí, whose work we liked, and we asked a Dutch couple, Simon Posthuma and Marijke Koger, known as the Fool, to paint it for us. They were talented, creative people, who wore outfits they had designed and made in velvet, richly decorated with beads and sequins. We must have got to know them through Robert Fraser, who owned an art gallery in Duke Street, or John Dunbar, Marianne Faithfull's ex-husband who ran the Indica Gallery in Mason's Court, St James's. They made amazing clothes for us all, and later for the Apple shop in Baker Street, which they also designed. On the night before the opening they took a bunch of art students to paint psychedelic murals on the outside of the building.

The painting they did for us at Kinfauns was stunning. It took months to complete and they stayed with us while they were working on it. I so wish we could have taken it with us when we moved but of course we couldn't.

We had also covered the outside of the house with graffiti. The walls had been plain white when we moved in, so we bought some cans of spray paint and spent many happy hours cheering them up. When friends came we would give them a can and they added a bit here and there. There were flowers and psychedelic patterns in every colour of the rainbow. Mick Jagger and Marianne Faithfull came to see us one day when we were out and wrote 'Mick and Marianne were here' in large letters on one of the walls. Sadly, when we left Kinfauns the new occupants painted over it.

In Esher we had a wonderful cleaner called Margaret. Whenever we had to go to Liverpool to visit George's mother she would have macaroni cheese ready when we got back. She used to love John Lennon visiting and would say to him, 'Have you got any of those lovely pills?' and John would give her an upper. Afterwards she would vacuum like a maniac – very different from her normal self. She was adorable. She believed that there was nothing beyond the sky and the clouds, and that the world was encased in a bubble. When she saw the moon landing and men walking on it, she refused to believe it was happening.

When George and I first got together I wasn't a good cook but always quite enthusiastic – I knew there was something better than school food and even Lilie's fare. I tried to make the sorts of things I imagined boys from the north would like – shepherd's pie, roast beef and Yorkshire pudding – and then George and I became vegetarian, which gave me a whole new interest. Someone gave us a book that talked about veal farming and how cruelly the calves were treated. They were kept in tiny crates in the dark, unable to turn round, and photographs showed them licking the metal bars. It was then that we decided we would eat no more meat.

Being vegetarian at that time was quite a challenge. There was so little to choose from, nothing ready-made and no meat-free equivalent of steak or sausages that you could cook with minimal preparation. I had to create things myself and discovered I loved doing it; I cooked for our friends, George's family and mine, and anyone who came to see or stay with us. We gave lunch and supper parties and I enjoyed buying the food. I would go into the health-food shop in Esher for grains and pulses, vegetables and fruit. I had hundreds of cookery books – for a while I read nothing else. I was vegetarian for about seven years but George remained so until the day he died and would not allow meat or fish to be cooked or eaten in his house.

We spent a lot of time in the kitchen – it was the heart of the house. I remember George sitting at the table with his guitar, writing the song that became 'My Sweet Lord'. When it came out as a single and went to number one, he was taken to court because an American group called the Chiffons recorded a song called 'He's So Fine', and the song's music publisher claimed that George had stolen it. It was tricky for him. I knew he had written it – I was there when he was working on it – but he had to take his guitar to court and play in front of the judge to prove that the melody was original and not based on their song. The judge found him guilty of 'subconscious plagiarism'. After that we never had a radio playing in the house in case he was unconsciously influenced by a song he had heard.

His guitars were always left around the house and in any spare moment he would pick one up and play. When John, Paul, Ringo or any other musician appeared – as they often did – they all played. But George would never play a complete song. He played what was in his head, or he would be working on new chords or a new song, I never knew which, and weeks later you would hear a song on tape. I loved listening to him, loved the sound of the guitar in the house. Sometimes I would start to talk and he'd be so deep in thought about the lyrics or the melody he was writing that he wouldn't answer. We'd be in the same room but he wasn't really with me: he was in his head. Most of the time I didn't mind. I'd think, Oh, good, he's writing a new song – he was always happiest when he was being creative.

Sometimes songs would come to him in the middle of the night and he would wake up in the morning and immediately start to play so he didn't forget it; he would change chords, then stop because something didn't sound right. John and Paul wrote most of their songs together – they sparked off each other – but George wrote on his own. He composed the melody first but as he was not formally trained he couldn't write the music down; he would play it and play it so it was fixed in his mind, then record it. The words came later. Sometimes I tried to help if he couldn't find a word to rhyme with another, but most of the time he did it alone, writing on the backs of envelopes, anything that came to hand.

He composed all over the world, wherever he happened to be, and he would play me a tape-recording of the things he had written – he didn't sing them to me with the guitar – and I always thought how much better it sounded like that than the finished product.

A lot of fan mail came to the house and when George's mother was down from Liverpool she would take it away and answer it. In the meantime it would stack up, mountains of envelopes, in cardboard boxes. I'll never forget coming home one day and finding the boxes all over the floor, the letters scattered far and wide. It looked as though we had been burgled. As I put it back I noticed that one envelope had been opened. It was addressed to Korky, our adorable white Persian cat – named after the character in the *Dandy* comic – and contained a ball of catnip, the herb cats go mad about. Clever thing, he'd found and opened his own fan mail.

Irritatingly, Korky seemed to prefer life in the girls' school next door, but perhaps that was because I was away so much – I was working regularly in Paris. I did a lot for *Elle*, and a few pages for American *Vogue*, where I met Diana Vreeland, its long-time editor-in-chief. Before that she had been fashion editor of *Harpers Bazaar* for twenty-five years and was a formidable woman. I was fascinated by her eyes: she put Vaseline on the bones above them. She wore her black hair scraped back and was very tall, thin and grand. I was working for Bailey on that shoot and because I was not eating much, I passed out on some steps outside the studio and missed my flight home. When I finally got back to Esher I found George's brother Pete and his wife Pauline installed in the house. They had come to have their holidays at Kinfauns. I was so annoyed; I made dinner for them and they wouldn't eat it because they said they only ate at 6 o'clock.

I became very fond of George's parents. They were quite short and very Liverpudlian. Harold drove buses and Louise worked part-time at a greengrocer's. She had always been supportive of George – she had bought him his first guitar when he was fourteen. She didn't object to the long hair, the winklepickers or the jeans he made tighter with her sewing-machine. George was their youngest child. His sister, also Louise, had emigrated to America but wrote often, telling him to get a proper job; his eldest brother, Harry, was a fitter and Peter a panel-beater. Harold had not wanted George to leave school so young: he thought education was the way to success. He had wanted him to take an apprenticeship like his brothers, and was afraid that he would never make a living as a musician. But his mother was all for it, and was one of the Beatles' staunchest supporters. All she wanted for her children was that they should be happy, and she recognised that nothing made George quite as happy as making music.

George was generous to his family – he loved them. He bought his parents a bungalow, which they were thrilled with. He took me to see the house they had had before, the one in which he had grown up, and it was in a very poor part of town. The bungalow always had that distinctive new-house smell, and had a nice little garden. We would go and see them for tea, but it wasn't tea as I knew it – not tea and biscuits or cake.

It was only when I went to his parents' house that I realised George had been brought up very differently from me. Because he and I always had a cup of tea in the afternoon and dinner at eight or nine in the evening I had assumed that this was the way he had always lived but, of course, he had not. His family held their knives like pens and 'tea' consisted of cold ham or pork pie, tomatoes cut in half, pickled beetroot and salad cream, with sliced white bread. They had it at six o'clock and later in the evening there was tea and biscuits. They drank little alcohol – his father had an occasional beer. I remember taking them with me on a trip to Paris, just the three of us, and giving them dinner on a boat on the Seine. They loved it.

Drink hadn't been a big part of my life before I met George. I might have had wine with Eric Swayne – there was a lovely restaurant called Bistro Vino just across the road from my flat and we ate there quite often – but I drank little. George wasn't a wine drinker until he arrived in London where Brian Epstein introduced him to it. When we went to places like Annabel's I would write down the names of some of the wines Brian ordered, which we had enjoyed, like Châteauneuf du Pape, Clos de Vougeot and Nuits St Georges.

Brian changed things for all of the Beatles, taught them more sophisticated ways. He came from Liverpool too, but a smart area – his parents owned a well-established furniture shop in which he had opened a music department, called NEMS, North End Music Store – and had been privately educated. He was also older than they were – twenty-seven when he started managing them – and more experienced in the ways of the world.

Unlike me, George was never hungry so we didn't eat much. We would have a cup of tea for breakfast, maybe fried eggs, then nothing for lunch. In the evening I was always ravenous. We were in the E-type one day, driving through Liphook or Hindhead, and stopped at a little tea room because I was starving. As we walked in an elderly lady said, 'It's three and six each, you know,' and we laughed because we must have looked as though we couldn't afford it.

George loved cars – all of the Beatles did. After the E-type he bought a silver Aston Martin DB5 and a Mini Moke, a little jeep-like car with no doors and no roof that was really fun in the summer; people would cruise up and down the King's Road in them, and George would often collect David and Boo from the station in it when they came to stay. He also bought a 1928 Rolls-Royce. My brother David remembers sitting in the bucket seat in the back of the DB5, asking me where Eric Swayne was and getting the most thunderous look from me. David worshipped George, who was his only male role model, and they would talk for hours. George would give him things to take to school, which would impress his friends, and if David liked a particular pair of trousers George wore, a shirt or a silk jacket, George gave it to him.

The combination of drinking a lot of alcohol and not eating enough took its toll on my body, and after a while I developed a kidney problem. It may have been something to do with the slimming pills, too, or the diet biscuits. Whatever the cause, it was very painful. My doctor, Tony Greenburgh, repeatedly gave me pills that would gradually improve things but the condition kept recurring. One day I heard about a weekend workshop being held in Wiltshire, somewhere near the Welsh border. I don't remember who was running it but there was some connection with Lord Harlech and, as George was away, I booked myself on to it.

I had met David Harlech many times; I knew his older children – Jane, Victoria, Alice and Julian Ormsby-Gore were friends, part of the King's Road set, and Jane married Michael Rainey who ran Hung On You, the boutique. I had been to the family house, Glyn, at Gwynedd in Wales, with them. There were always crowds of people there and David Harlech was a wonderful man. He had been British ambassador in Washington and a friend of the Kennedys. His wife had been killed in a car crash shortly before I met him and he was left to look after their five children on his own. He married again in 1969 and we were at the wedding, looking very hippieish. I was thrilled to meet the former Conservative prime minister Harold Macmillan.

On the way to the workshop I stopped at a chemist and filled yet another prescription for my kidney disorder. I arrived, not knowing a soul and thinking I'd made a big mistake. As we sat down for dinner the man next to me started to analyse my gesticulations. He said he hadn't been able to talk until the age of seven and had learnt to study people. Then someone else spoke and I realised my companions were healers. Another man asked how I was. I confessed that I wasn't feeling very well and he stopped me saying any more. He took out a crystal on a length of string, held it over me and, after a few minutes, said quietly, 'Yes, it's your kidneys.' I was amazed. I told him about the pills the doctor had prescribed, and he said, 'You can take them or not, as you like, but do *please* take these.' And he gave me a homeopathic remedy. I still don't know what caused the problem but I certainly know what fixed it. I took the remedy and have never had kidney trouble since.

★

In the summer of 1965 George was away on another long tour of America and I had my sister Jenny to stay at Kinfauns. I still had the flat in South Audley Street – but I spent little time there. The only problem was that George always seemed to be going away. Eventually he told Brian he'd had enough of touring. He hated it; they all hated it. They were sick of singing the same songs, which no one could hear because of the screaming; they were sick of the motorcades, the security, and the fans' insanity.

They were also sick of being away from home, particularly George. He became more and more lonely and phoned me every day, or if the time difference made it impossible he wrote. I couldn't have gone on tour with him because of my work, but Brian wouldn't have let me anyway because wives and girlfriends would have been too much for the security men. But Kenny Everett, the Radio 1 disc jockey, was in America with them, and every afternoon when we were sitting by the pool at Kinfauns we would turn on the radio and listen to the Beatles chatting to him.

At other times when he was touring I went away. In the summer of 1966 I asked Mary Bee and Belinda to come to the South of France with me. The Beatles' office arranged a flat for us in Monte Carlo, which, by a strange coincidence, belonged to Rudolf Nureyev – all the towels were monogrammed RN. The new sixties fashions we were wearing in London hadn't yet travelled further afield and everyone stared at us in our short skirts; we seemed to be the only people wearing them.

We felt awkward and uncomfortable so we hired a car and drove down the coast to St Tropez where no one turned a hair. It was much more fun than Monte Carlo, and we kept bumping into people we vaguely knew. One of them was Alexander Weymouth, then heir to the Marquess of Bath, who invited us to stay at his house in the hills for a few days. The rest of the time we stayed with my French friend ZouZou – I'd met her modelling a couple of years before – who took us to all the cool clubs where I gave the DJs the first pressing of 'Good Day Sunshine'. It was a lovely holiday – every morning the first one up would roll a joint and put on the Byrds, whose music filled the flat. The sun shone; we hadn't a care in the world.

George didn't want to meet new people or go to new places. He was happy to visit my old friends and our families, but he was wary of newcomers – unless they were musicians. One evening some months before we had been invited to dinner by a Mr Angardi, who ran the Asian Music Circle in London, and his English wife, who painted a large portrait of the two of us, for which we sat on several occasions. Mr Angardi wanted George to meet a sitar-player called Ravi Shankar. Ravi was well known in classical-music circles and a hero in his own country, India. They talked music all evening and George was awestruck.

Soon afterwards Ravi came to Kinfauns to give George a sitar lesson. At one point the phone rang and George put down the sitar, stood up and went to answer it, stepping over the sitar as he did so. Ravi whacked him sharply on the leg and said, 'You must have more respect for the instrument.'

The technique involved in playing the sitar is quite different from anything George had known before: he had to sit on the floor for hours, cross-legged, with the bowl of the gourd resting on the ball of his left foot. In no time at all his legs were in agony. However, he and Ravi became friends and a couple of months later Ravi invited George and me to India where he would be our guide for spiritual, musical and cultural lessons.

We flew to Bombay and I was overwhelmed by the noise, the heat and the mass of humanity. The road between the airport and the centre of the city was a seething tangle of cars, bicycles, carts, cows, dogs, tuk-tuks and people all going somewhere; the noise of car horns and bicycle bells was relentless. We stayed in the Taj Hotel, a grand Victorian building opposite the Gateway of India, and from

My parents' wedding at
Taunton in September 1942.

My mother *(centre, holding the dog)* and her twin brother,
John *(front left)*, with relatives at Howleigh House.

Colin, Paula, Jenny and me with Salome in Kenya before
our mother and Paula left for England.

The best bit about
having mumps
was that my
mother came to
visit me. I was so
thrilled to see her.

It was always fun on the rare occasions when Jenny and I modelled together.

I have no memory of this photograph being taken but I was given the print about five years ago by a friend who bought it at a Getty exhibition.

Me on a day off. George and I packed a basket one summer's day and went off into the countryside for a picnic with some friends.

Twiggy and me in Italian *Vogue*. The clothes were beautiful and we had such fun with our make-up.

When George was away on tour I invited his parents Harold and Louise to come to Paris with me.

The day we got married: 21 January 1966, at Epsom registry office.

Posing for a photo on our honeymoon. George didn't usually play with a cigarette in his hand!

Strolling along the beach in Barbados collecting shells with Venetia Cuninghame. She and her boyfriend joined us for the second week.

Sitting for Mrs Angardi, whose husband ran the Asian Music Circle. Sadly the painting disappeared from Friar Park.

The fireplace at Kinfauns which The Fool painted so beautifully.

Kinfauns, the bungalow in Esher, which we decided needed cheering up. Mick and Marianne arrived when we were out and left us a message below the window…

One of my favourite photos which George commissioned from American photographer Henry Grossman.

Paul, Ringo and John in Rishikesh. I didn't take many photos while we were there but I treasure the ones I did.

George in southern India in 1968. It was the last time I saw him looking so calm and relaxed.

Defiantly arriving at Kingston magistrates court after our drugs bust in March 1969. We had harmlessly smoked dope, but were treated as if we had been using hard drugs.

Friar Park on a very still day with its reflection in the lake. George's nephew, Paul Harrison – Harry's son – is on the stepping stones (*left*).

George, Ronnie and Krissie Wood, Kumar and Joss Stick, our Siamese cat, at Friar Park in the early morning. We had been up all night and were still going strong.

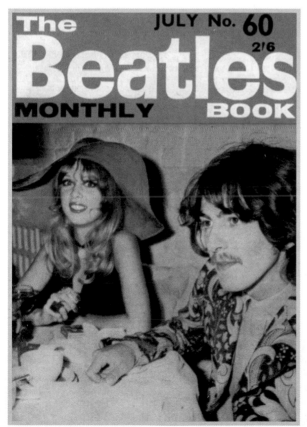

The Beatles
MONTHLY BOOK
JULY No. 60
2'6

George and me at a fashion show at the Arethusa restaurant in the King's Road. *The Beatles Monthly Book* ran for six and a half years.

Haight-Ashbury. They followed George as if he was the Pied Piper but then things suddenly turned nasty.

Frank Sinatra and George locked in conversation at the studios in Los Angeles, where we had just heard Sinatra record *My Way* with a full orchestra in one take.

our window, safely away from the mêlée, watched men and women going about their business. Ravi arranged yoga classes every morning, to teach George how to sit and hold the sitar, followed by several hours of lessons and practice with him and his other students.

After about a month we travelled together around India. Among many others, we met Ravi's spiritual guru, Tat Baba, who explained the law of *karma* to us both – the law of action and reaction, or cause and effect. Ravi was respected all over India: his students would bow down at his feet. He gave concerts across the country and people would sit, sometimes until four o'clock in the morning, to listen to him play, accompanied by Alla Raka on tablar and harmonium, while his students kept time. They counted the beat, which confused me: it was unlike western classical or even rock beat. I found it intensely moving: these were not just concerts – there was something profoundly spiritual about the experience. Ravi told us that sometimes he would go into a meditative state and not know consciously what he was playing.

We visited many jewels of India with him – the Taj Mahal, Jodhpur, Jaipur, Agra, Delhi, temples with ancient carvings of gods and goddesses in love, fighting and sometimes disguised as demons. We met some holy men who were more than a hundred years old, and sadhus who live in abject poverty. We visited the sacred ghats of Benaras, where people are cremated and have their ashes scattered in the Ganges. It was an astonishing sight to see bodies burning on the banks as we stepped out of the boat to walk up to a ghat. I was unable to look away, although I wanted to. We went to a festival of Kumbh Mela, the most sacred of all Hindu pilgrimages which attracts millions of people from all over India. We found ourselves in a crowd of about three thousand, most of whom had come on foot. We watched as the compound filled, pink dust rising, and in the distance I saw the maharajah riding an elephant, followed by a prince on a smaller one. They dismounted and sat on a dais where two *wallahs* kept them cool by wafting peacock-feather fans.

Meanwhile a man sat at our feet with a length of bamboo. Every now and then he would lean forward and stick his tongue into the hollow stick. Ravi told us there was a poisonous snake inside it: each time the man extended his tongue the snake struck, which gave him a high.

When everyone was assembled, we watched a religious play with wooden characters twenty feet high mounted on wheeled trolleys that moved back and forth across the arena. I felt as if I had been transported back two thousand years to Biblical times.

We ended the trip in Kashmir where we stayed on a houseboat, George and I, Ravi and his girlfriend Kamala. It was moored near a floating garden on Lake Dah and one night the man who owned the boat invited us to dinner at his house. As a Muslim, he didn't allow the women of the house to meet George or Ravi. When we arrived we were given tea, then Kamala and I were taken to meet the women. Communication was a bit limited as even Kamala didn't speak their language.

When we rejoined the men, we all sat down to dinner. Later the cook appeared and we heard his story. He had been bought as a child and castrated so that he could work with women in the kitchen.

The Beatles lived an unreal life and other musicians were the only people who shared it. They had found fame when they were so young – George was just seventeen when they were playing in Hamburg, Paul and John a couple of years older – and they had done nothing but work ever since. They hadn't had a chance to grow up in the way most people do, and from the moment fame hit, they had been so bombarded by fans and hangers-on, so cocooned by Brian Epstein, that they never knew whom they could trust.

In many respects they were still children. They had few real friends apart from each other, and when they were asked questions they could answer as one – they were so much on each other's wavelength. If one went to a gallery opening, they all went; if one bought a new car or a new house, they all did. If one seemed in danger of taking himself too seriously, the others knocked it out of him. They knew little about life and, with Brian looking after their every need, they had no reason to learn. Money was never a motivating force. They enjoyed the toys it bought them but they never had any idea how much they had. If they wanted something they asked Brian.

One December evening we were in London and George stopped the car and said, 'Let's get married. I'll speak to Brian.' He pulled up in Chapel Street, outside Brian's house, rushed in, leaving me in the car, came back fifteen minutes later and said, 'Brian says it's okay. Will you marry me? We can get married in January.'

'Oh, yes!' I said. 'That would be fabulous!' I was thrilled – but George had had to ask Brian's permission in case another tour was planned.

We were married on 21 January 1966. It was not the wedding I had dreamt of – I would have loved to be married in church, but Brian didn't want a big fuss. They all trusted him so implicitly that when he said it should be a quiet register office wedding George agreed. He also said it had to be secret – if the press found out, it would be chaotic. I had always thought I'd have a big white wedding, as all little girls do, then have children and live happily ever after – not be divorced like my mother. As a child I thought I'd do anything to avoid divorce – I even considered waiting until I was forty to marry because by that time I would have had my fun and there would be no chance of a marriage breaking up. But there I was, at twenty-one, marrying George, who was all of twenty-two. But I was so happy and so much in love, I didn't care. Divorce didn't enter my head: we would be together and happy for ever.

He didn't give me an engagement ring, but we did go to Garrard, the royal jewellers in Regent Street, to choose my wedding ring. There was a lot of fuss when we arrived: all the assistants were excited and the top man was called out from the back to serve us.

The ring I chose was a wide gold band that looked like a little brick wall made from yellow, pink and white gold. It was so unusual, flexible, and felt lovely on my finger. I didn't buy George a ring. He didn't want to wear one – few men did in those days.

I bought a Mary Quant pinky-red shot-silk dress, which came to just above the knee, and I wore it with creamy stockings and pointy red shoes. On top, because it was January and cold, I wore a red fox-fur coat, also by Mary Quant, that George gave me. She made George a beautiful black Mongolian lamb coat.

The ceremony took place early in the morning at Epsom register office, in Surrey, not the most glamorous place, and the room was very hot and stuffy. Brian Epstein was there and Paul McCartney, who was George's best man. Otherwise it was family – my mother, with her cousin Penny Evans, who had been around a lot while I was growing up, Colin, Jenny, Paula, David and Boo, George's parents and brothers. Uncle John, my mother's twin brother, gave me away.

He lived in Africa and although we children didn't see much of him as we were growing up, he was probably the main male influence in our lives. We adored him and Jenny and I both held him in higher regard than either our real father or our step-father. He was a writer. He had been stationed in the desert in Africa during the Second World War and afterwards worked for Reuters. Then he went to Singapore and wrote a book about it, and later returned to Africa, where he is still, aged eighty-three. He lives in Somalia, speaks the language fluently and is helping the Somalis to map their land. He is hardly paid a penny but he cares deeply about the people and can't bear the idea of coming back to Britain.

My mother thought I should invite Jock Boyd, my father, to the wedding so I wrote to him at an address in Devon. He had apparently been living there with a new wife for several years. I didn't know how to address him – Daddy, Jock, Mr Boyd? In the end I called him Daddy. I said, 'I am going to marry George, he comes from Liverpool, I'm sure you'd like him and if you'd like to come to our wedding, please do.' He wrote back saying he forbade me to marry someone so young whose family he hadn't met. He didn't come.

Uncle John not only gave me away, he saved the day. After the ceremony we all went back to Kinfauns for lunch and the photographer Brian had booked had a problem with his camera – he couldn't synchronise the flash. John came to the rescue with a little Instamatic he had just bought in Selfridges, and took the photos at the reception.

There was no shortage of pictures of us leaving the register office. We came out into the street to find dozens of press photographers lined up outside. So much for keeping the whole thing secret. We travelled to and from Epsom in a Rolls-Royce Princess, and after the ceremony David, who was then about twelve, walked out beside George and me. Not knowing wedding protocol, he jumped into the back of the car ahead of us. 'Wrong car,' said George, very quietly, so no one else could hear.

At the reception David sat between George's father and Paul McCartney, with (the other) Mrs Harrison one place away. David and Boo should have been at school but came to the wedding instead. They went to the most horrible schools. Bobbie had little money but felt that the boys would be better off away from my mother – I now discover – and persuaded the council to foot the bill for two boarding-schools. Even at that age David was very independent and a bit of a rebel – and, out of school, thought he could safely have a cigarette. What he hadn't bargained on was George's mother, who told him to put it out at once.

When Paul realised that David and Boo were bored, he took them outside in search of fun. In a disused loo, with hundreds of fan letters waiting for Mrs Harrison's attention, they found George's bow and arrows. Paul showed the boys how to use it. David pulled back the string, and Paul watched the arrow score a direct hit on the bonnet of his gleaming Rolls-Royce.

After our wedding we had to endure a press conference that Brian had set up. It was so terrifying that I have almost blanked it from my memory. Lots of reporters asked questions about when George had asked me to marry him and our plans for the future. George said he had proposed on the day we met, on the train filming *A Hard Day's Night*, and I said I hadn't thought he was serious. He then said he'd asked me out and I'd turned him down. And I blurted out that we'd like three children but not immediately: there was plenty of time.

We spent our honeymoon in Barbados in a fabulous rented villa called Benclare at Gibbs Beach, on what is now the Sandy Lane Estate. It was perched on a hill with a sweeping lawn to the main road, views of the sea and a full staff. One day we were out in the garden and the maid said, 'Oh, look, there's the Queen of England!' Sure enough, there she was, driving past in an open-topped car waving to everyone, with Prince Philip sitting beside her, head buried in a newspaper. We spent beautiful sunny days exploring the island, playing in the sea and having romantic dinners at home to the sound of the ever-present tree frogs. We lounged on the beach, went to the famous Sandy Lane Hotel, swam, talked and walked, and I was so happy I thought I might burst. It was bliss to have George to myself, no work pulling either of us and no fans making life a misery.

We didn't know anyone on the island and there were few tourists at that time, but gradually word got out that we were there so we posed a couple of times for the local press, and then the local dignitaries wanted to be photographed with us. We made a few friends including the eccentric George Drummond, of the banking family, who lived there. He showed us around the island and gave parties for us to meet other locals. A lot of people still lived in the old wooden chattel houses, built on blocks so they could be lifted up and moved, with shutters on every window, and painted blue, pink or yellow. The island was full of life and colour, cascading bougainvillaea in every shade, flame red trees, smartly dressed school children in uniform, pretty brown, black and white goats.

After a week some friends who were in New York came to join us – Terry Howard was the creative director of an advertising agency and his girlfriend, Venetia Cuninghame, was a model – another face in the *Birds of Britain* book. One day we took them up to an old hotel on the northern tip of the island, where it was very wild and windy, and in those days undeveloped. It is the point at which the Caribbean meets the Atlantic, so there are big seas and strong currents. The owner had invited us to a picnic lunch. There was a huge swimming-pool, overlooking the sea and, as everywhere in Barbados, a beautiful sandy beach. We said we'd like to be on the beach rather than by the pool, so we went down some stone steps that led to it from the hotel garden and found a perfect spot on which to lie and sunbathe.

The sand was silky soft but so hot in the midday sun that we couldn't sit on it for long. Soon we raced into the sea to cool down. George and I swam a little further out than the others, but as we headed back towards the shore we suddenly discovered we were making no progress. We were about sixty yards from the beach, swimming and swimming but moving nowhere. George and I looked at each other, and he said, very calmly, 'Just keep swimming. Don't panic.' We could see Terry and Venetia at the water's edge but they were blissfully unaware of our predicament and probably wouldn't have heard our shouts over the noise of the waves. Every time a wave came we tried to use it to inch a little further but then the fierce undertow took us out to sea again. Eventually, after about half an hour, we made it and collapsed, exhausted, on to the sand.

We were desperate for something to drink and ravenously hungry – as if by a miracle, a waiter appeared at that precise moment with a huge jug of lemonade, tinkling with ice, and a silver platter laden with delicious things to eat. Horror of horrors, no sooner had he put them down on the sand beside us than a huge wave whooshed up the beach and swallowed our lunch, tray and all. The sea was ferocious in that northern part, which, I now know, was why the hotel had such a glorious swimming-pool.

Recently I was in Barbados and went back to see the beach. Forty years on the hotel is in ruins, the swimming-pool too, but I found the stone steps to the beach, overgrown and unused, and felt a shiver run down my spine.

CHAPTER SIX

A New Direction

G eorge was away on tour yet again and I was sitting with my friend Marie-Lise at the kitchen table in Kinfauns. It was February 1967, and we had the Sunday papers spread out in front of us. I had a yearning to take up chanting, meditation or something spiritual – I suppose after the experience of India – and she felt much the same. Something was missing from our lives, we decided. So there we were, combing through the papers, when we came upon an advert for transcendental-meditation classes in London. Perfect. Off we went to Caxton Hall and enrolled in the Spiritual Regeneration Movement. In the course of a long weekened we were initiated and given our mantras.

TM is an ancient Indian practice that was brought to the West in the 1950s by Maharishi Mahesh Yogi as a means of ultimately achieving enlightenment. It is a simple technique. You are given a mantra, a single word, which you keep secret, to say over and over again to yourself. The idea is that in repeating the mantra you clear your mind so you can give it and your body a brief rest from the stress of modern life. You sit with your eyes closed, completely relaxed for twenty minutes, repeating your mantra, to make yourself feel calmer, more creative, focused and more successful. The benefits are cumulative. Day by day, life is supposed to get better and better. I loved meditating and I found the effects remarkable: I really did feel more alert and energetic. It did what it said on the bottle – it was life-changing. I couldn't wait to tell George.

As soon as he came home I bombarded him with what I had been doing and he was really interested. Then, joy of joys, I discovered that Maharishi was coming to London in August to give a lecture at the Hilton Hotel. I was desperate to go, and George said he would come too. Paul had already heard of him and was interested, and in the end we all went – George, John, Paul, Ringo, Jane and I. Maharishi was every bit as impressive as I thought he would be, and we were spellbound.

At the end we went to speak to him and he said we must go to Wales where he was running a ten-day summer conference of the Spiritual Regeneration Movement in Bangor. It started in two days' time. We leapt at it. I persuaded my sister, Jenny, to join us. Mick Jagger and Marianne Faithfull came, also Cynthia Lennon. John had been doing an awful lot of drugs, which Cynthia didn't like, and I think she was worried about the effect they were having on him, and about their marriage. When he came back from the Hilton lecture full of enthusiasm about Maharishi, who was against drugs, I think she hoped it might lead to something she could share. Maharishi said that through meditation you could attain a natural high more powerful than any a drug could give you. Maureen had just had a baby so she couldn't come.

We were travelling to Bangor in the same train as Maharishi and caught it by the skin of our teeth. We had travelled up from Surrey in John's Rolls-Royce and arrived at Paddington to find pandemonium at the station, hundreds of people – passengers, press, police, photographers and fans. And we were on our own. For the first time, Brian was not in charge, and although he had sent his assistant, Peter Brown, to see us off, we were like children allowed into the park with no nanny. John said it was 'like going somewhere without your trousers on'.

Brian had seemed interested in what Maharishi had to offer but it was a bank-holiday weekend and he was committed to spending it with friends at his house in Sussex. He said he would join us later. Neil Aspinall and Mal Evans, the two roadies who had looked after the Beatles since the Cavern Club days and went everywhere with them, were not there either so we had to carry our own baggage and fight our way through the crowds on to the platform.

In the rush Cynthia was left behind – she was probably carrying the suitcases while John, empty-handed and thoughtless as ever, made a dash for it. And so the train pulled away and I shall never forget the sight of Cynthia running down the platform shrieking at John to wait. But Peter Brown arranged for Neil Aspinall to drive her to Bangor in his car and she arrived not long after the rest of us.

On the way down, John, George, Paul and Ringo signed autographs for fans and we went to see Maharishi in his first-class compartment. He was sitting cross-legged on the seat, which one of his followers had covered with a white sheet, and seemed to be doing an awful lot of giggling. He was a rather rotund little man in a white robe, with long hair and a big beard that was white at the tip. He had had no idea who the Beatles were, simply that they were very famous, but he promised that TM, in which he would initiate them at Bangor, was simply a method of reaching a spiritual state and that his meditation had to be practised for just half an hour every morning. Then it was like a bank – no need to carry all your money around with you, you'd pop in now and then and take out what you wanted. 'What if you're greedy,' asked John, 'and have another half-hour's meditation after lunch, then slip in another half-hour after tea?' Everyone laughed.

When the train pulled into the little seaside station at Bangor, hundreds of people were waiting, a combination of screaming fans and press. We wanted to go on to a stop further along the line and take a taxi back to avoid the inevitable scrum but Maharishi insisted we stay close to him. He marched up to the press and agreed to hold a conference that afternoon, little realising, I think, who the press were actually interested in.

When we were shown to our rooms in the teacher-training college where the conference was being held, I felt as though I was back at boarding-school – Spartan dormitories with the regulation chest of drawers and lino on the floor. That night we went into Bangor in search of a restaurant and found the only one that was open late, the Chinese. Fine. In we went. A couple of hours and many bottles of wine later, we discovered that none of us had enough money to pay the bill. We weren't used to paying restaurant bills. Or any others, for that matter.

The next day, Maharishi gave an introductory seminar to his three hundred-odd devotees, seated cross-legged on the floor, and afterwards the impromptu press conference took place. Reporters were swarming all over the college and there was no one to keep them in check. I am sure they had little idea who Maharishi was and perhaps thought the Beatles were pulling a stunt. But the Beatles said that not only were they deadly serious, they were no longer going to take drugs, in accordance with Maharishi's teaching. Just a month before they had put their names to a petition in *The Times* calling for cannabis to be legalised. 'It was an experience we went through,' said Paul. 'Now it's over. We don't need it any more. We think we're finding new ways of getting there.'

The petition had been in protest at Mick Jagger and Keith Richards receiving custodial sentences after the infamous drugs raid on Redlands, Keith's house in Sussex, in May. The previous Sunday, the *News of the World* had run a story that quoted Mick Jagger admitting he had frequently taken drugs. The paper had made an expensive mistake: it wasn't Mick who'd been overheard talking in a nightclub, it was Brian Jones, and Mick sued for libel. The following week, acting on a tip-off, the police raided the house in the early hours of the morning, knowing that Mick Jagger was there and drugs were in the house. The tip-off, it transpired, had come from the *News of the World*. George and I had been at Redlands that evening. Marianne Faithfull was there and also Robert Fraser. There was an American drug dealer, too, known as the Acid King, and a few others. At about three o'clock in the morning George and I drove home. No sooner had we left than thirty policemen burst into the house with a warrant to search it for drugs.

Drugs were still new and the police were still quite naïve. Robert Fraser produced a bottle of pills from his coat pocket, which he said had been prescribed by his doctor for a stomach problem. An officer said he had better take a few to have them tested. He left Robert with about twenty-four. They were pure heroin. They also found amphetamines and cannabis. Keith, Mick and Robert were arrested and spent a night in Lewes jail. That Sunday, the *News of the World* had the entire story – including the detail that 'a famous couple had left earlier'. They had obviously been waiting for us to go, presumably so that a Beatle wouldn't be implicated.

Robert went to jail for six months for possessing heroin. Mick was sentenced to three months for possessing four pep pills, which he had bought legally in Italy, and Keith got nine months for allowing cannabis to be smoked on his property. Mick did one night of his sentence before he was bailed; Keith spent three at Her Majesty's pleasure and came out saying he intended to prosecute the Queen for allowing cannabis to be smoked on her property – he had been offered half a dozen joints in prison and 'they were fab'.

When word got out that the tip-off had come from the *News of the World*, fans stormed the newspaper building and hurled Molotov cocktails. *The Times*, not noted as the most liberal of newspapers, attacked the judiciary in an editorial written by the editor, William

Rees-Mogg, under the headline 'Who Breaks a Butterfly on a Wheel?'

Drugs were a part of our lives at that time and they were fun. We didn't take anything hard – none of us used heroin, and we'd had no idea that Robert did – but we took acid regularly. Everyone did, and it was perfectly legal. We also took uppers and downers and smoked cannabis. Our dentist, John Riley, had turned us on to acid. He and his girlfriend invited John, Cynthia, George and me to dinner at his house in Hyde Park Square one evening some time in 1965. We knew him quite well and had been to a few clubs with him in the past. The four of us went to London in my little Mini Cooper S – George had bought me a fabulous orange one for my birthday.

We had a lovely meal, plenty to drink, and at the end George said, 'Let's go.' We were planning to see some friends playing at the Pickwick Club.

John Riley's girlfriend jumped to her feet. 'You can't,' she said. 'You haven't had any coffee yet. It's ready, I've made it – and it's delicious.'

We sat down again and drank the coffee she was insistent we should have. But then we were really keen to get away and John Lennon said, 'We *must* go now. These friends of ours are going to be on soon. It's their first night, we've got to go and see them.'

And John Riley said, 'You can't leave.'

'What are you talking about?' said John Lennon.

'You've just had LSD.'

'No, we haven't.'

'Yes, you have,' said our host. 'It was in the coffee.'

John Lennon was absolutely furious. 'How dare you fucking do this to us?' he said.

George and I said, 'Do what?' We didn't know what LSD was.

John Lennon was the only one of us who knew because he had read about it in *Playboy*. He said, 'It's a drug,' and as it began to take effect we felt even more strongly that we didn't want to be there. I wondered if the dentist, who hadn't had any coffee, had given it to us hoping the evening might end in an orgy.

We were desperate to escape. John Riley said he would drive us and we should leave our car with him. 'No,' we said. We piled into my Mini, which seemed to be shrinking, and drove to the club where our friends were playing. All the way the car felt smaller and smaller, and by the time we arrived we were completely out of it. People kept recognising George and coming up to him. They were moving in and out of focus, then looked like animals. We clung to each other, feeling surreal. Soon we moved on to the Ad Lib Club – we knew it and might feel better if we were in familiar surroundings, we thought. It wasn't far from the Pickwick so we walked and on the way I remember trying to break a shop window.

The Ad Lib was on the top floor, above the Prince Charles Theatre in Leicester Place, and we thought the lift was on fire because there was a little red light inside. As the doors opened, we crawled out and bumped into Mick Jagger, Marianne Faithfull and Ringo. John told them we'd been spiked. The effect of the drug was getting stronger and stronger, and we were all in hysterics and crazy. When we sat down, the table elongated. Hours later we decided to go home. We climbed into the car again and this time George drove – at no more than ten miles an hour, concentrating hard, all the way to Esher. But it felt as though he was doing a thousand miles an hour and I saw some goalposts and said, 'Let's jump out and play football.'

The journey took hours and it was daylight by the time we got home. We went into Kinfauns and locked the gate so that the cleaner wouldn't come in and find us, put the cat into a room on her own and sat down. The drug took about eight hours to wear off, but it was very frightening and we never spoke to the dentist again. George said, 'It was as if I had never tasted, talked, seen, thought or heard properly before. For the first time in my whole life I wasn't conscious of ego.'

I had always thought John Riley was rather odd. No matter what he was going to do in our mouths, he would give us intravenous Valium. All of the Beatles went to him and we took it for granted that this was what happened – no one questioned it. We would go into a deep sleep and wake up not knowing what he had done. I watched him trying to revive George once by slapping his face. It was sinister – he could have been doing anything to us while we were out.

After that experience, acid became part of the creative process for the Beatles. They had been taking other pills since Hamburg days – George used to tell me about how they had to play for hours on end and to stop them falling asleep the nightclub owner used to feed them pills. At the time we thought nothing of it. We didn't consider that they might be harmful. They were just fun. They could be scary but most of the time they made us feel like a million dollars, see wonderful psychedelic images and hear everything much more acutely. George used to say that when he took LSD he felt as though a lightbulb had gone on in his head. Every sensation was heightened.

The police didn't share our view. I think the Establishment felt they were losing control, that the young were being corrupted by their decadent long-haired, hippie heroes. A lot of the Beatles' songs were clearly drug-induced but the Beatles were clean-cut: everyone loved them – even our parents' generation. The Rolling Stones were the bad boys, overtly sexy, dissolute and dangerous. If only they had known . . .

In the summer of 1967 George was working in Los Angeles for a couple of months. We rented a house on Blue Jay Way and met so many fantastic people. Joni Mitchell came over and invited me to hang out with her while George was busy. She was great fun and took me to a studio belonging to a friend of hers where she and some other musicians sat down and played together. One day David Crosby, of the Byrds, invited us to his place in the hills. We arrived to find a swimming-pool full of naked people. Not knowing anyone – or, indeed, what to do – we went into the house until David arrived, naked, with a joint in his hand. He soon realised we were not going to join in so he put on his shorts. Next thing, the pool attendant arrived and didn't bat an eyelid, just got on with his job. LA is wild, I thought.

Most exciting of all, one evening we were invited to meet the great Frank Sinatra. We turned up at the studio where he was recording and, through the glass wall of the control room, watched while he sang 'My Way' accompanied by a full orchestra. At the end of the song he came out to hear it back and meet George. We were then ushered into limos and driven down Sunset Boulevard to a restaurant. We glided in, as smooth as silk, and sat at a table already prepared with a bottle of whiskey, or bourbon, in front of each of Frank's crew – all short, wide men in large suits. I found the ones I sat next to very difficult to understand.

We also went to see my sister Jenny, who was living with a friend in San Francisco. We flew there in a private Lear jet with Derek Taylor and Neil Aspinall and were met by a limo, then picked up Jenny, and we all went to have lunch. Afterwards we thought it would be fun to go and have a look at Haight-Ashbury, the district that had been taken over by hippies. Musicians like Jefferson Airplane, Grateful Dead and Janis Joplin lived there, and it was the LSD capital of America. On the way, Derek produced a tab. Would we like some? Since we were going to Haight-Ashbury, it seemed silly not to.

The area is named after the intersection of two streets, Haight and Ashbury, and as we approached, the driver said he wouldn't drive down the street itself, he'd park among the side-streets. It seemed a little odd but we didn't argue. We got out of the car, the acid kicked in and everything was just *whoah*, psychedelic and very . . . I mean, it was just *completely fine*. We went into a shop and noticed that all these people were following us. They had recognised George as we walked past them in the street, then turned to follow us. One minute there were five, then ten, twenty, thirty and forty people behind us. I could hear them saying, 'The Beatles are here, the Beatles are in town!'

We were expecting Haight-Ashbury to be special, a creative and artistic place, filled with Beautiful People, but it was horrible – full of ghastly drop-outs, bums and spotty youths, all out of their brains. Everybody looked stoned – even mothers and babies – and they were so close behind us they were treading on the backs of our heels. It got to the point where we couldn't stop for fear of being trampled. Then somebody said, 'Let's go to Hippie Hill,' and we crossed the road, hoping the lights were red, and went into a park. Then somebody said, 'Let's sit down here,' and we all sat down on the grass, our retinue facing us, as if we were on stage. They looked at us expectantly – as if George was some kind of Messiah.

We were so high, and then the inevitable happened: a guitar emerged from the crowd and I could see it being passed to the front by outstretched arms. I thought, Oh, God, poor George, this is a nightmare. Finally the guitar was handed to him. I had the feeling that they'd listened to the Beatles' records, analysed them, learnt what they'd thought they should learn, and taken every drug they'd thought the Beatles were singing about. Now they wanted to know where to go next. And George was there, obviously, to give them the answer. Pressure.

George was so cool. He said, 'This is G, this is E, this is D,' and showed them a few chords, then handed back the guitar and said, 'Sorry, man, we've got to go now.' He didn't sing – he couldn't have: he was flying. We all were. I was surprised he could even do that.

Anyway, we got up and walked back towards our limo, at which point I heard a little voice say, 'Hey, George, do you want some STP?'

George turned around and said, 'No, thanks, I'm cool, man.'

Then the bloke turned round and said to the others, 'George Harrison turned me down.'

And they went, 'No!'

And then the crowd became faintly hostile. We sensed it because when you're that high you're very aware of vibes, and we were walking faster and faster, and they were following.

When we saw the limo, we ran across the road and jumped in, and they ran after us and started to rock the car, and the windows were full of these faces, flattened against the glass, looking at us.

That was a turning-point for George. We had always thought of drugs as fun, a means of expanding your mind and consciousness. What we saw at Haight-Ashbury was an eye-opener. Those people had dropped out, were sleeping rough and taking all kinds of drugs – some of which were ten times stronger than LSD. STP was one, as George later discovered from Mama Cass Elliot. There was nothing remotely artistic or creative about those people: they were like alcoholics or any other kind of addict, and it turned George right off the whole drug culture. He stopped taking LSD, and took up meditation.

So, Maharishi and his teachings had come into our lives at the right moment – or, at least, into George's life – and not just by providing an alternative to drugs. George was unsure why he was so famous. He knew he was a talented musician but he also knew that there were dozens of talented musicians, some more talented than him, yet he was the one who was world-famous, who couldn't walk in the street without being mobbed or sit in a restaurant without someone pestering him for an autograph. He was looking for an explanation and Maharishi offered a practical way of accessing the spirituality and mysticism he had glimpsed on our trip to India with Ravi Shankar.

By Sunday morning in Bangor, everyone had been initiated into transcendental meditation and believed we had found a new way of living. Then the telephone rang and the world as we knew it came to an end.

Brian Epstein was dead. It was the most shocking, dreadful moment. Paul took Peter Brown's call. Brian had been found dead in his bed at his house in Chapel Street. He was thirty-two years old.

105

At that point there was no explanation. We were stunned when Paul, ashen-faced, repeated what he had been told. It had to be a mistake. Paul and George were in complete shock. I don't think it could have been worse if they had heard that their own fathers had dropped dead. The unthinkable had happened. Brian had found them, believed in them, moulded them, turned them into millionaires and made them famous the world over. He had looked after them, pandered to their every whim, protected them, guided them, advised them. He was their friend, their enabler, their hero. He was irreplaceable. We knew, in the cold hard light of a Bangor morning, that life would never be the same again.

We were outside, just after breakfast, when we heard the news. We had been on our way to Maharishi who was going to talk to us privately – and suddenly that seemed the right thing to do so we kept the appointment. We needed someone wise and spiritual to tell us what to think. We were lost. I even thought, idiotically, Maharishi is so amazing, maybe he can bring Brian back to life. He couldn't, of course, but he was calm. He talked about reincarnation, but he said, too, that negative feelings would impede Brian's journey. His spirit was with us, and to release it, we must be joyful for him, laugh and be happy. It was hard to feel any joy that day, but it was an enormous help to have someone to turn to, who knew with such certainty how we should cope. I can't help thinking it was no coincidence that we were with Maharishi when Brian died. Someone up there was looking after us.

Brian had died of an overdose of a bromide-based drug, which he had been taking to help him sleep. The police inspector called to the house, after Brian's secretary, housekeeper and doctor had broken down the locked bedroom door and discovered the body, reported finding seventeen bottles of pills in his bathroom cabinet, his briefcase and beside his bed. The question was whether he had died on purpose. We knew that Brian took sleeping pills. He took all sorts of drugs and drank far more than was good for him, but we all did.

However, you shouldn't drink alcohol on top of sleeping pills: it was suggested that Brian had taken some pills, woken up later and drunk something, then taken more pills, forgetting what he had already swallowed.

I cannot believe he committed suicide. On the other hand, I don't think he was happy and, fundamentally, probably never had been. He was gay, and I think he found it difficult: he was attracted to the wrong sort of people, rough trade who would treat him badly, then leave him. Much of the time he was lonely and depressed. For all their closeness, he had never really socialised with the Beatles. He had held mad, wild, mind-blowing parties at his house in Belgravia and at Kingsley Hill, his country house near Heathfield in Sussex, to which we had all gone, but for most of the time he left us to do our own thing – and we left him to do his. We had noticed that he had become a little loose in his social life – I got the feeling he no longer cared about anything as much as he once had.

The year before, George and I had been to the South of France with him again for a week, and that had been typical of the old perfectionist Brian. He had every little detail worked out, each meal, each restaurant, each place we would visit. He even laid on a plane to take us to a bullfight in Arles. But in the last year of his life, when our lives changed so dramatically, he had let things go. We knew he was taking far too many drugs, but we didn't know that he was spending most days in bed, only emerging from his flat at night, or that he had scarcely been seen in the office for months. I suppose we were so absorbed in our own lives, as children are, that we didn't stop to wonder how Daddy was.

I don't know whether any of us cried when we heard the news that Sunday morning, but I know I did during the memorial service at the New London Synagogue in St John's Wood a few weeks later. We didn't go to the funeral, which was family only in Liverpool, but George sent a single sunflower; Brian's business partner, Nat Weiss, threw it into the open grave. At the memorial his mother, Queenie, looked frail and broken. Her husband, Brian's father, had died a little over a month before.

Already George was full of Maharishi's teachings: 'There is no such thing as death,' he said to reporters, that Sunday morning in Bangor, 'only in the physical sense. We know he's okay now. He will return because he was striving for happiness and desired bliss so much.' And a little later, he said much the same thing: 'There's no such thing as death anyway. I mean, it's death on a physical level, but life goes on everywhere.' George found it comforting to believe that Brian's soul would be back one day – and I agreed with him.

The real sadness for Brian, I think, was that when the Beatles stopped touring, they no longer needed him so much. And in August 1967, when he died, they hadn't been touring or done a live performance for a year. For a long time they had hated playing to vast, screaming audiences, but the crunch had come in Manila, at the end of a tour of Germany, Japan and the Philippines. Brian Epstein and Peter Brown had been having breakfast in the coffee shop of their hotel in Tokyo when someone came to tell them that Mrs Marcos, the wife of the Philippines' president, wanted to invite the Beatles to lunch during their visit to her country.

Brian said, 'We don't do that. We don't go to official functions.' This was because the last time they had gone to one – at the British Embassy in Washington in 1964 – it had been a fiasco. It was after a concert at the Coliseum, their first on American soil, and the embassy was swarming with reporters as well as guests. Everyone had had too much to drink and kept grabbing the Beatles to demand autographs. Someone cut off a chunk of Ringo's hair, then John swore and walked out. Brian had decided that in future they would do nothing that he hadn't arranged.

When the Beatles flew into Manila, their bags were confiscated. They were terrified they would be busted for carrying drugs – their fears were unfounded. The day after the concert, someone arrived at their hotel and said he had come to take them to the palace for lunch.

Brian explained that they had declined the invitation. 'But you have to go,' said the emissary. Brian was adamant that they would not, whereupon he received a call from the British ambassador suggesting he reconsider. Brian dug in his heels and they didn't leave the hotel. All the while the story on national television, which George and the others were watching in their suite, was that the Beatles were expected at the palace but had not yet shown up. Then, as time passed, the news became 'Beatles snub First Family'.

The next morning they were due to leave and woke to find that all security had been removed, there was no room service and every facility was unavailable. There was no car or taxi to take them to the airport. Eventually they found two vehicles: Neil, Mal and Tony Barrow, the Beatles' press officer, went in one and the Beatles, Brian and Peter in another. When they arrived at the airport no one would help with the bags and the crowd were booing. The young people were screaming and trying to grab them but the older ones were punching them, throwing bricks and kicking them.

When they found their way to the right gate, they were put into a glass room on display to people on the mezzanine floor. The security people who had confiscated their bags on the way into the country came in to shove them around. The thugs were wearing guns and the Beatles' entourage were frightened. When Mal, a big bloke, was knocked over it turned nasty. They were leaving on a KLM flight to India and were worried that it would take off before they could get aboard.

On the plane, finally, a call went out for Mr Epstein and Mr Evans to get off. Brian sorted it, but it cost him everything the group had earned in Manila. The stress brought him out in hives.

That was when George said he never wanted to go on tour again. Being mobbed because people loved you was one thing; being mobbed because they hated you was another. The only good thing that came out of Manila was the beautiful emerald ring George brought home for me with some gorgeous black pearls.

The last live performance they gave was at Candlestick Park, San Francisco, in August 1966. From then on the Beatles wrote songs and recorded albums. And Brian's role changed. He had never been needed in the recording studio – that was the domain of George Martin, the Beatles' record producer. Although they still relied on him to fix and arrange everything in their personal lives, his day-to-day contact with them diminished. He had plenty of other people to look after, but the Beatles were becoming independent. Brian's empire, NEMS Enterprises, was huge and he had signed up many other artists, including Cilla Black, Gerry and the Pacemakers and Billy J. Kramer, but the Beatles were special. For five years they had been his life and suddenly they were almost gone.

Shortly after Brian's death, a couple wrote to George and John saying that Brian was trying to make contact with us. The wife was a medium and could conduct a séance. But, they said, it was vitally important that we told no one about it because some Venusians would join us, and if anyone got wind of their visit, the military would try to kill them. There had been a lot of sightings of Venusians recently, they said, and they would be travelling in their V6 spaceship. We thought this sounded exciting, so John, Cynthia, George and I drove to East Grinstead, in West Sussex, where the couple had converted an enormous country house into a health spa.

While we waited for the Venusians to arrive, the wife explained that she had previously lived in London. One day a little person had appeared in the window and said, 'You have been sent here to help people whenever you can.' So, she and her husband had bought the house and turned it into a health spa to fulfil her destiny.

We waited and waited. There was no sign of the Venusians. Were we sure we hadn't told anyone? Yes. Then the husband sat in front of a big old-fashioned radio, like something out of a 1940s movie, put on earphones and fiddled with some knobs, saying things like 'V6, V6, come in, V6 . . .' The Venusians, he announced, had said they weren't coming after all, but they would contact us at another time. He and his wife were so disappointed, but we dared not look at each other for fear of cracking up.

We were ushered into a big dark room where we sat round a circular table. Suddenly the wife was talking in a weird voice as though she had been taken over by a spirit. She talked about people on the other side, people who were coming forward, who wanted to speak to us. She had Brian with her, she said. He was saying he was all right, we were not to worry about him – and he wanted us to know that he had not committed suicide. I so wanted to believe her, and so did George, I think, but she got a few things wrong for me: she was pretty accurate in the things she told Cynthia, but John pooh-poohed the whole thing. When it was over, and the spirits had left her, she looked drained.

Her husband told us that because the Venusians hadn't come, they wouldn't charge us, and we said goodbye. Outside, we howled with laughter.

When Brian's death cut short our time in Bangor, Maharishi had invited us to stay with him at his ashram in India. Every year he held a course for Westerners who wanted to become TM instructors. None of us did, but we wanted to study it some more, and I think the Beatles thought their fans might copy them, which meant they would be using their influence on young people in a good way.

In February 1968, with half the world's press, we set off for Rishikesh, a small town in the north of India in the foothills of the Himalayas. Short though it had been, the experience in Wales had filled us with excitement about where Maharishi and Indian spirituality might lead. George and I, my sister Jenny, John and Cynthia flew out to Delhi together and Paul, Jane, Ringo and Maureen arrived a few days later.

When we had been there for four weeks, Magic Alex arrived. He was a young Greek who had attached himself to the Beatles, and Jenny was renting a room in his house. His name was Alex Mardas and his father was one of the Greek colonels who had overthrown King Constantine in the 1967 *coup d'état*. He had invented some weird electrical gadgets that appealed to the Beatles, John in particular, and made things for the Apple boutique, which had opened just before we left for India. At one time he was keen that the Beatles should buy a Greek island so we went to Greece and stayed on a boat hopping from island to island – all I remember about the holiday is that some of us took acid, and we didn't have to go through Passport Control because Alex's father was so important.

Jenny was coming to Rishikesh with us partly because she and I loved doing things together and partly because, coincidentally, while George and I had been discovering Indian philosophy with Ravi Shankar, Jenny had been going through a similar process at home. She had just broken up with Mick Fleetwood, and was missing him and us when she decided that the beliefs with which she had grown up made no sense any more. One day she had come across a shop off the Charing Cross Road that was full of books on Eastern philosophy. When she had seen what they were saying about life, death and reincarnation, she had suddenly recognised that God was everywhere, inside each one of us, and that everything was a circle. When we got back from India she told us what had happened to her. We, of course, had had exactly the same experience.

At that time Jenny and I seemed to know exactly what the other was thinking. We often dreamt about each other, and eight out of ten times we would phone and discover that what had gone on in the dream had happened in real life. It was quite uncanny – a time of psychic closeness between us. Our simultaneous move towards Eastern philosophy was an extension of this.

Our lives were also running in parallel. Jenny had left school and become a model, as I had. Occasionally we worked together, which was fun, but where I was almost exclusively a photographic model, she worked in-house for a designer, so the opportunities for us to do so were rare. She, too, had fallen in love with a musician. Mick

Fleetwood was the drummer in Fleetwood Mac, so Jenny was part of the rock 'n' roll scene, as I was. Their recent split was not permanent: her relationship with Mick was always on and off. He had first seen her when she was fifteen – at the Coffee Mill, in Notting Hill, where she and her friends used to go after school – and had decided then that he would marry her. She was seventeen when they started going out together, and they married in 1970 when Jenny was twenty-three.

The plan was that we would stay at the Academy of Meditation in Rishikesh for two or three months. It was a long time for me to be out of circulation as a model, but George had never liked me working and I was making an effort to cut down on the jobs I took. I never knew quite what it was about it that he disliked. I suspect he was simply a product of his upbringing and wanted his wife to be at home with the kids, waiting for him with a meal on the table when he came in from work. My career took me away from home and out of his bed at an ungodly hour; it made other men look at me which he might not have liked – he was quite chauvinistic – and perhaps he worried that if I became more famous, it would fuel the public interest in us that he was always trying to escape. But when I gave up modelling I lost an important part of my identity, my feeling of self-worth, my independence and my self-confidence.

From Delhi, we took taxis for the six-hour journey to Rishikesh. The road was full of bicycles and ox-carts, donkeys and sacred cows. It was a hotch-potch of noise, and the smell of dung and spices hung in the air. As we left the city the dust rose, and through it we saw women working in the fields in bright saris, red and yellow, purple and green. We passed fields of wheat, mountains and rivers – it was an amazing drive.

Rishikesh nestles beside the Ganges at the point where the river cascades out of the Himalayas into the plains. The ashram was at the top of a hill overlooking the town and the river; the air was clear and clean and filled with the scent of flowers. It was about eight or ten acres, surrounded by a high perimeter fence and padlocked gates. Inside we were shown Maharishi's little bungalow, the post office, a communal dining area, a lecture theatre and a series of stone chalets, where we stayed; they had flat roofs on which we sunbathed.

Maharishi and the elders greeted us and we were shown to our rooms. Initially George and I shared one. It was sparsely furnished, with two skimpy beds, but we kept disturbing each other in our meditation so we ended up with a room each; John and Cynthia were next door to us to begin with but they were not getting on well – John had met Yoko Ono – and after a week or two he moved into a room on his own. I felt so sorry for Cynthia: he received notes from Yoko in the post almost every day saying things like, 'If you look up at the sky and see a cloud, it's me sending you love.'

Every day was much the same. We would wake in the morning, to the piercing sound of peacocks calling, and go to breakfast in an open dining area, covered with canvas held aloft on bamboo sticks. The cooks were a couple of twenty-one-year-old Australian boys, who were on their way round the world and had heard the academy needed help. Everything they cooked was vegetarian and delicious. It reminded me of the chapattis and beans the Kikuyu had made in Kenya. They produced porridge and toast for breakfast, which we would eat watched by hundreds of big black crows in the trees – they were waiting for us to leave so that they could swoop down and peck at our leftovers. Sometimes monkeys jumped on to the tables, grabbed a handful of food and bounded off. Ringo had spent years in hospital as a child: he couldn't eat onions, garlic or anything spicy so had brought with him a suitcase of Heinz baked beans.

After breakfast we were given our itinerary for the day, which mostly amounted to meditating and attending lectures given by Maharishi. These were held in a large covered area with a platform that was always covered with flowers when he spoke. For me one of the greatest revelations was the concept of reincarnation, which he espoused. It hadn't occurred to me that there might be a continuation of life in a different sphere. I had thought that when we died, that was it. Over the years, as friends have died, this belief has been a great consolation to me.

There were probably about sixty of us at the ashram, an interesting collection of people from across the world – Sweden, Britain, America, Germany, Denmark – and everyone was so nice. Despite that, we felt cut off from the rest of the world so it was always exciting when letters came in the post – my mother wrote regularly with news of home – or when others joined us. One of the newcomers was Donovan, with his manager, 'Gipsy Dave'. We had known Donovan for some years. He and the Beatles had recorded together, and he'd contributed to the *Yellow Submarine* album. He had fallen in love with Jenny – for whom he wrote 'Jennifer Juniper'. Mike Love, lead singer of the Beach Boys, also turned up, as did the actress Mia Farrow, with her brother Johnny and sister Prudence.

Maharishi's lectures were fascinating. He talked about the ideas behind meditation and what we should be trying to achieve, about life and astral travelling, how this can happen when you're meditating. It's like an out-of-body experience, and it happened to me once at Rishikesh. I felt as if I was in one of the other rooms, then realised I was in my own. It happened to George, too, and we compared notes. Sometimes Maharishi gave our group private lessons, just him and us, including Donovan, sitting out of doors. Afterwards we would go to our rooms to meditate, at first for a limited time. Gradually we were allowed to spend as long as we wanted meditating, and if we were going to do so during mealtimes we had to let someone know so that food could be left outside the room. The longest I managed was seven hours, from five in the afternoon to midnight.

Every so often a tailor would appear and we would get him to make clothes for us. We all wore pyjama trousers and big baggy shirts, and the boys grew beards. It was baking hot during the day so you had to wear loose, flowing Indian clothes. After four in the afternoon it could get quite cold, and when it rained there was no hot water. One evening Maharishi organised boats to take everyone on a trip down the river while two holy men chanted. Then George and Donovan started to sing, and we all joined in with a mixture of English and German songs. It was so beautiful, with mountains on three sides of us. In the setting sun the one to the west turned a deep, deep pink.

George, John and Paul wrote several songs while we were there – several went into the *White Album* – and Donovan taught them his finger-picking technique on the guitar. Someone was always playing a guitar and there would be discussions and singing, a nice little hubbub of social activity. And if it was anyone's birthday, and there were a surprising number while we were there, including George's twenty-fifth and my twenty-fourth, there would be cake and a party. At George's everyone put red and yellow paint on their faces and wore garlands of flowers, and an Indian musician came to play for him. The same musician played on my birthday, and gave me a beautiful *dilruba* – an Indian string instrument – with a bird's head engraved at the neck. John drew me a picture of us all meditating and wrote 'Happy Birthday Pattie love from John and Cyn' on it, and Cynthia, who was an accomplished artist, made me a lovely painting.

While the Beatles were recording the *White Album*, George wrote a song called 'Something', which he released as his first single. He told me, in a matter-of-fact way, that he had written it for me. I thought it was beautiful – and it turned out to be the most successful song he ever wrote, with more than a hundred and fifty cover versions. His favourite was the one by James Brown. Frank Sinatra said he thought it was the best love song ever written. My favourite was the one by George Harrison, which he played to me in the kitchen at Kinfauns.

Prudence Farrow didn't have such a good time at the ashram. She overdid the meditating – we couldn't get her to come out of her room. She stayed in it for something like two weeks, as if she was in a trance. We took it in turns to visit and talk to her, but to no avail. She was trying to reach God faster than anyone else. We were worried and so was Mia. Even Maharishi was concerned. When she finally came out, he told her she must meditate only in short bursts. John wrote a song for her, 'Dear Prudence', and the boys would stand outside her room and sing it to her.

Ringo and Maureen only stayed two weeks. Maureen had a phobia about flies – which at the time I thought silly – and she couldn't have come to a worse place: there were all sorts of flying insects. Ringo looked so sad when they left, but I think they also missed their children, who were very young – and he was probably tired of baked beans.

Paul and Jane left after about a month. Paul was keen to get back to London and Apple, the business the Beatles were about to launch. The Apple shop had opened just before we left but there was an office to find and a new manager to replace Brian. He had always been more interested in business than the others and I guess a month of meditating was enough for him.

The two who were most engrossed in Maharishi's teachings were John and George. They would meditate for hours, and George was very focused. I loved meditating, but I can't sustain that sort of intensity for long. Sometimes I would leave George meditating and make a foray to Mussoorie and Dheradun, Tibetan trading posts. At that time China was slowly taking over Tibet, whose people were being pushed out of their country as their culture was destroyed.

I bought a few trinkets – a prayer wheel and lots of pretty Tibetan beads – and sometimes I would walk down to the Ganges with a couple of friends. There were lepers on the other side of the river, begging, and a man sat meditating in the middle on a pointed rock. If I had seen lepers in Oxford Street I'd have been upset, but in India they and the man on the rock were just part of the scenery.

As the days got hotter the cool water in the river was delicious. It moved so fast that you could sit on it, quite literally, and it would take you along as if you were on a chute. George disapproved – he thought it far too frivolous. He never knew that one day when I was in the river I lost my wedding ring. I panicked. George would be furious. Johnny Farrow was with me and we looked and looked, I was convinced in vain, but miraculously, after about twenty minutes, he had it in his hand. Maybe it was a sign.

And then everything went horribly wrong. Mia Farrow told John she thought Maharishi had been behaving inappropriately. I think he made a pass at her. John threw a hissy fit. 'Come on, we're leaving.' Then Magic Alex claimed that Maharishi had tried something on with a girl he had befriended. I am not sure how true that was. I think Alex wanted to get John away from Rishikesh – he seemed convinced that Maharishi was evil. He kept saying, 'It's black magic.' And perhaps John had been waiting for an excuse to leave – he wanted to be with Yoko. Whatever the truth, they left.

We stayed on but the next night I had a horrid dream about Maharishi, and when George woke me the next morning, I said, 'Come on, we're leaving.'

He, Jenny and I went south to Madras: George didn't want to go straight from two months of meditation into the chaos that was waiting for him in England – the new business, finding a new manager, the fans and the press. Instead we went to see Ravi Shankar and lost ourselves in his music.

CHAPTER SEVEN

The Tears Begin

We had learnt to meditate at the feet of a master – despite the allegations, George and I still regarded Maharishi as a master – we had been shown the way to spiritual enlightenment, we had returned from Rishikesh renewed and refreshed, and yet from the time we left India our lives and our relationship seemed to fall apart.

I was delighted to be home and eager to tell my friends all about our trip. George retreated into himself. He had become very intense in India: the experience seemed to have answered some of the nagging questions he had had about his life but it had taken some of the lightness out of his soul. He continued the meditation and the chanting, and his prayer wheel was never far from his hand. To begin with, so did I, but he became obsessive about it. Some days he would be all right, but on others he seemed withdrawn and depressed. This was new: he had never been depressed before, but there was nothing I could do. It wasn't about me, but I found that my moods started to mirror his. Because I kept a diary, I discovered that we went into deep despair at the time of the full moon, and that it was particularly bad with every fourth – so bad, indeed, that at times I felt almost suicidal. I don't think I was ever in any real danger of killing myself, but I got as far as working out how I would do it: I would put on a diaphanous Ossie Clark dress and jump off Beachy Head.

And there were other women. That really hurt. In India George had become fascinated by the god Krishna, who was always surrounded by young maidens, and came back wanting to be some kind of Krishna figure, a spiritual being with lots of concubines. He actually said so. And no woman was out of bounds. I was friendly with a French girl who was going out with Eric Clapton. She was always flirtatious with George, but so were a lot of girls and he, of course, loved it. Then she and Eric broke up – Eric told her to leave – and she came to stay with us at Kinfauns.

It was 1 January 1969, and George and I had seen in the new year at Cilla Black's house. She was an old friend of the Beatles, one of the originals from Liverpool, and gave fantastic parties. We arrived home in good spirits but then everything went swiftly downhill. The French girl didn't seem remotely upset about Eric and was uncomfortably close to George. Something was going on between them, and I questioned George. He told me my imagination was running away with me, I was paranoid.

Soon I couldn't stand it so I went to London to stay with Belinda and Jean-Claude. Six days later George phoned me to say that the girl had gone and I went home.

I was shocked that George could do such a thing to me. It might have been different if I had been a stronger, more confident person: I might have guessed that, with his infidelity, he was just being a boy and would get over it, that it didn't mean he didn't love me, but my ego was too fragile and I couldn't see it as anything other than betrayal. I felt unloved and miserable.

But ours wasn't the only relationship in trouble. Shortly after we came back from India, Jenny, Donovan and Gipsy, his manager,

Magic Alex and Cynthia went off for a fortnight's holiday in Greece. John had urged Cynthia to go – so that he could move Yoko Ono into their house and his life.

He had met Yoko, a Japanese artist, at the Indico gallery in London. It was a way-out place and she had been holding an exhibition there, The Unfinished Paintings and Objects Show, to which John had been invited. John Dunbar, the gallery's owner, had told her to chat him up as a potential sponsor. I don't think she knew who he was, but John was intrigued. She was everything that Cynthia – and probably every other woman he had ever met – was not. She was anarchic, original, afraid of nothing – and she didn't fall into the stereotype of the subservient woman that John had been used to.

John said he had never known love like it; and she seemed to take the place of everyone else in his life. It was as though he no longer needed the Beatles or any of his friends. She left her second husband, by whom she had a daughter, Kyoko, John walked out on Cynthia and their son Julian, and after their respective divorces they married in Gibraltar in March 1969. They spent their honeymoon in in a hotel bed in Amsterdam, protesting about the Vietnam war.

Meanwhile Paul and Jane's relationship, which everyone had thought would end in marriage, had also spectacularly hit the buffers. Jane came home unexpectedly from New York and found another woman in the house, an American girl – and did what I should probably have done with George. She went and got her mother, and between them they moved her stuff out of the house in St John's Wood. Not long afterwards, Paul met Linda Eastman, an American photographer, in the Bag o' Nails, a club behind Liberty's department store, which stayed open late and the boys often went there when they had been recording late.

Linda was in London photographing rock groups for a book called *Rock and Other Four Letter Words*. She came from a wealthy family – her father, Lee Eastman, was a New York lawyer and her mother was independently wealthy through Linders' department stores. She had a daughter, Heather, from a previous marriage and was reluctant to commit again, but eventually Paul persuaded her.

George's moods, I think, had much to do with what was going on between the Beatles. After Brian Epstein's death they were like orphans, so underlying tensions and resentments began to surface. George felt excluded: John and Paul had always been the songwriters and he had had to fight to get any of his songs on to an album. As he became older and more confident about his talent, he recognised how unfair this was, but they were powerful characters. I don't think I knew half of what was going on – George would start to say something about Paul then stop. He appeared unable or unwilling to share his thoughts with me; he wouldn't tell me he felt left out – although I am sure he did. He kept his hurt, frustration, anger, or whatever it was, to himself. We had once been so close, so honest and open with one another. Now a distance had developed between us. At times I couldn't reach him.

Apple was another bone of contention: they were musicians, not businessmen, but for tax reasons they had been persuaded to start a company. The name Apple Corps was Paul's idea. He had just bought a Magritte from Robert Fraser, which was simply a big green apple with 'Au revoir' written across it (Paul was disappointed that no one got the pun – corps, core.) Apple was essentially a record-production company, with other divisions to handle the Beatles' other activities, like music publishing, books, films, television and the shop; most were run by old friends. The accountant had been urging Brian, long before his death, to do something to minimise the tax the Beatles were paying – 85 per cent at that time – and because of an issue over renegotiating their contract with EMI, they suddenly had a mountain of money. If they didn't invest it, it would go to the taxman. Apple was launched in New York a couple of months after we came back from India.

Simultaneously, the Beatles announced the formation of the

Apple Foundation for the Arts, inviting anyone who thought they had talent in any artistic field to apply for funding. They put an ad in a newspaper saying, 'Send us your tapes and they will not be thrown straight into the wastepaper basket. We will answer.'

The offices were bombarded with every manner of artistic endeavour – not just tapes, but clothing, paintings, drawings, novels, plays, poems, sculpture, designs – everything you could think of – and most of it was rubbish. Much was delivered in person by a variety of extraordinary characters, who believed that the Beatles would help them make their fortune. Once they even had a bunch of Hell's Angels on the doorstep, complete with motorcycles, who had flown in from America. And there was a nerve-racking moment at the Christmas party when an Angel became obnoxious and Peter Brown had to reason with him. 'Well, that was strange,' said Ringo, with his gift for understatement.

Originally the Apple offices were above the shop in Baker Street but so many people and packages kept arriving that they soon needed more space. Eventually, in July 1968, they settled permanently into a five-storey Georgian building at 3 Savile Row, in the heart of London's bespoke-tailoring district. Magic Alex set about building what he promised would be a state-of-the-art recording studio in the basement. Sadly, it didn't turn out quite like that, and they had to go back to using the EMI studios in Abbey Road. That was just one of many ways in which they were pouring money down the drain.

No one would ever be able to step into Brian Epstein's shoes. Robert Stigwood, whom Brian had brought in to NEMS as a partner to look after some of the other musicians on his books, had assumed he would take over as the Beatles' manager but they quickly put a stop to that. Another contender was Allen Klein, who managed the Rolling Stones. To begin with, the Beatles weren't convinced that they needed a manager. Brian's genius, apart from managing their private lives, had been for organising tours and live performances but those days were over. For the future they needed someone to take care of business and run the office. That job fell to Peter Brown, who became Apple's business administrator and personal fixer, and Neil Aspinall, who had started out as the Beatles' roadie and became managing director in charge of Apple's artistic and creative side.

Peter Brown was another Liverpudlian; he and Brian had met in the late fifties and become friends. They had both been in retail, working in neighbouring shops. Peter had been doing management training in a department store across the road from where Brian managed NEMS in his father's shop; when he went to open a second branch, he asked Peter to take his place in the first. Soon after, Brian left the family business to manage the Beatles, and in 1963 they moved to London, leaving Peter in Liverpool. It was not long before he realised how much fun he was missing, and at the end of 1964, he arrived in London to join Brian as his executive assistant.

Peter was great and, a little older than the rest of us, became another father figure. He was always very kind to me. Whenever George was busy or away – which he was on most of my birthdays – Peter would take me to lunch at San Lorenzo or Inigo Jones, or we'd go to the theatre, Covent Garden or Glyndebourne. I once went to Jamaica with him and his boyfriend, Gary. He always says he remembers the holiday because of the size of suitcase I took with me. It was tiny, and he was astonished that, night after night, I appeared dressed to the nines in a different outfit. The secret was that I had lots of silk, which packs down to nothing.

12 March 1969 is ingrained on my memory. It was the day Paul and Linda were married at Marylebone register office. It was also the day on which our worst nightmares came true. We didn't go to the wedding – Paul hadn't invited any of the Beatles, perhaps because feeling among them was so bad at that point. It was quite late in the afternoon and I was on my own at home in Esher. We were going out to a Pisces party that evening, given by an artist friend, Rory McEwan. He was a marvellous painter and an old friend of Princess Margaret. George was at the Apple office in London and I was

expecting him home so that we could drive to Rory's house together.

Suddenly I heard a lot of cars on the gravel in the drive – far too many for it to be just George. My first thought was that maybe Paul and Linda wanted to party after the wedding. Then the bell rang. I opened the door to find a crowd of uniformed policemen, one policewoman and a dog standing outside. At that moment the back-doorbell rang and I thought, Oh, my God, this is so scary! I'm surrounded by police.

The man in charge introduced himself as Detective Sergeant Pilcher, from Scotland Yard, and handed me a piece of paper. I knew why he was there: he thought we had drugs, and he said he was going to search the house. In they came, about eight policemen through the front, another five or six through the back and there were more in the greenhouse. The policewoman said she would follow me while the others searched and didn't let me out of her sight. I said, 'Why are you doing this? We don't have any drugs. I'm going to phone my husband.'

I rang George at Apple. 'George, it's your worst nightmare. Come home.'

'What are you talking about?' he said.

'The police are here. Come home.'

He said he would sort something out – he was always very calm – and in the meantime he would send a friend round so I wasn't on my own.

After a while Pete Shotton, one of John Lennon's best friends from school, arrived. It was a great relief to see someone who wasn't dressed in blue, so I said, 'Let's have a drink.' He and I started tucking into the vodka and tonic.

Suddenly Sergeant Pilcher appeared. 'Look what Yogi, our dog, has found!' He produced a block of hash.

I said, 'Are you mad? You brought that with you.'

He denied it. 'Yogi found it in one of your husband's shoes,' he said triumphantly.

'This is a joke,' I retorted. 'If we had a lump of hash like that we certainly wouldn't keep it in George's shoes. If you'd said at the start you were looking for cannabis, I would have told you it's in the sitting room on the table in a pot. But you said you were looking for drugs. I thought you meant heroin or something dangerous. Why are you doing this? Don't you realise the implications? George and the other Beatles have a lot of fans and if they get to hear through the press, which they will, that George smokes dope, lots of kids will do the same.'

Sergeant Pilcher replied, 'I want to save you from the evils and peril of heroin.'

I said, 'I'd never touch heroin. Even if you put it in front of me, I'd never touch it. I don't believe you. I know you've planted this on us.'

So there we were, no George, just me and Pete Shotton with our vodka and tonic and all those policemen, one of whom clearly thought he was on a mission to save the world.

'Now what are you all going to do?' I asked.

And they said, 'Any chance of a cup of tea?'

'Well, I'm not going to make it.'

So the policewoman made tea for them and then they were standing around with it, not knowing what to do. One asked if they could watch television. So some did that, and one of the others said, 'Have the Beatles been doing any new music?'

'Yes,' I said, 'but you're not going to hear it.'

Then Pete asked them about being in the drugs squad. What drugs, he wanted to know, had they taken themselves so that they knew what they were looking for? One policeman said he'd been searching a house and had run his finger along someone's mantelpiece, licked it – and found himself on an LSD trip.

Eventually George arrived and found us in the middle of this policemen's tea party. He was still calm but he wasn't happy. The police were obviously excited to meet him. They stood to attention and were almost elbowing each other out of the way to get closer to him while Sergeant Pilcher went into his 'I am arresting you . . .' bit. George had Derek Taylor, the Beatles' press officer, with him and a lawyer called Martin Polden, who worked for Release, set up by Caroline Coon and Rufus Harris after Mick and Keith's bust to give free legal advice to anyone in that situation. Busts were happening more and more frequently and people were being far too harshly treated by the police and the courts.

The day after Jenny had left for India, Magic Alex's house, where she had a room, was raided and the police found a pipe Colin had brought her from Morocco, which she had smoked once and decided she didn't like. The lab found traces of cannabis in it and the day she got back from India they were on the doorstep to arrest her. They took her to the police station and were joking in the car about Rishikesh. 'Why did you want to go to India?' they said. 'Couldn't you have just gone to see the local vicar?' She was taken to court and given a year's conditional discharge – but since Alex owned the house and she was simply renting a room, he could also have been charged. I think they left him alone because of who his father was.

After Sergeant Pilcher had cautioned us we were taken to Esher police station to be processed and fingerprinted. The local police were flabbergasted: they knew us and were appalled to see us being marched in by all those London policemen. I don't think they'd used the fingerprinting machine before – it took them about twenty minutes to find it and even longer to work it. We were formally charged but released on bail. We got home feeling gloomy, so George said, 'Come on, let's go to the party.'

The first person we saw when we arrived at Rory McEwan's house was Lord Snowdon. Thinking – in vain – that he might be able to pull a few strings, George rushed over to him. 'Can you help us? The most awful thing's just happened.' Meanwhile I went downstairs and couldn't believe what I was seeing. Princess Margaret was standing with my youngest sister Paula, who was in the process of handing the Queen's sister a joint she had just lit. After everything we'd been through that evening, it was too much. I leapt at her and said, 'Don't!' When I told them what had happened, Princess Margaret and Lord Snowdon beat a hasty retreat.

Sergeant Pilcher had been making a bit of a name for himself and, apart from wanting to rid the world of drugs, I think he quite enjoyed the celebrity. He had led the Redlands raid on Keith Richards and had also busted Donovan. He went on to arrest a whole range of musicians, including Brian Jones. A few months before he busted us, he raided John and Yoko's flat. He turned up at midnight with five other policemen, one policewoman, two dog-handlers and two dogs – Yogi, once more, and Boo-Boo. The dogs arrived considerably later than the press, who had plainly been tipped off.

John and Yoko were half naked in bed, and when they refused to open the door, Pilcher and his men tried to get in through the windows. John and Yoko were terrified, but John had been warned by a reporter on the *Daily Mirror* that Pilcher was planning to get him and had cleared everything out of the flat. He was confident there was nothing to find. But he had forgotten about a pile of his belongings that Anthony, his driver, had brought from Weybridge. Among them were a couple of things with some cannabis in them, which the sniffer dogs found. John and Yoko were charged with possession and wilful obstruction of police officers, arrested and taken to Marylebone police station.

Three weeks after our bust we appeared in court and, as I recorded in my diary, 'fined £500 – the bastards'. The real problem about being convicted, for John, Yoko and us, was that afterwards it became difficult to get into America and New Zealand. The day after we were arrested, the US Embassy seized our passports and thereafter they had a code in them that told the immigration authorities we had a criminal record for drugs. The States took such offences seriously and every time I wanted to go to America – and when Jenny moved to Los Angeles, it was quite often – I had to go through rigorous tests and examinations, explaining exactly why I wanted to go there and, most humiliating, I had to sit in the narcotics lounge with all the other drug offenders when I arrived in America.

John's conviction was equally damaging. A deportation order was served on him when he and Yoko were living in America, which took four years to resolve, and meant he couldn't leave the country for fear of not being allowed back in; Yoko was convinced that that contributed to her losing custody of her daughter, Kyoko. But Sergeant Pilcher got his comeuppance. Not only did John immortalise him as 'semolina pilchard' in 'I Am The Walrus', but years later, after he had retired to Australia, he was brought back and sentenced to four years in prison for corruption.

One aspect of that whole episode still puzzles me. We were busted in the late afternoon – and discovered long afterwards that Pilcher had chosen that day because he'd thought we would be at Paul and Linda's wedding and the house would be empty. The home secretary, James Callaghan, had given him such a hard time for his handling of the John and Yoko bust that he had wanted to get us without attracting attention.

Earlier that day I had been in London and something odd had happened. I was driving down Sydney Street on my way to Ossie's shop, and at traffic-lights a boy appeared at the side of the car and asked for a lift. I said, 'No,' and drove off, parked my car and went into Ossie's. When I came back, someone had left a packet of cigarettes under my windscreen wiper with his name and number written on it. I took it off, threw it into the car and drove home to Esher. When I got home I opened the cigarette packet and found a small lump of cannabis. I chucked it on to the bed and forgot about it. I suppose the police took it as evidence. I never knew whether the two incidents were connected, but it was weird.

After a while, all of the Beatles had grasped that they were not businessmen. They had found some good artists – including

James Taylor, Mary Hopkin and Jackie Lomax – but Apple was haemorrhaging money and they needed someone to take charge before they went bankrupt. The office was like the best-stocked bar in town, and Scotch, VSOP brandy, vodka, wine, champagne, cigarettes, whatever anyone wanted was dispensed liberally to all, from the office juniors to friends, other musicians and anyone who happened to drop in.

Derek Taylor's office was on the top floor and he always had interesting people with him – writers, artists, musicians – and they entertained the Beatles like courtiers. Visitors didn't stop at drinks: they walked out with typewriters, hi-fi speakers, television sets – anything that wasn't screwed down. Security was non-existent because it had never occurred to anyone that it might be necessary. As George said, 'We've been giving away too much to the wrong people. This place has become a haven for dropouts. The trouble is, some of our best friends are dropouts.'

Derek Taylor came from Manchester but, crucially, had been born in Liverpool. He had started as a journalist in the Manchester office of the *Daily Express*. In 1964 the paper had sent him to Paris to interview the Beatles and they all got on well. Brian had liked him too, and when George was briefly contracted to produce a weekly column for the *Express*, Derek did the writing and they became quite close. Brian then hired him as the Beatles' press officer. Later he started his own PR company, went to Los Angeles for three years and worked for the Beach Boys and Warner Bros, then came back to work for Apple in 1968. He, Joan, his wife, and six children moved to Ascot and they were great friends of ours. I remember being at their house watching *Monty Python's Flying Circus*, all of us doubled up with laughter. Derek knew the Monty Python team and I think it was he who first brought Eric Idle to our house.

Being the Beatle who took most interest in the business, when Peter Brown needed a signature, Paul was the one he went to. He was easiest to get hold of, living in London, and the one most prepared to come into the office, so Apple was created somewhat in his image. Then Yoko came along with some firm ideas, and John complained that he wanted things changed but it was too late. Paul had also brought in his father-in-law and Linda's brother on the legal side, which delighted Peter, but the others were resentful and felt that Paul was taking over.

John wanted Allen Klein, a small, round, ruthless American accountant who had managed the Stones, to manage him. Klein had made the Stones a fortune – far more than the Beatles, even though they'd sold fewer records – and Mick had once sung his praises. But he had fallen out with Klein. They had parted company but Klein had managed to keep the rights to many of the group's earlier songs. When Mick heard the Beatles were about to meet Klein, he wanted to advise them against him. He rang Peter Brown and told him that the Beatles should not meet with Klein because he could not be trusted.

Peter insisted that Mick should tell the Beatles so himself, and set up a meeting. But John, in his perverse way, invited Klein to be there too. Mick left. The upshot was that John, George and Ringo hired Allen Klein, while Paul stuck with his in-laws. Klein promised them all sorts of riches but in the end the relationship soured, as it had with the Stones, and the Beatles ended up suing him.

While Klein was around, though, he looked after our every need – and was very influential. George and I went to New York for a week in December 1970: George had just made his first solo album, *All Things Must Pass*, and wanted to be sure it was cut properly before it was released on to the American market. Afterwards we planned to go on to Jamaica for a holiday. We flew directly from New York to Montego Bay where a Customs official was horrified to see that my smallpox vaccination was three months out of date. A nurse promptly gave me a jab, but they couldn't understand how I'd got into America without an up-to-date certificate. The answer was that one of Allen Klein's heavies had met us at the airport in New York and rushed us through Immigration and Customs without anyone checking anything.

By the end of 1970 the Beatles as such had virtually ceased to exist. Many things led to the break-up, and Brian's death certainly played its part; John's obsession with Yoko contributed too. The four had never allowed anyone into the recording studio with them, but Yoko not only sat by John throughout every session, he consulted her about the music they were making, which upset Paul. She even moved a bed in because they often recorded through the night. The others were furious but there was nothing they could do about it – John was wrapped up in her. But Yoko aside, they were angry with each other and beginning to go in different directions creatively.

John was writing more challenging music than he ever had before and becoming more political. He and Yoko had the Plastic Ono Band and he was also making some rather strange films. George was working on his own albums, also recording with the Krishnas, Jackie Lomax, Doris Troy, Billy Preston and other bands. Ringo had developed a taste for country music. Paul was composing the ballads he had always written and was making his own albums with Linda. The four were establishing their own identities and, having been so close for so long, finding it an uncomfortable process.

One of John's films, called *Erection*, about a hotel being built in Brompton Road, was shown at the Cannes Film Festival and we went to support him, although he and Yoko weren't there. Cilla Black and her husband Bobby came with us, also Mark Bolan, lead singer with T. Rex, his wife June, and Roger Shine, a friend of Ringo's, with his girlfriend. We stayed on a sumptuous boat with a crew of thirty-two. There were valets to unpack our suitcases and we each had an entire suite. Ringo conveyed to the chef that he would like chips with everything, so whenever we ordered a glass of wine, along came a bowl of chips. If challenged the waiter would say, 'But Monsieur Starr says that everything he orders must have chips.'

There had been terrible rows during the recording of *Let It Be*, which dragged on for six agonising weeks at the beginning of 1969. It was filmed as part of a fly-on-the-wall documentary for television, directed by Michael Lindsay-Hogg at Twickenham Studios. It was fraught with difficulty. At one point George and Paul came to blows and George walked out. Lindsay-Hogg managed to persuade him to come back and they finished the recording at the Apple Studios in Savile Row, then played the title number on the roof to an invited audience.

The situation reached boiling-point in September. John arrived at Kinfauns unannounced, as he often did, with Yoko and told George he was planning to leave the Beatles. It seemed to have come out of the blue. I thought Yoko must have been behind it, wanting to take John in a different direction. George was very angry.

Also that day George heard that his mother had been ill for eight weeks and was in a critical condition. She hadn't wanted us to know in case George was busy, but I have no doubt her illness was another reason for his black moods. His brother, Harry, had telephoned with the news, and when we arrived at the house in Warrington it was clear that he hadn't been exaggerating. Lying in her bed, Louise Harrison reminded me of my grandmother the last time I'd seen her, just days before she died. Her skin was covered with goose-pimples and she was rambling about people in the room whom we couldn't see.

Her GP hadn't done anything other than give her some pills; he thought she was suffering from dementia and hadn't thought to examine her. When we saw him he asked George for an autograph. We immediately found another doctor, who sent Louise straight to hospital for X-rays. Four hospitals later, we discovered she had a brain tumour. It was inoperable, but a surgeon drilled a hole in her skull to release some fluid and relieve the pressure. Then she had two weeks of radium treatment. We were told her chances of survival were fifty-fifty, and it was sad to watch George try to comfort his father when he himself was so low. Gradually, though,

Louise improved. We stayed with her for those two weeks and in the end, although still in hospital, she was up and dressed, watching television and telling jokes.

The illness had set in a couple of months after we had sat up until three or four in the morning at Kinfauns watching Neil Armstrong take his first steps on the moon. I believe that threw Louise into 'Future Shock', a concept Alvin Toffler wrote about in a book of that title – that people can be psychologically affected by too much change in too short a time or, to use the phrase he coined, from 'information overload'. According to his theory, someone like George's mother, who had lived through the war years, then seen her youngest son become globally famous, had been through such a lot that the idea of men walking on the moon was too much for her. Louise wanted to believe it had been done in a film studio.

She died about a year later. It was hard on George because he had adored his mother. But he was also concerned about how his father would cope. He, of course, was devastated. After the funeral he came to live with us, and later George took his father to Los Angeles with him. Suddenly the old man blossomed: he was amazed to find that so many people wanted to meet him; it gave him a whole new lease on life.

For some time my mother had been saying it was a shame that I hadn't become pregnant – perhaps I should see my doctor, she suggested. I made an appointment with my GP, who sent me to see a gynaecologist at a hospital in Chelsea, where I was kept in overnight while they did tests. 'Received a beautiful injection,' I wrote in my diary. It would have been around my thirty-second birthday, and I had never used any form of contraception – the only time I did was soon after this when I went on the pill for a month, thinking that women were always more fertile when they came off it. I'd always thought I'd become pregnant naturally, but it didn't happen. The specialist discovered that one of my tubes was partially blocked but the other was clear and, in his opinion, I should have been able to conceive naturally. I wasn't desperate for children and I imagined that something would happen sooner or later so I didn't panic.

George was working very hard, things were not going well with the Beatles and he was bringing home bad vibes. We would argue and bicker, never reaching any conclusion so we were left feeling irritated with one another. He spent more and more time away from home – sometimes he wouldn't get back until four or five in the morning, at others not at all.

When he wasn't recording he would be at the Apple offices, which I knew were full of pretty girls – and George was sexy, good-looking, witty and famous, an irresistible combination. He had never used aftershave or cologne in the past, but since we had come back from India he had taken to wearing sandalwood oil, which I imagined was to attract other women. But if I accused him of any-thing he would deny it. He made me feel I was being unreasonable, nasty and suspicious.

My diary is full of entries about my unhappiness and the disintegration of our relationship. On 24 July it simply says, 'Silence reigns and my cheeks get wet.' I felt so helpless. At George's insistence I had virtually given up modelling. I thought he had wanted me at home so we could be together, but as often as not I had just the cat for company. Maybe I should have stood my ground and fought for what I felt was my due, but I didn't have the confidence. And the more George retreated into himself, the less confident I was. I busied myself with other things and saw my friends and family.

I let it be known that I was available for modelling again, and did a show for Ossie Clark at Chelsea Town Hall, which the Beatles came to watch. One of my outfits was a long strapless chiffon dress that barely covered my nipples – I was terrified they might pop out and cause a row with George. Then I went to Milan with Twiggy and Justin de Villeneuve, and did some cover shots for Italian *Vogue*. Twiggy and I did our own makeup and did it identically, with little freckles pencilled over our noses falling on to our cheeks. Anna Piaggi, the fashion editor, loved us and ran us over five pages. I did some British *Vogue* covers with David Bailey; then Jenny and Paula, my sisters, and I did a job together for the one and only time. It was for *Vogue* with Patrick Lichfield, a nice picture of us with kites on Hampstead Heath.

I also took up flying. I had a few lessons in a Cessna at a little airfield near Esher called Fairoaks. I gave it up in the end because maths was involved and numbers had always been beyond me. I also did a cookery course, which I enjoyed, and George gave me a knitting machine so I took knitting lessons. I had been inspired by Twiggy who also had one and could run off wonderful sweaters. I found it terribly difficult. I knitted George a Fair Isle one and that was it.

I also went to art classes in Richmond with a friend called Sheila Oldham. She was married to Andrew Loog Oldham, who managed the Stones for quite a while. We became passionate about Perspex and were terribly creative, especially after lunch and a joint, or so we thought. One day I arrived at her house and she asked me how I wanted to feel. She had all these pills and said, 'I've got up, down or sideways.' I couldn't decide so she chose some for me and I had mine and she had hers, and we drank whatever we drank and soon we were pretty high. It was a nice day and we were talking in the sun, and her little boy Sean was playing.

Later we went down to the basement of her huge house in Richmond and she started work. She was chucking paint around – all very Jackson Pollock – setting fire to it, then putting it out. Suddenly rather more than she had intended caught fire and we were so out of it . . . I grabbed Sean and ran upstairs with him, leaving Sheila to deal with the fire, which she did. I was so stoned I couldn't drive – I could hardly walk or talk – so Sheila drove me home. George was furious that she had let me get into such a state. For his next birthday I gave him a Perspex sculpture, which he seemed to like.

I took such pleasure in buying him presents. When I was modelling I would always come back from Paris or Rome or wherever with something special. For Christmas I once gave him what looked like the most extravagant, expensive present, beautifully wrapped. We watched, tension mounting, as he ripped off the paper. Inside he found a black leather box embossed with gold and inside a little brush, with a note: 'For the man who has everything – a belly-button cleaner'. He loved it! One year I bought him a Dobro guitar, which has a metal body. I was so thrilled to find one and drove to Hastings to get it. He loved that too.

That Christmas George gave me a Nikon camera with three lenses. I had bought a small Pentax when I was with Eric Swayne, but this one took my photography to a new level. I'd hung out with so many photographers that I knew how important lighting, composition and shutter speeds were. I was fascinated by the process and loved being on the other side of the lens. I took photographs of the cat, my family, our friends, other musicians who came to the house, the places we travelled to and the people we saw. It grew into a passion and eventually I created my own darkroom.

I also started buying and selling antiques. Jenny and I took a stall in the antiques market in the King's Road, and specialised in art nouveau. We called it Juniper – because of 'Jennifer Juniper' – and ran it for about a year. Jenny looked after the stall and I did the buying. I drove all over the country finding *objets d'art*, including a set of Fabergé menu-holders, paintings and knick-knacks of the period. John Jesse, who was married to Mick Fleetwood's sister, introduced me to art nouveau at a time when few people prized it and I could buy it quite cheaply; the jewellery was recognisable and we knew that if it had a signature it was more valuable. Our stall was next door to an antiquarian bookseller. We didn't make much money because we didn't charge enough. I was always so pleased when someone liked what I had bought that I would almost give it away.

Lots of people still came to our house, mostly old friends of mine, family and musicians. Among the latter group a new face began to appear – that of Eric Clapton. He had played on a couple of albums with George, had been in the Yardbirds, John Mayall and the Bluesbreakers, Cream and Blind Faith. I first met him at a party Brian Epstein gave after a Cream concert at the Saville Theatre, which Brian had just bought. Eric was held in awe by his fellow musicians for his guitar playing, and graffiti declaring that 'Clapton is God' had been scrawled on the London Underground. He was incredibly exciting to watch. I was in a box next to Tony King, who worked for the Beatles, and he kept saying, 'Oh, my God.' He looked wonderful on stage, very sexy, and played so beautifully. But when I met him afterwards he didn't behave like a rock star: he was surprisingly shy and reticent.

He and George had become close friends; they played, wrote music and recorded together. At that time his girlfriend was a model called Charlotte, but I was aware that he found me attractive – and I enjoyed the attention he paid me. It was hard not to be flattered when I caught him staring at me or when he chose to sit beside me or complimented me on what I was wearing or the food I had made, or when he said things he knew would make me laugh or engaged me in conversation. Those were all things that George no longer did.

In December George and I, Ringo and Maureen went to see Eric playing with Delaney and Bonnie and Friends at the Albert Hall. Delaney and Bonnie were an American husband-and-wife team and just the best band. It was an electrifying show, and afterwards we went on to the Speakeasy, in Margaret Street. It was a great place – really funky, not as smart as Tramp, the Crazy Elephant or the Ad Lib. The best musicians went there and we'd stay until it was almost daylight – they would put the chairs on the tables and still we stayed.

That night, a guy I knew called Denny Laine sang a beautiful song called 'Go Now'; I was feeling really chilled until his girlfriend grabbed me and gave me a tongue sandwich. It was so shocked, but she was drunk, as we all were, and later became one of the Marquess of Bath's wifelets so I'm sure she didn't fancy me. 'A fantastic night to remember,' I wrote in my diary – and it wasn't that kiss that had made it special.

A few days later Delaney and Bonnie and Friends were playing in Liverpool and I took Paula with me to see them; once again, there was a fantastic party afterwards. Paula was then seventeen and a bit of a wild child; my mother was finding it difficult to cope with her. She was so pretty – the prettiest of us all – creative, lively and outgoing, not cripplingly shy like Jenny and me. As a little girl, when our step-father was living with us, she was utterly adored and always had the biggest present at Christmas; but she clearly remembers even at that young age thinking that when she opened her present, whatever it was, it wouldn't be enough. She was born with an addictive personality; her attitude to the Christmas present was like the alcoholic for whom one glass is never enough – and as a teenager she was well on the way to having a problem.

She had always wanted to be an actress and had been sent to a children's drama school. George and I went to see her on stage a couple of times, and she had parts in a couple of children's television series, including *Swallows and Amazons*. Potentially she had a good career ahead of her. And then it started to go wrong. She and my mother started to fight over clothes: she wanted to wear really short skirts and other things that Mummy thought she was too young for. Eventually Paula was sent to boarding-school but that was a disaster and only made things worse. As soon as she left school, she went to live with an actor boyfriend. Poor Mummy was frantic. Then, to add to her worries, that night in Liverpool Eric fell for Paula. After the show we all went to a restaurant and everyone was quite drunk and raucous. When the rest of us went back to the hotel, we left Eric and

Paula dancing. George was furious with him. He was protective of Paula.

The next night Delaney and Bonnie and Friends played in Croydon, and again Paula and I went to watch, and again there was a wild party afterwards, this time at Eric's magnificent Italianate manor house, Hurtwood Edge, about an hour's drive away. Everyone was exhausted, but it was a fantastic night. Soon afterwards, Paula moved into Hurtwood Edge.

CHAPTER EIGHT

Friar Park

G eorge and I had been together for five years, married for three and, although we still loved each other dearly, life was not idyllic. Emotionally, 1969 was an up-and-down year and one of the activities that kept me busy was house-hunting. George had decided he wanted to move. I was always very happy at Kinfauns – and certainly our happiest years together were in Esher – but he had had a bad experience with the school next door and wanted to get away.

The school had wonderful parkland, which we were allowed to use, with beautiful old trees, lakes and rhododendrons. George had gone there once on acid and sat under the trees with the sun shining. An old watchman had come up to him about ten minutes before closing time and said, 'Get out and go away.' George said, 'All I want to do is look at the trees,' but the man threw him out. George was upset, his feelings probably heightened by the drug, but his reaction was 'Okay, I'll buy my own park.' He wanted a large garden and a house big enough for him to convert part of it into a recording studio.

I had no budget: we never discussed or thought about money. If we needed something we'd ask Brian Epstein, then Peter Brown and, latterly, Allen Klein. I just had instructions to find the right house. And it took a long time. For about a year I drove around the countryside, looking at one grand house after another. Sometimes George came with me but most of the time it was Terry Doran, his assistant and general factotum.

Terry had been around as long as I had known the Beatles. He had been Brian's friend originally, but had known the whole gang since Liverpool days. He had started off in the motor trade – immortalised in the song 'She's Leaving Home' – and came to join the rest of them in the early sixties. With his broad Scouse accent, he had phoned Bradshaw Webb, an upmarket car dealer in Cheyne Walk, and said, 'If you treat your customers anything like you treat me you're fucked – you'll never sell another car. I want to speak to the chairman.'

The chairman sent him a first-class rail ticket and asked him to work for the company, so he did. He sold Brian a Maserati – Brian was colour-blind and driving with him was terrifying because he used to stop at green traffic-lights and go on red.

Brian soon saw how lucrative the motor trade was and set Terry up in business with a showroom in an old cinema at Hounslow. It made good money: he sold everyone their Ferraris and Lamborghinis, Aston Martins and Minis – not only Brian and the Beatles but the Stones and just about every other musician you care to name. Brian liked it when he did cash deals. Afterwards they would go off to the White Elephant with the money to gamble, and as they walked in, the manager would say, 'Good evening, Mr Epstein. How much would you like tonight? Forty thousand?' But Brian never put anything back into the business and eventually it went under.

Then Terry went to work for John Lennon, who said he'd keep

him as long as he made him laugh – but when John married Yoko and they moved into Ringo's flat in Montague Square, the job came to a natural end and George asked Terry to work for us in Esher. I adored him. I called him Teddy, which had been his childhood nickname. He was a real hippie with hair like Bob Dylan's, and he was so kind and funny, someone I could always talk to when George was being difficult or withdrawn. He was there all the time, and always good-natured with David and Boo when they came to stay. I remember racing out of the house screaming one day when they were in the swimming-pool because I thought they were about to kill Terry, who couldn't swim.

We searched and searched, and finally we found the perfect house. It was called Plumpton Place, near Lewes, in East Sussex, and had been designed by Edwin Lutyens, with a garden by Gertrude Jekyll. You went in through a big gate with little gatehouses on either side, then crossed a bridge over a moat, which spilt into a lake, which spilt into another. A woman showed us round and in every room the wallpaper was decorated with birds. In the garden she had an aviary with about two hundred budgerigars, plus the odd robin and sparrow that had found its way in. She said she had started with just a few but they had bred over the years. We fell in love with the house and put in an offer – but she turned it down. She said she didn't want rock 'n' roll musicians buying her lovely house and sold it to the local doctor instead. He realised what a treasure he had bought and sold it to Michael Caine (who had once lived with my friend Edina Ronay), who sold it on to Jimmy Page, the heavy-metal guitarist who founded Led Zeppelin.

It was back to the drawing-board. Then one Sunday Perry Press, our estate agent, spotted a tiny ad in the *Sunday Times*, placed by some nuns, for a house called Friar Park, near Henley-on-Thames, Oxfordshire. They wanted £125,000. I went to see it with Perry one day towards the end of 1969, when the clouds were low. As we went up the drive a magnificent Victorian Gothic pile appeared before us like something out of a fairytale. Built of red brick and stone, it stood proudly on a hill and was the most beautiful place I had ever seen in my life.

I raced back to Esher, told George and Terry about it, and we all went to see it the next day. When he saw it George flipped, and we put in an offer straight away for £120,000. Eventually we bought it for £140,000 – but this for a house on three floors with twenty-five bedrooms, a ballroom, a drawing room, a dining room, a library, a huge kitchen and hall, intricate carvings, formal gardens of ten or twelve acres and a further twenty acres of land. There were two lodges and a gatehouse. It was certainly big enough for George to have his recording studio – and to lie under the trees in the sunshine without being moved on.

The house had been built in 1898 on the site of an old monastery by Sir Frank Crisp, a wealthy London solicitor, microscopist and horticulturalist. He must have been an amazing man – deeply eccentric with a strong sense of humour. There were towers, turrets and pinnacles, large traceried windows and gargoyles. The light switches were friars' faces and you turned them on and off with the noses. All over the house puns about friars and little sayings, some in Latin, some in English, had been carved into the walls. Just outside the dining room there was a carving of a little boy eating and above him the legend, 'Eton boys a Harrowing sight.' Another, over the entrance to the walled garden, cautioned, 'Scan not a friend with a microscopic glass; you know his faults so let his foibles pass.' How wise.

When we bought it, Friar Park was owned by the Salesian Sisters of St John Bosco, a Catholic teaching order that had run a school there for twenty-odd years – Jane Birkin had been a pupil. The school had closed and six nuns and a monk were living alone in the huge house. If they hadn't sold it, the sisters said, they were planning to demolish it, which would have been a tragedy. It was very run-down but in its heyday it must have been spectacular – also the gardens, which Sir Frank had opened to the public. People used to come from far and wide to visit the Elizabethan garden, the Japanese garden, the vegetable garden, the lakes, the topiary, the maze and the massive greenhouses where he grew peaches, nectarines and apricots. It had taken him twenty years to create it and he delighted in showing it off. George was particularly tickled to discover that he'd had signs up saying, 'Don't keep off the grass.'

We became passionate about restoring the house and garden to their former glory. We found lots of maps of the estate and booklets, printed in the 1920s and 1930s, describing how it had been, and we discovered there had been lakes in the garden. Recently they had been used as a dump for Henley's rubbish. I suspect the nuns saw that as a way of making a bit of income. The wonderful gardens were overgrown and full of rusting iron and old bedsteads.

Sir Frank had travelled extensively and brought back to his garden ideas from all over the world. He had built an Alpine garden with a miniature Matterhorn made from twenty thousand tons of granite he had brought from Yorkshire. He had made a network of underground caves leading from the house and in each one he had hung distorting mirrors, like the ones you see in fairgrounds, and as you walked on you came across another filled with little red gnomes and fairies, and another with glass vines and bunches of grapes. It took months to excavate the lakes and patch them up but when we filled them with water we discovered that stepping-stones led from one to the other, and beneath the top lake there were more caves, which were only accessible by boat. You had to row along a very dark passage that led to an enormous replica of the Blue Grotto at Capri, blue from the blue glass he had laid in the garden above the top of the cave. If you rowed on you came to another cave full of stalagmites and stalactites, then on to a third where the walls were covered with glistening mica.

Inside the house you went into a small vestibule with beautiful floor tiles, through two oak doors into a huge hall with a grand, sweeping staircase that had a lamp at the bottom in the shape of a magnificent copper eagle. Wooden pillars extended from the hall to a minstrels' gallery above, and as you walked up the stairs you could see that the first pillar had, on three sides, carvings of a day in the life of a farmer. At five a.m., with a few rays of sunshine, he's getting out of bed; at six, his wife's stirring the porridge; at seven he's off to work in the fields, and on, to the last scene of night-time stars. The fireplace in the hall was twenty feet high with a painted panel on either side of it – one was the Tree of Life, the other the Tree of Destiny – and a beautiful stained-glass window reached to the second floor.

In the dining room the walls were covered with embossed leather, depicting flowers, plants and golden peacocks. At either end there was more stained glass, big windows designed by Edward Burne-Jones, and a huge fireplace between them. It was quite dark and I remember John and Yoko coming to see it. John said it was so dark he didn't know how we could live in it. George suggested he took off the sunglasses he was wearing.

The ballroom was pale blue, creamy white and gold, with cherubs on the ceilings. Somebody said that the nuns had plastered little skirts on the cherubs to make them decent.

The whole house, though, was in a state of terrible disrepair. There was grass coming up through the dining-room floor, the weather had damaged the wall coverings and a lot of the lead had gone from the roofs. The wiring, plumbing and central-heating systems needed to be replaced. In fact, the whole house had to be gutted from top to bottom, then have its beautiful, quirky features carefully restored.

In March 1970 we moved in – George, Terry and I – and immediately brought in an architect called David Platt, who oversaw the project, starting with the top floor. The house was basically uninhabitable but we stayed there for a few weeks while the Middle Lodge was done up, then moved into the Lodge for a few months until the top floor of the main house was ready. Those first few weeks were so freezing – I don't remember ever being so cold, not even with the aunts in Northamptonshire when I was a child. The only two rooms we could warm were the kitchen, a huge room with a lovely big scrubbed-pine table that seated twenty, and the hall, where there was a big fireplace. At night we used to pile up the fire in the hall with logs and sleep in front of it in sleeping-bags, wrapped in hats, coats, scarves, gloves, anything we could find.

One night as we were sitting in front of the fire we heard a noise upstairs. I had a torch so I strode up the stairs and, to my horror, saw a burglar climbing in through one of the first-floor windows. I was so indignant. I shouted, 'Burglar!' and everybody scattered in different directions to look for him. Fortunately he ran away.

It was in the big old kitchen one morning that I opened a letter addressed to Pattie Harrison, Friar Park. It had 'express' and 'urgent' written at top and bottom. Inside I found a small piece of paper. In small, immaculate writing, with no capital letters, I read: 'as you have probably gathered, my own home affairs are a galloping farce, which is rapidly degenerating day by intolerable day . . . it seems like an eternity since i last saw or spoke to you!'

It began, 'dearest l.' He needed to ascertain my feelings: did I still love my husband or did I have another lover? More crucially, did I still have feeling in my heart for him? He had to know, and urged me to write – much safer – and tell him: 'please do this, whatever it may say, my mind will be at rest . . . all my love e.'

I read it quickly and assumed it was from some weirdo. I did get fan mail from time to time – when I wasn't getting hate mail from George's fans. When I showed it to George and others in the kitchen at the time, 'Look at this really weird letter,' they laughed and dismissed it as I had.

I thought no more about it until that evening the phone rang. It was Eric. 'Did you get my letter?'

'Letter?' I said. 'I don't think so. What letter are you talking about?' And then the penny dropped. 'Was that from *you*?' I said. 'I had no idea you felt that way.' It was the most passionate letter anyone had ever written to me and it put our relationship on a different footing. It made the flirtation all the more exciting and dangerous. But as far as I was concerned it was just flirtation.

Jenny had come to stay for a few days as soon as we moved into Friar Park – and suffered those freezing nights in the hall – also Chris O'Dell, a pretty blonde American girl who had been working at Apple. She came home with George late one night. He had asked her to live with us for a bit to help with the house – and I confess I was miffed. I was convinced he was playing around big-time and that any girl who came into our lives was an immediate threat. Whatever nice noises they made to me, I knew that they wanted George. As a result, I had virtually no girlfriends. Jenny was the only one I knew I could trust. So when Chris walked in through the front door, looking like Goldie Hawn and chatting confidently with George and Kevin, the new roadie, I guessed he had brought her home because he intended to sleep with her.

Chris and I got on well together; we cooked, went into Henley to do the shopping and hung out together, and it was all good fun. I liked her, I wanted to be her friend and she clearly wanted to be mine. That made me even more frightened: I knew that if George came on to her I would lose her. I decided to bite the bullet. 'Chris,' I said, 'I'd really like to be your friend and – I'm sorry, I've never said this to anyone in my life before – you will only be my friend as long as you don't let George have you.'

'Okay,' she said, 'that's a deal. I'd rather be your friend.' And we still are friends. And, of course, George tried – she told me, so she was clearly someone I could trust.

From time to time during the spring and summer of 1970 Eric and I saw each other. One day we went to see a film called *Kes* together, and afterwards we were walking down Oxford Street when Eric said, 'Do you like me, then, or are you seeing me because I'm famous?'

'Oh, I thought you were seeing me because *I'm* famous,' I said. And we both laughed. He always found it difficult to talk about his feelings – instead he poured them into his music and writing.

Once we met under the clock on the cobbled Guildford high street. He had just come back from Miami and had a pair of bell-bottom trousers for me – hence the track 'Bell Bottom Blues'. He was tanned, gorgeous and irresistible – but I resisted. On another occasion I drove to Ewhurst and we met in the Hurt Woods. He was wearing a wonderful wolf coat and looked very sexy, as he always did. We didn't go to the house, probably because someone would have been there. A lot of people lived at Hurtwood Edge: the Dominos were there – they were Eric's current band – also Paula, Alice Ormsby-Gore and various musicians or friends who needed a roof.

Eric had started going out with Alice, Lord Harlech's youngest daughter, at about the same time as he'd started going out with Paula. The two girls were the same age and they were friends; how he juggled them I don't know. Another girl, a model called Cathy, was around at the same time. He met Alice through David Mlinaric, the interior designer, and took her with him to Hurtwood Edge when he first went to view the place. She was only sixteen, which I think Eric thought a bit young but he was seriously attracted and a year or so later she moved in with him. Like Paula, I think she was very much in love with him. The convent girl in me found the situation uncomfortable but at the same time strangely exciting.

Another of our secret meetings took place in London one afternoon. The Dominos had finally left Hurtwood Edge and moved into a flat in South Kensington, which that afternoon was empty. Eric took me there because he wanted me to listen to a song he had written. He switched on the tape machine, turned up the volume and played me the most powerful, moving song I had ever heard.

It was 'Layla' – about a man who falls hopelessly in love with a woman who loves him but is unavailable. He had read the story in a book he had been given by a mutual friend, Ian Dallas. Ian had given me a copy too. It was called *The Story of Layla and Majnun* by the Persian writer Nizami. Eric had identified with Majnun, and was determined that I should know how he felt. He had written the song at home and recorded it in Miami with the Dominos.

He played it to me two or three times, each time watching my face intently for my reaction. My first thought was Oh, God, everyone's going to know who this is. I felt uncomfortable that he was pushing me in a direction I wasn't certain I wanted to go. But the song got the better of me, with the realisation that I had inspired such passion and such creativity. I could resist no longer.

That evening I was going to the theatre with Peter Brown to see *Oh! Calcutta!* the Kenneth Tynan revue that had caused a stir. It was the first time full-frontal nudity had been seen on the British stage. By this time Peter had left Apple and was working for Robert Stigwood in America so I hadn't seen him for a while. Afterwards we were going to a party that Robert was holding at his house in Stanmore, North London. George didn't want to go to the theatre and said he wasn't interested in the party either, so Peter was my date.

After the interval I came back to my seat to find Eric in the next seat. He had spotted me in the theatre and persuaded a stranger to swap places with him. Afterwards, he drove himself to the party and I went with Peter, but we were soon together. It was a great party, and I felt elated by what had happened earlier in the day, but also deeply guilty.

Much later in the evening, George appeared. He was morose, and his mood was not improved by walking into a party that had been going on for several hours and most of the people there were out of it. He didn't want to speak to anyone, just to find me. He kept asking, 'Where's Pattie?' but no one seemed to know. He was about to leave when he spotted me in the garden with Eric. It was early morning, just getting light, and very misty. He came over to us and said, 'What's going on?'

To my complete horror, Eric said, 'I have to tell you, man, that I'm in love with your wife.'

I wanted to die.

George was furious. He turned to me and said, 'Well, are you going with him or coming with me?'

And I said, 'George, I'm coming home.'

I followed him to his car, we got into it and he sped off. When we got home I went to bed and he disappeared into his recording studio.

The next time I saw Eric, he turned up unexpectedly at Friar Park. George was away – I don't know whether Eric knew that in advance – and I was on my own. He came in and we had a glass of wine together. Then he said he wanted me to go away with him: he was desperately in love with me and couldn't live without me. I had to leave George right now and be with him.

'Eric, are you mad?' I asked. 'I can't possibly. I'm married to George.'

And he said, 'No, no, no. I love you. I have to have you in my life.'

'No,' I said.

At this point he produced a small packet from his pocket and held it out towards me. 'Well, if you're not going to come away with me, I'm going to take this.'

'What is it?'

'Heroin.'

'Don't be so stupid.' I tried to grab it from him but he clenched his fist and hid it in his pocket.

'If you're not going to come with me,' he said, 'that's it. I'm off.' And he went. I hardly saw him for three years.

He did as he had threatened. He took the heroin and became quickly addicted. And he took Alice Ormsby-Gore with him. He already did a lot of drugs, but they were the ones we all used – marijuana, uppers, downers and cocaine – and he drank quite heavily too. His dealer had been insisting recently he bought heroin when he supplied him with cocaine and he had been using it infrequently for about a year, but not often enough to make much of a dent in his hoard. He had amassed a big pile and now set about using it. He and Alice retreated into Hurtwood Edge and pulled up the drawbridge. He didn't leave the house, he didn't see friends, he didn't answer the door or the telephone, and the two of them sank into virtual oblivion.

By this time Paula had gone. She had been with Eric in Miami when he was recording *Layla and Other Love Songs*, and he had invited her into the studio to hear him sing 'Layla', the last track to be laid down. The minute she heard it she realised it was about me. She had always had a nagging suspicion that he was only with her because she was the next best thing to me and I was unobtainable. Hearing 'Layla' confirmed it. She packed her bags and took her broken heart home. She had been seriously in love with Eric, but he destroyed her pride, her self-esteem and her confidence – which were already fragile. On top of that her big sister, traditionally the nurturer in the Boyd family, was the last person to whom she could turn for comfort.

She went off to stay, first, with Bobby Whitlock, who played with Delaney and Bonnie and the Dominos, then bounced from one relationship to the next, one marriage to the next. Her first husband, Andy Johns, was a sound engineer who worked with the Rolling Stones (as did his brother Glyn); he and Paula had a son called William. Then she married David Philpot, a rug dealer, and had two daughters, Emma and Cassie, but that relationship didn't last either. She embarked on a life of drink and drugs, which has been a constant source of worry for us all but my mother in particular. Sadly, it destroyed not just her youth but her potential to develop her talent into a career.

Eric disappeared into Hurtwood Edge. I tried to telephone but Alice always answered so I hung up. Instead I turned my attention to Friar Park and my husband. For a brief period the project united us, but the house was so enormous, and there were always so many people living in it, that we never had the intimacy we had enjoyed at Kinfauns. Most of the time, even when he was in the house, I didn't know where he was. At meals, if he was there, too many other people were at the table for us to have any real conversation; and even though we shared a bed he was often in his recording studio or meditating half the night.

The house took about four and a half years to restore. It was a lot of work and George put a huge amount of money into it. He poured more into the garden. Friar Park lifted his spirits. He and Terry spent hours in the garden, discussing what needed to be done and how they were going to do it. George's attention to detail was second to none. At Kinfauns I had felt that, although it was George's house, I had a say in it. I felt we had had an equal partnership. At Friar Park I didn't. I felt it was George's house and he would make the decisions. I did a lot of the furnishing but I never felt the house was truly 'ours'.

David Mlinaric helped with the interior decorating. I had met him with David Harlech and the Ormsby-Gores at their house in Wales. He had also done Eric's house in Ewhurst. George and I knew and liked his work but we did quite a lot of the inside ourselves. I commissioned Kaffe Fassett, a friend of mine, to make a big tapestry of ancient musical instruments to hang in George's recording studio; a young artist called Larry Smart did a *trompe l'oeil* at the end of an upstairs corridor. I bought lots of fabulous Tiffany lamps – there was one with dragonflies around the edge and another with tulips – and went to the Furniture Cave in Lots Road, Chelsea, to buy cheap sofas, then had them resprung and reupholstered. Terry bought a billiard table for forty pounds from a working men's club in Chipping Norton that was closing down. But the real pleasure was going out to find serious pieces of art nouveau. We had lots of big rooms to furnish and I had a wonderful time hunting out the perfect pieces for each one.

George and I had a beautiful bedroom – and as soon as it was finished we moved back into the main house. It was above the kitchen and the library and had huge windows that looked out over the lawns towards the lake. We knocked three rooms into one so we had a bedroom, dressing room and bathroom – with a deep Victorian bath – that ran into one another. That bathroom was mine – George had his own at the top of a spiral staircase – and we bought the most beautiful art-nouveau doors and hung them between the bedroom and my bathroom.

I remember flying to Hollywood in a hurry because MGM were holding an auction and I wanted some art-nouveau chandeliers. Our bed was designed by Louis Majorelle. It was mahogany, beautifully carved, and came from Lillian Nassau, a shop in New York that specialised in art nouveau. We also bought a huge cabinet that we put in the hall, and a table for the kitchen. The table was slightly paler than mahogany, oblong with rounded corners, carved flowers and leaves on the legs.

The original kitchen had been a big, big room at one end of the house with stone floors, huge sinks and a butler's pantry. For a long time we cooked and ate there, but we made a new one between the dining room and the library. I spent months finding wonderful old tiles for the walls – I went all over the country to reclamation companies and building renovation sites looking for them, and Jenny helped. Sometimes we chiselled them off walls ourselves. The kitchen, dining room and library were south-facing rooms, with enormous french windows opening on to the garden. A gravelled walk ran along the front of the house with a stone lip, then lawns, with stone steps that led down at either end of the house to a lower level and a round pond, then further down to the lakes.

The library was a sweet little room – the smallest in the house – with wood panelling, a fireplace and a really good feel. Terry was convinced there was a ghost in the house but I never sensed one and neither did George. The library was where I would sit if I was on my own. I loved books; I bought a lot about art and cookery. George wasn't a great reader, except of Indian spiritual writings. He read the teachings of Paramahansa Yogananda again and again and could quote them at length. 'Create and preserve the image of your choice,' he would say.

He became increasingly obsessive about meditating and chanting. He would do it for hours, usually in the temple he had made in an octagonal room at the very top of the house with Persian rugs on the floor. It became his sanctuary. The other was the recording studio, which he had designed on the first floor; he converted the wine cellars into an echo chamber.

I had great plans for the house: I imagined we would host wonderful charity parties with music and ballet for hundreds of people on balmy summer evenings and our friends would visit, but gradually I realised that George didn't think like me. He just wanted to be in his recording studio, surrounded by other musicians and a few old and close friends and family.

When he had first seen the house, he'd thought we might turn it into a spiritual institution, which would be our life's work and payment for the privilege of owning such a glorious place. Then he had doubts about whether we should buy it at all. I wrote in my diary, 'G got up with naughty spoilt depression. Now he doesn't want Friar Park. A bad air of destruction around.'

I don't know whether it was to fulfil his spiritual dream or as a means of providing cheap labour, or a combination of the two, but shortly after we moved into the house George decided to invite three Hare Krishna families to live with us. The idea was that the men would do gardening and the women would look after us and cook. I wasn't sure about this arrangement but George thought it would be wonderful: we could chant together and there would be good vibes in the house.

He had become quite involved with the Hare Krishnas. On our trip to India with Ravi, we had been to Brindaban, which is full of Krishna people – Krishna had lived there four thousand years ago – and George was blown away by chanting with them. But I think these families came through Apple. They had turned up at the offices with all the other lost souls and wannabes, and George had invited them to Friar Park.

To begin with, it was fine. They were a mixture of English and Americans, they were young, they had children and they all dressed in orange. They lived on the top floor of the house and every morning at seven they would start cooking pungent-smelling food. Then they would take over the dining room for their chanting; I joined them sometimes, but I began to feel that what I considered my home had been taken over. And while they may have been spiritual and belonged to a spiritual group, at the end of the day they were just people. And as they were big fans of the Beatles and George, they were quite nice to me, particularly Syamasundara, the head of this Hare Krishna chapter.

What finally got to me was that they didn't look after their children. One had a toddler who was left to wander around on his own until one day he fell into the pond. Luckily someone saw him and pulled him out, but he was in a bad way and I called the doctor, who raced round to revive him. Then it happened again. Once again, I called the doctor: he came but this time he said he was not prepared to turn out a third time: they had to take responsibility for their children, because he wasn't going to do it for them.

When I relayed what he had said they were angry, and I was too. 'You've *got* to look after your children,' I said. Their response was, 'Krishna looks after them.'

Well, that was it. I spoke to George about it, but he liked having them there – and what he wanted counted more than what I wanted.

I felt more and more alienated, and my only allies were Terry,

Chris O'Dell and Jenny, but then Chris went back to London and in June 1970 Jenny married Mick Fleetwood.

Eventually, in 1973, George bought the Krishnas a house in Hertfordshire. They renamed it Bhaktivedanta Manor, and it is still the UK headquarters for the International Society of Krishna Consciousness. They created a nice vegetable garden for us among other things, but I found them invasive, and I didn't like their attitude to their children. But they left a lasting reminder. Syamasundara went to South India because he'd heard that a ruby mine was for sale and being a miner he was curious. And because the mine owner was so pleased with the sale, he sent Syamasundara back to England with a sack of ruby chips for George, with some larger bits and one or two nice pieces that George gave to me. One was an emerald surrounded by diamonds attached to an uncut ruby necklace. He also gave me a handful of rubies that I thought I would have made into necklaces to give to my nieces when they reached eighteen. He couldn't think what to do with the rest, so he scattered them among the gravel on the path to the swimming-pool.

At one point we had eight gardeners working on the garden, not counting the Hare Krishnas, and Beth Chatto, the well-known garden designer, came in to advise us on planting and the oxygenating species we would need in the lakes. (I loved flowers and thought there was nothing nicer than filling the house with them, but George would never allow me pick anything from the garden or the greenhouse: it had to stay as it was. He insisted I went into Henley to buy flowers from a florist.) Maurice, our gardener in Esher, became head gardener and lived in one of the lodges. George's eldest brother Harry, his wife and two children lived in the gatehouse, and the third was kept for guests if they preferred to sleep there rather than in the house. George respected Harry. He was a garage mechanic but when George asked him to oversee the work being done in the grounds he was happy to come south. His brother's fame didn't faze him: he simply said, 'He's our George,' and ignored it.

When the caves had been excavated we had a big party and my youngest brother Boo, aged fourteen, was given the job of rolling the joints for everyone. Terry showed him how to do it and he sat there doling them out to our friends – people like Bobby Whitlock, Bobby Keys – a saxophonist who played with George and Eric – Harry Nilsson, Donovan and the Stones. All sorts of people spent the evening cosying up to him and saying, 'Hey, Boo, let's have another.'

Suddenly someone said they thought the police were coming up the drive. Boo, thinking he mustn't let me get into any more trouble after the drugs bust in Esher, threw the entire huge bag of marijuana into the bushes. No police materialised, only our guests saying, 'Hey, Boo, let's have another.' To his acute embarrassment, he had to confess what he had done. Our friends spent the rest of the night scouring the bushes for marijuana.

Boo loved George and he loved the kudos of having him as a brother-in-law. He also loved the crushed-velvet trousers that George gave him – David and Boo both fitted into George's trousers – which gave him an edge when it came to wooing the girls at the school across the road from my mother's house. But he was not influenced by George as David was. David hero-worshipped George. One of his first memories is of listening to George and Mummy discussing religion, and when he was about thirteen he remembers George, some friends and me coming to stay with my mother for the weekend at her house near Tiverton, and going on an outing across Bodmin Moor to climb Brown Willy, Cornwall's highest hill. It was a long walk and everyone became rather bored, but while the rest of us went back to the car, George sat at the top of the hill, prayer wheel in hand, with David and told him about Babaji, a divine guru, who was an incarnation of Krishna and had a perfect physical body that he could materialise and dematerialise at will.

Not long afterwards when David was visiting us in Henley, George gave him a copy of *The Autobiography of a Yogi* and urged him to read it. David devoured it. Next came a copy of *The Prophet* by

Kahlil Gibran. David was very affected by both books. He had been brought up a Christian, with Sunday visits to church, but now he was drawn to Hinduism. George had a tough job: David had adopted him as spiritual mentor now, as well as male role model.

By the age of seventeen David's beliefs had changed again and he found comfort in the Chard Full Gospel Church. He went on to become a minister in the charismatic Bath City Church, then moved to a church in Hampstead. Finally, after decades of devoted service, he became a life coach.

George bought my mother a house near Axminster in Devon. It was called Old Ruggs, and our friends went there almost as much as we did. They went to see my mother and whoever else was at home. It was such a lovely house – grey stone with a thatched roof and big rooms with enormous flagstoned floors. But Mummy was convinced it was haunted and only stayed for two or three years.

We drove down to see her in a black Radford Mini that George had at that time, which my brothers were wild about – particularly after he had it sprayed in psychedelic colours. It came to a sorry end: George lent it to Eric, and Alice wrapped it round a lamp-post.

CHAPTER NINE

Leaving George

Cooking was my thing. Having given up modelling full-time, and with no children, I needed to find some role for myself, some *raison d'être*. Preparing wonderful meals for George and all the people who came to Friar Park became a passion. I was good at it and loved the whole process. I took cookery books to bed with me and woke up in the morning knowing what new dish I wanted to create. Driving into Henley and buying all the ingredients was a pleasure. I loved finding new shops and buying the best of everything, finding new brands, new tastes, specialist cheeses, unusual vegetables, different-shaped pastas, exotic varieties of wild rice, fruit, nuts and pulses, olive oils, vinegars and spices. I loved bringing it all home and unpacking it, laying it out on the kitchen counter, and the business of washing and chopping. Then at last the cooking: I was insane about getting the sauces smooth, and I loved combining tastes and textures to see what worked, and creating delicious, nutritious and exciting dishes. As we were vegetarian, it was a challenge to keep meals interesting, but I threw myself into it.

I never knew how many people I was feeding but we had some great dinner parties: George seemed to love my food, there would be plenty of wine, and afterwards everyone would sit around and smoke dope. From time to time there might be some cocaine, which had crept into our repertoire. George developed an interesting and extreme relationship with it. He was either using it every day or not at all for months at a stretch. Then he would be spiritual and clean and would meditate for hour after hour, with no chance of normality. During those periods he was totally withdrawn and I felt alone and isolated. Then, as if the pleasures of the flesh were too hard to resist, he would stop meditating, snort coke, have fun, flirting and partying. Although it was more companionable, there was no normality in that either.

I think owning that huge house and garden created confusion in him. It was a constant reminder of how rich and famous he was, and that gave him a sense of power, but in his heart he knew was just a boy from Liverpool who was talented and had got lucky. He had embraced spirituality with an obsessive intensity, yet he wanted to experience everything he had missed by becoming famous so young. He once told me that he felt something in life was evading him. But he wouldn't – perhaps couldn't – go out and be normal.

I remember Boo once asking George if he wanted to go to the pub for a drink. The guys who protected him froze; George never went to the pub. 'No,' I said. 'George never goes to the pub because of the Beatlemania.'

Boo said, 'Come on, he's got to be able to go to the pub. How else does he enjoy himself?'

And George said, 'All right,' and off they went. He wasn't mobbed and he had a really good time. It was the first time he had done anything so normal for years.

George really didn't like going out – he hated being recognised –

162

so we stayed in that great house and became gradually detached from reality. We didn't listen to the radio because George wouldn't let us, and we didn't have newspapers, and the people who came to see us were either musicians or worked for Apple.

In Esher everything had been easy, relaxed and fun, but in Friar Park it was different. Maybe there was just too much to do, but the house and the garden became an obsession with George. He found out everything there was to know about Sir Frank Crisp, how and why he built that extraordinary house and garden, why he wanted to re-create the Blue Grotto of Capri and build a mini Matterhorn in the Oxfordshire countryside. He wanted to get inside Sir Frank's mind and fit into his old boots, and he seemed to want to do it alone. I can be obsessive, but then I get bored and need a change. George stayed with it, and his obsession grew. Also, it wasn't me he wanted to discuss his ideas for the garden with: it was Terry. He gave me a little area to work on where I did lots of planting, but I didn't feel included in his thinking or his plans. I wasn't his partner in anything any more.

It was the same with the spirituality. He had left me behind – or maybe I had chosen to be left behind. I didn't want to chant all day. George did it obsessively for three months, then went crazy. He wanted to reach the spiritual place to which he aspired, but the pleasures of the flesh were too tempting. Derek Taylor was on a plane with George who was chanting in his seat when a stewardess asked if he'd like a glass of wine. Furious at the intrusion, George told her to 'Fuck off'.

Ravi Shankar was a frequent visitor. George adored him, so when Ravi asked if his nephew Kumar Shankar could come to stay the answer was 'Yes.' But Kumar didn't know whether he should be helping in the garden or giving the engineer a hand in the studio so one day George must have said, 'Why don't you cook some *dhal* or something?' Kumar cooked and that night produced the most wonderful Indian meal. From then on he took over in the kitchen.

George, of course, loved everything to do with India so this was his idea of heaven. Once when Mummy was staying with us and George emerged from his studio, she said, 'You must be hungry, darling. Let me make you an omelette.' He told her, yes, he was hungry but he didn't want an omelette: 'Kumar is going to cook me an Indian meal.'

I felt crushed. He had taken away my one pleasure, the one thing that made me feel I had done something worthwhile with my day, something creative – which being surrounded by musicians all the time was an important part of my self-esteem. In depriving me of the satisfaction of cooking for him and his friends, I felt he was telling me, in a roundabout way, that he didn't want me around.

George also had a secretary called Doreen. She didn't live at Friar Park and I can't remember where she came from, but she was in the house every day. She and Kumar were friends and they would go out together on their days off. She dismissed me, ignored what I said, treated me as if I was a nobody in my own home and my wishes and opinions were insignificant. It was uncomfortable to be in my own house and know that two other people, who were there all the time, one living in it, didn't like me. But it was not a conversation I could have with George: we didn't communicate on any level any more. He was surrounded by yes-men. When I challenged him about it he said, 'Well, I'd hate to be surrounded by no-men.'

There is no doubt that he was going through a difficult time. Having had such a structured life as a Beatle, he was on his own and uncertain of what the future might hold. When he eventually decided to do an album, which was *All Things Must Pass*, he was nervous about it – but he didn't talk to me. He went to Chris O'Dell and Terry. Terry became our go-between. I confided in Terry, too. We were living in a surreal world with a very creative and eccentric person. Between ourselves we referred to George as Geoffrey; then we could discuss him freely and no one would know whom we were talking about. To gauge his mood, we would ask whether his hands were 'in or out of the bag' – meaning his prayer bag. If they were in it, he was in spiritual mode and incommunicado; if they were out, there was a chance of talking to him.

When *All Things Must Pass* was released in America George and I went to New York and stayed for about five weeks. There, we saw Paul and Linda, who were also making a record. We went on to stay with Bob Dylan, his wife and five children at their country house in Woodstock, two hours from New York. It was early November and the autumn colours were glorious – reds and golds, oranges and yellows. The last time I had met Bob had been at Kinfauns in the summer of 1969, when he had been in England to play at the Isle of Wight festival – pop festivals were new at that time – and was coming to supper in Esher the night before. Terry and I had prepared a great feast, David and Boo were there and several other people.

George had gone to meet Bob at the airport but his plane was late and he had to go straight to the Isle of Wight. We were so disappointed but he phoned the next morning and told us to join him there so we set off – George, me, Terry and Mal, the roadie, and caught the ferry from Southampton. Bob, his wife Sara, Al Aronowitz (who had introduced Bob to the Beatles on the famous night he turned them on to marijuana) and the Band met us; they were staying in some grand house and we were in a hotel where there was a tennis court. Having been in my school's team, I suggested we play. Bob said, 'Yeah, that's a great idea,' and everyone played together, which meant about seven people on each side of the net.

Bob had done little performing since a motorcycle accident two years before, and as I watched him on stage he looked a little fragile. Afterwards he came back to Esher with us so David and Boo got their autographs after all.

While we were in New York we went to a couple of big dinner parties, to George's horror and my delight. One was given by Ahmet Ertegün, the co-founder of Atlantic Records, the other by Robert Stigwood. George hated parties, unless they were exclusively for his friends. Put me into a room full of people and I come to life. Sometimes George and I, both Pisceans, were like the symbolic fish swimming in opposite directions. George seemed torn between the deep beneath us and the glitter on the surface, and I was so dazzled by what sparkled above that I couldn't look down for fear of what might be lurking there.

From New York we flew to Jamaica – just the two of us for a change. We had planned originally to go to Los Angeles but a New York journalist had warned George against it. Charles Manson's trial was under way and his defence team was claiming that Manson had been influenced by the Beatles' music when he murdered Sharon Tate. So we went to Jamaica and it was a disaster from the start, beginning with the smallpox problem. Immigration then said, probably because we were white, British, long-haired and had money, that we had to report back to Montego Bay two days later, a journey of seventy miles, to see someone from the Tourist Board. There was no explanation. The man just said, 'That's what I say.' As I told my diary, 'There were such bad vibes everywhere. We stayed in a hugely expensive hotel at Frenchman's Cove. It rained every day except one.'

Our room, which came with a butler and a maid, was in one of about a dozen bungalows in the grounds and we were given a little golf cart to get to and from the main building. After dinner we would go back to our bungalow and George would play his guitar. One night when it was raining I walked outside and recorded it all – the sound of him playing, and the sound of the rain and the jungle and the noises of the night. It was an amazing combination.

The next time I heard from Eric was in January when he wrote to me from a cottage at Llanddewi Brefi in Wales; it had been two months since he had walked out, vowing to take the heroin. On the title page from a pocket-sized copy of the novel *Of Mice and Men*, he'd written:

dear layla

for nothing more than the pleasures past i would sacrifice my family, my god, and my own existence, and still you will not move. i am at the end of my mind, i cannot go back and there is nothing in tomorrow (save you) that can attract me beyond today. i have listened to the wind, i have watched the dark brooding clouds, i have felt the earth beneath me for a sign, a gesture, but there is only silence. why do you hesitate, am i a poor lover, am i ugly, am i too weak, too strong, do you know why? if you want me, take me, i am yours . . .

    if you don't want me, please break the spell that binds me.
    to cage a wild animal is a sin, to tame him is divine.
    my love is yours.

It was signed with a heart and was the same distinctive handwriting with no capital letters.

That one short note stirred up feelings I had spent two months suppressing. I wrote and told him what he wanted to hear.

How are you? I hope the Welsh air has been soothing your mind and warming your heart. Oh, I so long to spend some time with you there . . . it would be beautiful to be together, just for a while.

If the stars should suddenly change their course and I can come to Wales I'll send a telegram. Please write to me and let me know how long you will be there and at Glyn

[Lord Harlech's house]. Please take care of yourself.

Moons full of love

L

              Magnificent is space today!
              Cast bridle, spurs and reins away
              And let us race on steeds of wine
              To skies enchanting and divine!

As though two angels overcome
By fever's wild delirium,
Through morning skies of limpid blue,
Let us that far mirage pursue!
Gentle the winging of our flight
As we the cunning whirlwinds ride
In rapturous and shared delight.
Charles Baudelaire

As soon as I had posted the letter I had terrible doubts and immediately wrote a postcard. It simply said,

Hullo,
Please forgive and forget my bold suggestion.
Love L

His reply came by return of post on the dust-jacket of a book of Scottish ballads and was written in green ink. My letter had come as a nice surprise he said, but 'now that i have been here for a week my expectations (fantasies if you like) have gradually withdrawn into themselves to await a period of greater comfort, perhaps? my dear one, i would not dream of asking you down here now that i have uncovered the full portent of such an existence.' The cottage, he said, was damp and primitive and his vain attempts at lighting a fire would only have warmed a quarter of the room. 'bold suggestions indeed, hah! it was rather significant that i received both communications on the same morning. something like watching a boomerang in flight.' He said he understood my situation and didn't know what to recommend. Then, portentously,

i don't think, even if we were the last ones left alive, that you could be happy with me, and as for me i think i am content to remain alone until someday i am free to be discovered . . .

i love you even though you're chicken.

p.s. baudelaire, too, was ultimately a pesimist [*sic*].

p.p.s. the thing about pessimism is that in most cases it's nothing more than a front behind which a body can hide its most sweet yet painful hopes. please forgive mine

Nothing came of our fantasies and I didn't see or speak to him again until August 1971. George had persuaded him to come out of Hurtwood Edge briefly to perform in the Concert for Bangladesh that he had organised in Madison Square Garden, New York. Ravi Shankar had inspired it. He had told George about the catastrophe in Bangladesh: three million people had been killed in the war with Pakistan and ten million had fled to India where they were starving. He said he was thinking of doing a concert to raise $25,000 for the UNICEF fund to help the refugees and asked whether George might be able to help. George was immediately fired up and, with the Beatles' ethos that 'if you're going to do something, you might as well do it big and make a million' still pumping in his veins, decided to stage a major extravaganza – the first ever pop concert for charity. With the help of an Indian astrologer he settled on 1 August as the most favourable day for him to make a major impact. He then rang his friends and pulled together the most incredible collection of musicians – Bob Dylan, Ringo Starr, Leon Russell, Billy Preston, Ravi Shankar and Eric Clapton.

George knew that Eric was in a bad way but his addiction was unspoken. He thought that if he got him on stage, even propped up with drugs, it would become an open secret and maybe he would open the door a little to his friends, who might be able to help. But everyone knew that if Eric was to have a chance of getting through two performances, one in the afternoon and another that evening, he would need a supply of heroin when he arrived in New York – obviously he couldn't travel with it. I remember discussions about finding a really good one for him, called White Elephant. It had to be very pure because he never injected – he was terrified of needles – always snorted it, as if it was cocaine, from a gold spoon he wore round his neck.

Alice found it. She always did the scoring, as she did everything Eric wanted. At Hurtwood Edge, she went to London to do the sordid business of getting supplies while Eric stayed at home. If ever they ran short, she would give him her share and take something else. She was drinking at least two bottles of vodka a day so he could have the heroin, yet he would accuse her of doing the reverse.

That day he and I scarcely spoke. He was surrounded by people, then on stage, and he was very out of it; I am not sure he really saw me. It was a shock to think that he had done this to himself because of me. At first I felt guilty, then my feelings would swing violently the other way and I was angry that he should have asked me to choose between him and my husband.

When the concert was over Eric and Alice went back to the horrors of their self-imposed prison at Hurtwood Edge and took up where they had left off. Once again they closed the doors on their friends and the world and left the phones to ring unanswered.

Alice's father and Pete Townshend of the Who eventually got through to Eric and persuaded him to seek treatment. David Harlech must have been worried sick about his daughter but he had been incredibly supportive and patient throughout the three years of Alice and Eric's addiction. And Pete Townshend had been the only friend who had refused to take no for an answer and been to the house so often that eventually Eric had seen him. If anyone else managed to get in Eric had hidden upstairs. But Eric confided in Pete, and as good as asked for help.

David Harlech suggested that Townshend put together a charity concert in London. Eric was again persuaded to perform, alongside Townshend and Ronnie Wood (guitars), Rick Grech (bass), Steve Winwood (keyboards) and Jim Capaldi (drums), all friends. He didn't look well: his addict's diet of junk food and chocolate had made him put on weight.

I was sitting in the audience at the Rainbow, Finsbury Park, with George, Ringo, Klaus Voormann, Elton John, Rory Gallagher, Joe Cocker, Jimmy Page and Ahmet Ertegün. As I heard the opening wail of 'Layla', the first number of the evening, then the lyrics, my blood ran cold. He might have been wrecked for the last three years, but he hadn't forgotten how to tear at the heart-strings with his guitar. All the emotion I had felt for him when he disappeared from my life welled up inside me. The show, billed as his comeback, was a triumph.

The Rainbow concert reminded Eric there was an alternative to his life as an addict but it was still another year before he agreed to accept treatment. David Harlech persuaded him to see Dr Meg Patterson, who specialised in heroin addiction and practised what she called neuro-electric therapy, which involved sticking things like acupuncture needles into the earlobe and passing an electrical current through them. She came to Hurtwood Edge initially, then he stayed with her and her family at their house in Harley Street while the treatment lasted.

Four weeks later, he went to spend a month farming with Frank Ormsby-Gore in Oswestry. They became very good friends and the physical outdoor work did him a power of good. He was mucking out, baling hay, chopping logs, sawing trees, and soon he was tanned, fit and ready to take on the world. However, he and Frank also went to the local pub and became drinking companions. Eric went straight from heroin to alcohol.

I had met Meg Patterson soon after Eric finished his treatment, and she had warned me that this might happen. I didn't notice the problem immediately. When he returned from Wales he became a regular visitor to Friar Park and professed his love for me with increasing vigour. Letters arrived almost daily, in which he pleaded with me to leave George and come to him.

Meanwhile George and I had been stumbling along, with things going from bad to worse. I don't know what his feelings were about Eric when he reappeared in our lives. We had been so stoned on the night of Robert Stigwood's party that he might have forgotten about the confrontation in the mist, but I don't think so. He never spoke about it but after that night I think he felt he could be as blatant as he liked in his pursuit of other women.

In the spring of 1973 we were supposed to go on holiday to Portugal together. The day before we were due to leave he said he wasn't feeling well and couldn't go. I told him he looked fine, but he insisted, so I cancelled the flights. Then I was invited to the Bahamas by Sheila Oldham, my artist friend. George clearly didn't want to go away with me so I decided to go on my own and take Paula and her baby, William, with me.

Paula was in a bad way. She and her husband, Andy, were living in a flat in Little Venice and one day she confessed to me that she had been so stoned and so out of it that she couldn't remember whether she had last fed William an hour or a day ago. I thought if I could get her away from Andy, who was also using, I might be able to sort her out.

My thoughts about George were right. He didn't want to go on holiday with me and ended up going to Spain, supposedly to see Salvador Dalí, with Ronnie Wood's wife, Krissie. Ronnie, then bass guitarist with the Faces, and Krissie were friends. They lived in Hampton Court but often came to stay at Friar Park. I was desperately hurt: another of my friends was sleeping with George. When I challenged him he denied it, and tried once again to make me feel as though I was paranoid.

When Paula and I met at Heathrow for the flight, I asked her what heroin was like. She said, 'Try some,' so, always up for anything, I did. I went into the loo, and when I came back I felt truly amazing.

'Did you like it?' Paula asked.

'Yes, it was kind of extraordinary.'

'I'm never giving you any more.'

I said I hoped she never would *have* any more. Furthermore, I hoped she didn't have any illegal substances on her as we had to go through strict Customs on arrival in the Bahamas. She assured me she didn't.

Sheila picked us up at the airport and took us to Paradise Island by boat where Paula and I were given the Polynesian House to stay in. It was pretty, straw-thatched, and had its own swimming-pool.

As soon as we had dumped our bags Paula said, 'I did have some with me, and a syringe.' She pulled out a package from under her shorts.

'Hand it over to me now,' I said, 'because this is it. I hope you told your doctor to give you something to help when you come down. I'm not a nurse and I don't know what I'm doing.' She gave me the syringe and I told her I'd bury it in the sand.

Off I went. I waited a bit, then brought it back surreptitiously and hid it with my T-shirts.

The days went by. We did yoga every morning and she seemed to be getting on quite well, William was happy and everything seemed good. But I had to hide her from my friends, Sam and Sheila, because I couldn't trust her. When I went to see them I would tell Paula to stay in the house. And they kept saying, 'Where's Paula?' and I kept saying, 'She's got a bad cold.'

After about a week she panicked and wanted the syringe for one last hit. It was pathetic: she was desperately digging in the sand, digging, digging, digging for the syringe. I couldn't bear to see her like that so I dug too, and pretended to find it. She filled it, and after she had used the last of the heroin, we destroyed it.

Then Andy rang to find out how she was, and wanted to come out too so I could clean him up. I thought this would be fantastic – little William might stand a chance – but Andy was far more difficult than Paula. He wanted to stay up all night drinking vodka, and then he would wander off into the sea. I was terrified he would drown and had to watch him all the time. He was hard work but gradually he got better, and he was so much nicer when he was clean; they were both on tremendous form. But I was worried that Andy would find it difficult to stay clean when he got back to the Stones. I asked him whether he thought he'd be tempted and he said, 'Maybe.'

'Andy, how can you say that? I'll have wasted ten days!'

'Sorry, but it might be difficult for me to say "No".'

At least Paula was clean – for the time being.

In the midst of all of this we had a call from Ronnie Wood. He was on tour and said he might come to see us for a few days. It was such a relief to have someone else to party with, someone who was light and fun, who enjoyed life and didn't need looking after. He didn't seem upset that his wife was with George – just thought it was funny that they'd gone to see Salvador Dalí. Ronnie was, and is, the most adorable man and maybe at that moment, some fun, laughter and a pair of comforting arms were what I needed.

In hindsight I wonder whether George's pursuit of other women was a challenge: perhaps he was hoping to provoke me, hoping to make me put my foot down and reclaim him. At the time I saw it as rejection, and ever since the day my mother left me in Kenya while she sailed to England with Bobbie and Paula, I have lived in fear of being abandoned. When things reached such a pitch with George that I thought our marriage was past saving, I left before he had a chance to leave me.

The final straw was his affair with Maureen Starr, Ringo's wife. She was the last person I would have expected to stab me in the back. But she did. I discovered from some photos Terry had had developed that she had been staying in the house with George one weekend when Jenny and I had gone to Devon to see my mother. He had given her a beautiful necklace, which she wore in front of me. Then I found them locked into a bedroom at Friar Park. I stood outside banging on the door and saying to George, 'What are you doing? Maureen's in there, isn't she? I know she is,' but he laughed.

He was supposed to be in the studio and everyone was waiting for him. Eventually he opened the door, and said, 'Oh, she's just a bit tired so she's lying down.' I went straight up to the top of the house and with the help of Phil and Andy, the studio engineers, lowered the OM flag that George had flying from the roof and hoisted a skull and crossbones instead. That made me feel much better.

Maureen wasn't even prepared to be subtle. She would turn up at Friar Park at midnight and I would say, 'What the hell are you doing here?'

'I've come to listen to George playing in the studio.'

'Well, I'm going to bed.'

'Ah, well, I'm going to the studio.'

The next morning, she'd still be there, and I'd say, 'Have you thought about your children? What are you up to? I don't like it.'

'Tough.'

That whole period was insane. Our lives were fuelled by alcohol and cocaine, and so it was with everyone who came into our sphere. Friar Park was a madhouse. Chris O'Dell was there, madly in love with an American; Ronnie and Krissie Wood would arrive, she with a basket that contained beautiful clothes; Eric was pursuing me; Terry was tearing off to London to see bands playing in clubs and returning at three or four in the morning. We were all as drunk, stoned and single-minded as each other. Nobody seemed to have appointments, deadlines or anything pressing in their lives, no structure and no responsibilities, except in the evenings when Chris and I would sometimes cook dinner.

One evening when John Hurt, the actor, was with us, Eric was due to come over and George decided to have it out with him. John wanted to make himself scarce but George insisted he stay. He remembers George coming downstairs with two guitars and two small amplifiers, laying them down in the hall, then pacing restlessly until Eric arrived – full of brandy, as usual. As Eric walked through the door George handed him a guitar and amp – as an eighteenth-century man might have handed his rival a sword – and for two hours, without a word, they duelled. The air was electric and the music exciting. At the end nothing was said but the general feeling was that Eric had won. He hadn't allowed himself to get riled or to go in for instrumental gymnastics as George had. Even when he was drunk, his guitar-playing was unbeatable.

Cocaine was a seductive drug because it made you feel euphoric and good about yourself. It took away your inhibitions and made even the shyest, most insecure person feel confident – usually over-confident. And we had so much energy – everyone would talk nonsense for twice as long, and drink twice as much because the cocaine made you feel sober. Every pleasure was intensely heightened and prolonged. Like everything, done in moderation it was fine. Done to excess it was not. George used coke excessively and I think it changed him.

Smoking marijuana changed us too, but it wasn't destructive. Dope in the sixties – a very different drug from the skunk kids smoke today – was about peace, love and increasing awareness. It was the basis of flower power; it was innocent. Cocaine was different and I think it froze George's emotions and hardened his heart.

Ringo didn't have a clue what was going on until I rang him one day and said, 'Have you ever thought about why your wife doesn't come home at night? It's because she's here!' And he flew into a rage.

George continued to pretend that nothing was going on: 'I'm not sleeping with her.'

'You must be. What else are you doing?' And he would leave me feeling as though I was becoming paranoid, going quietly mad. I didn't say, as I should have done, '*Enough!* Get that woman out of my house.'

I suppose I didn't really think of it as my house. I felt very undermined and unloved and George was so terribly difficult to talk to. If you spoke to him you didn't know whether you would get an answer in the middle of his chanting or whether he would bite your head off. He had become worse in the last year – maybe because Eric kept coming around and making it obvious that he wanted to see me. George must have sensed we were having an affair but he never said so. I felt he wanted to break us up, he wanted to get rid of me. I felt we were like chopsticks joined together and cracking apart; something had to happen.

The 1973 New Year's Eve party was at Ringo's, and George, Terry and I were all ready to go when I realised I'd left something behind. I dashed upstairs to the bedroom – and saw the car lights disappearing into the night. They'd gone without me. I got into my car and drove towards Ringo's but there was thick fog around Ascot and so much traffic that no one could see a thing and we hardly moved. Suddenly all the cars stopped because it was midnight and everyone got out of their cars to wish each other a happy new year – complete strangers were hugging one another.

When I finally arrived George said, 'Let's have a divorce this year.'

On our wedding anniversary, 21 January 1974, I wrote in my diary: 'Wedding anniversary. Joke!'

Ringo realised that things were bad between George and me and offered me a job, which helped take my mind off my problems. He was playing Merlin the Magician in a musical comedy he made with Harry Nilsson called *Son of Dracula*. He asked me to take the stills shots. The film was produced by Apple Films and was so bad that it was hardly ever shown.

At home the madness continued. Until one day George, Chris O'Dell and I went to Ringo and Maureen's house where George, in front of everyone, proceeded to tell Ringo that he was in love with his wife. Ringo worked himself up into a terrible state and went about saying, 'Nothing is real, nothing is real.' I was furious. I went straight out and dyed my hair red.

On 22 June that year, my little brother Boo was married to Monique in Devon, and I went down for the wedding. We had both been invited but George didn't come. Boo and I had been shopping in the King's Road the previous week and had bought him a lovely suit to wear on the big day and a shirt; the suit had to be altered so I said I'd bring everything with me. Boo was worried I'd forget the shirt and as soon as I arrived he asked if I'd remembered it. 'Don't worry, Boo,' I said, 'it's in the car.' Then he asked how the suit looked. I'd left it at Friar Park.

It was about ten o'clock at night, in Bampton, Devon, and the wedding was at ten in the morning. Boo freaked. 'Don't worry,' I said. 'I'll get George to send it down in a helicopter.' We went into a public telephone box and rang George, who was furious. Alfie, his driver, brought it down overnight. To complete the fiasco, Paula and Andy were so drunk that they missed the ceremony.

'Return to find lunacy inspired by Eric with Pete Townshend and Graham Bell [another musician]' is what I wrote in my diary about the following day. I arrived home in the evening to find them all locked in conversation. I made some soup, which we ate amid forced jollity, then Eric took me aside and pleaded with me once more to leave George. We were alone together for what felt like hours, and he was so passionate, desperate and compelling that I felt swamped, lost and confused. But now I had to make a choice. Would I go to Eric, who had written the most beautiful song for me, who had been to hell and back in the last three years because of me and who had worn me down with his protestations of love? Or would I choose George, my husband, whom I had loved but who had been cold and indifferent towards me for so long that I could barely remember the last time he'd shown me any affection or told me he loved me?

That night Eric left and went off almost immediately to America on tour with the band who had made *461 Ocean Boulevard*. On 3 July I told George I was leaving him: it was late at night and I went into the studio and told him we were leading a ludicrous and hateful life, and I was going to Los Angeles to stay with Jenny and Mick. When he came to bed, I could feel his sadness as he lay beside me. 'Don't go,' he said.

Half of me wanted to stay, and to believe him when he said he would make it better, but I was at the end of my tether. I must have weighed about eight stone and I was really, really thin. I said, 'I'm going.'

The next day, with a great sadness in my heart, I packed some things, said a tearful goodbye to Friar Park and our two Siamese cats, then flew to America.

A week later Eric phoned and asked me to join him on tour. Eight days later I met him in Boston and he played the Boston Gardens that night. By the end of the week I was writing, 'At last I can feel the lost woman in me.'

If only that could have remained true.

CHAPTER TEN

Eric

What I had felt for George was a great, deep love. What Eric and I had was an intoxicating, overpowering passion. It was so intense, so urgent, so heady, I felt almost out of control. Having made the decision to leave my marriage, I knew I had to be with him, go everywhere with him, do everything he did, keep up with him in every way. Which, on that tour of America in 1974, meant drinking.

I had never been allowed to go on tour with George so had no idea what to expect, but standing at the side of the stage night after night, amplifiers booming, lights up, music exploding in my head and vibrating through every part of me, was an incredible sensation – deeply sexy. For the first time I understood what a high musicians get when they're in front of a stadium full of fans, adrenaline pumping. And looking out at the thousands of screaming, waving, swooning people who had come to see Eric, my Eric, and seeing their reaction every time he played the opening chords of the song he had written for me was mind-blowing. They went mad. At the end when the band left the stage and everyone was calling for an encore, the audience would hold up candles or lighters, and watching twenty thousand flames sent shivers down my spine.

When Eric was playing in Memphis, and staying for a couple of days, Roger Forrester, who was looking after him, came into our hotel room and said, 'Stevie Wonder wants to meet you.' Next we had a phone call. 'Elvis wants you to go to the cinema with him.' Wow, I thought. What's happening? First Stevie and now the King! Then there was a knock at the door. 'Oh, hi, Stevie, come in.' We chatted to him, had a few drinks, and the next night we had a few drinks with Elvis, then went to see a film.

I had met Elvis once before, with George, and he had looked a lot better then than he did this time. He was now well on the way to being bloated and was surrounded by henchmen, who stopped us as we made for the row Elvis was sitting in and told us to sit five rows back. Not so good. We found ourselves watching some boring old 1950s movie. At the end Elvis said, 'Do you want to see another? We're going to the theatre next door.' It was a five-screen complex. We had visions of going from one to the next watching more boring fifties movies, so we made our excuses and left.

In Los Angeles one night, standing with Jenny at the side of the stage, I spotted Peter Brown in the wings on the other side. It was wonderful to see him after so long, and at the party afterwards we sat on a swing on the beach and talked all night. To me, Peter was a father figure – the only one I had left. It was such a relief to be able to speak freely to someone who knew George about what I had done. Peter understood the situation, and it wasn't the sort of conversation I could have had with my mother. Peter knew about George's infidelity, the chanting and everything else. He thought I was right to have left him. He said I had been too loyal and that George hadn't deserved it. It was comforting to hear that, particularly from someone whose views I respected.

The tour was gruelling: twenty-six shows, from coast to coast, playing to huge audiences; some of the venues seated seventy thousand and they were all packed. We were living out of suitcases, checking in and out of hotels and airports, getting on and off buses, in and out of limos and partying until well into the night after each gig. I found it exhausting. For Eric, after three years of addiction, it was shattering.

He coped by drinking himself close to oblivion. He began in the morning and drank all day until four o'clock when Roger made him stop temporarily. At that time Roger was working for Robert Stigwood, but eventually became Eric's manager. He reckoned that if he could stop Eric drinking at four, he had enough time to sober him up with showers and coffee before the show. After that he made sure Eric had only cold tea and 7Up to drink. Eric's normal poison was Courvoisier and 7Up, which looked much the same as cold tea, and by that stage in the day he couldn't tell the difference.

The plan didn't always work. There were times on that tour when Eric was so drunk on stage that he played lying flat on his back or staggering around wearing the weirdest combination of clothes that somehow looked stylish.

One night, on a later tour in Australia, Roger got cross with Eric. I had found them with a couple of strippers in our hotel suite in Adelaide. A man on the street opposite had been touting for trade and Eric had shouted from the balcony, 'Send two up here, will you?' I walked in to find Roger and him lying on the bed watching the strippers and went berserk: how could they exploit women in that way? Eric said he couldn't agree more, that it had been Roger's idea, and Roger took the flak.

At the next gig Roger exacted his revenge. Instead of mixing the 7Up with cold tea, he mixed it with Sarson's malt vinegar. He could barely contain his delight as Eric took the first gulp on stage, uttered a strangled scream and spat it over Alfie O'Leary, the roadie, who was standing in the wings with a bucket.

Alfie was a great character. He came from the East End of London and his family were friends of the Kray twins. He was the size of a small mountain and his main job was to protect Eric on the road – he would flatten anyone who stood in Eric's way – but he was sweet-natured and would have done anything for Eric. He looked after Hurtwood Edge when we were away once, and I'll never forget coming home and asking Alfie to go to Cranleigh for some wine. 'Sure,' he said, 'what sort do you want?'

'Some St Emilion would be good.'

He went into the shop and asked for something called 'thanks a million'.

Back in England after the American tour, I rang George to say I was coming to Friar Park to collect my clothes, photographs and various other things I had not taken with me when I had left three or four months before. George was there, and he was very sweet but looked so sad. I felt so guilty and wondered whether I had done the right thing. In that beautiful house, with the furniture, and the gardens and the lakes, everything we had spent so much time making right, the memories flooded back of laughter, lovely parties and the good times we'd had.

As I walked in through the kitchen doors, which led out on to the lawns, my lilac-point Siamese appeared with a deep, guttural miaow. 'Hello, Rupert!' I said, as he wound his sleek body round my legs.

George couldn't believe it: Rupert had disappeared the day I left and he hadn't seen him since. As I picked him up and he lay in my arms, purring like a steam engine, I remembered that before I had gone I had cuddled Rupert then taken him for a walk in the gardens and told him everything. I had explained how unhappy I was and that the time would come when I had to leave, but I promised I'd see him again. It was hard to say goodbye a second time.

After the twenty-six-gig American marathon Eric needed a holiday so we went to Montego Bay in Jamaica to stay in a house called Goldeneye, which had belonged to Ian Fleming, who wrote the James Bond novels. It had just been bought by Chris Blackwell, who founded Island Records. Subsequently he turned it into a luxury resort, but when we were there the house was full of original 1940s furniture in mint condition, and had its own beach. We had the most glorious time except . . . every morning the gardener would arrive with the biggest, fattest joint for Eric, then take him to the 'tea shop'. In fact, it sold rum and they would spend the day smoking dope and drinking. Eric would come back in the evening and pass out. Then the maid would ask, 'Is it dinner for one again, madam?'

Eric was clearly an addictive personality: he had moved from heroin to alcohol without blinking, as Meg Patterson had warned. I think he was basically shy and he used drink to enable him to be the personality, the life and soul of the party, that everyone had come to expect. And I tried to keep up, to be what he wanted me to be.

I had never drunk so much in my life, but I assumed that that was what happened on the road and, always up for a party, I drank when the boys did. It seemed like jolly good fun, and in those first heady months I was so happy, carried away with the thrill, the excitement, the passion. But, ultimately, it wasn't satisfying. I wasn't a musician, so I didn't feel I was contributing anything and consequently I didn't feel good about being out of it so much. I didn't feel I had the right to be wrecked each day.

Eric was a working-class boy, like George, but in other respects their backgrounds were different. George came from a stable, loving family and had no insecurities on that account – he loved his family, and couldn't have been more welcoming or generous to my own. Eric's mother, Pat, had given birth to him when she was sixteen after a wartime affair with a Canadian wing commander called Edward Fryer. He was stationed with the Canadian air force at Ripley in Surrey, which was where Pat lived, but he had a wife at home to whom he returned, leaving Pat to bring up their baby alone. Her mother and step-father, Rose and Jack Clapp, supported her, but an illegitimate child was socially unacceptable in the 1940s, so when she met Frank McDonald, who became her husband and the father of three more children, she had to choose between marriage and her baby son. It was an impossible decision for any woman to make but she married, then went to live in Germany and, later, Canada. Eric was left with his doting grandparents in the village of Ripley where, to avoid stigma, he was brought up as their own child, believing that his mother was his elder sister. 'Clapton' had been the name of Rose's first husband, who had died.

It was not until Eric was nine and Pat reappeared in his life that he learnt who his real mother was. He was angry – and I think that anger was always inside him, colouring his relationships with women. He never trusted them and he couldn't understand the concept of having a platonic friendship with a woman; if no sex was involved, he didn't see the point. It made him intolerant of any friendships I had. He was insanely jealous of anyone who diverted my attention from him – which included my family. He also became obsessed by the need to find his father. Eventually a journalist in Toronto traced him, but by the time Eric had tracked him down, Edward Fryer was dead. However, the search had not been in vain because Eric discovered where his musical talent had come from: his father had played piano and saxophone.

When Eric was a boy Rose and Jack lived in a two-bedroom house on the village green, and although they didn't have much money they showered him with expensive toys, which made the other local boys envious. It was their way of compensating him for having no mother. He had lots of friends – many of whom were still close when we were together – but as a child he was solitary. It was not until he was given a guitar at the age of thirteen that he discovered the perfect way to express himself.

By the time I knew Eric his grandfather was dead, and Rose was living in a house that Eric had bought for her in Shamley Green, not far from Ripley and Hurtwood Edge. He was very close to her, which Pat had found difficult to come to terms with when she had returned to Ripley; there was some jealousy between the two women. I tried to encourage Eric to make friends with his mother. She was riddled with guilt at having abandoned him as a baby, and she was depressed: her son Brian, Eric's half-brother, was killed on a motorcycle in Toronto soon after Eric and I got together.

I liked Pat but she couldn't rewrite the past, and although Eric softened to some extent, I don't think he ever entirely forgave her. Rose was the one he adored. He would visit her every week, sometimes twice, and she came to lunch with us most Sundays – also his aunt, uncle and their children, and sometimes Pat too. As often as not, his old friends from Ripley were also there. He would meet them in the pub and they would come home for lunch. My role as cook had been re-established and I was back to never knowing how many people I was catering for.

Unlike George, Eric had no social graces when it came to mealtimes. He would only sit at the table until he had finished his food and then he would get up, regardless of whether others were still eating, and go to watch TV or play the guitar. For him eating was functional: it was not an opportunity to enjoy good food, wine and conversation, not the high spot of the day as it was for me.

With Eric I slid back into eating meat. When we were in America he and I went to Disneyland and I was so hungry I was driven to it. The Americans are such carnivores; there was nothing there for me to eat except Iceberg lettuce. The only alternative was a hamburger the size of a plate. It was the first meat I had eaten in seven years and after half of it I felt as though I'd eaten a brick.

That Christmas we had turkey, and as we were sitting down to it at Hurtwood Edge, George burst in, uninvited. He was horrified to see me eating meat and berated me – but then we laughed and he had some Christmas pudding with us, and some wine, and it wasn't awkward at all. I couldn't believe how friendly he and Eric were towards each other.

He had come over to see what we were up to. And the sad thing was, I realised later, he wasn't doing anything on Christmas Day and must have been lonely. I know he was hurt and angry that I left him but not long afterwards he met Olivia Arias, and from then on things were easier all round.

She worked for Dark Horse, his record label in Los Angeles, and I liked her, but I was hurt when they married in 1977 because George didn't tell me. I said nothing to Eric but he knew instinctively that it had upset me and wrote a song about it – 'Golden Ring', on the *Backless* album. When I went back to Friar Park some time later, when Dhani, their son, was about six, I was interested to see that the house was as I had left it. George asked how I felt, coming back to my old home. He hoped I wasn't uncomfortable.

Hurtwood Edge was in the most terrible state when I arrived, but it felt much more like real life than Friar Park had. It was beautiful: it had a square tower and a huge hall with a black and white marble floor, and big arched windows overlooking the terrace. It looked rather like an Italian villa, with a garden designed in the thirties by Gertrude Jekyll and views for forty miles. But everything was on a smaller scale than it was at Friar Park, and cosier: there were only six bedrooms, and some were dinky. For years the house had been a kind of commune – bats circled round our bedroom – but when I appeared everyone, apart from the bats, was told to go. They left behind a complete mess but a lot of it was Eric's: books, boxes and records, all out of their covers, were strewn all over the place, with piles of paper, unopened letters and unbanked cheques. Eric, I discovered, was not a naturally tidy man and didn't look after any of the lovely things he had. He had a large collection of leather shoes and a wardrobe of expensive clothes. The shoes were scuffed and dirty and the suits no better. The bedroom carpet was lamb's wool, and filthy, and the bath was full of his jumpers and shirts – that was where he stored them. The kitchen was a health hazard: it was very 1950s with lino on the floor, lots of Formica, an old gas cooker and a mouse that scuttled about whenever I came in. There was a lot of work to be done.

After a couple of years, I reshaped the kitchen, and put in an Aga and new units, but I had to get permission from Roger Forrester before I could spend any more money on the house. And he blocked my plans for the beautiful, romantic garden, laid out immaculately with rhododendrons, redwood trees and rare plant species. There was a fantastic wisteria walk supported by round brick pillars, the colour ranging from deep purple at one end through paler shades to white at the other. Another walk was lined with azaleas that came into bloom in stages so that throughout the spring the whole garden smelt heavenly. I wanted to bring in a designer and a few extra gardeners to change it a bit because it hadn't been very well looked after but Roger said, 'No.'

There was just one gardener, Arthur, whose wife worked in the house. They were from the Isle of Wight, lived in a flat above the garage at the top of the drive, and adored Eric. When I arrived I said, 'Arthur, these are the vegetables I would like to grow.' He smiled and said, 'Yes,' then went on growing what he'd always grown. I bought some chickens, and one day I noticed a broken egg outside the hen run. 'Arthur, how could that have happened?'

'Rats. They work in pairs,' he said. 'They go underneath the wire netting, into the compound, into the henhouse and take an egg. Then one rat lies on his back with the egg between his paws and the other pulls him under the netting by his tail. They tuck in when they get to the other side.'

Eric loved animals, and when he was away, Arthur was always there to look after them. When I first arrived Eric had a huge ginger cat called Fast Eddy and a Weimaraner called Willow. For one birthday he bought me an Airedale puppy, which I called Trouper because she was one; she had the most hilarious sense of humour and always looked as though she was laughing. She would race about the garden, then suddenly put out her front paws and raise her haunches on straight woolly legs. She was gorgeous, like a teddy bear. One Christmas I bought Eric a donkey called Matthew, who lived in the field.

Eric wouldn't move unless Roger approved – theirs was another father-son relationship, like the Beatles and Brian Epstein. All of those musicians were like little boys in long trousers. Eric was charming to everyone and agreed to everything. He never had to display negativity because if he didn't like a situation he'd got himself into, Roger would deal with it. If someone asked him to play on their record, he would say, 'Yes,' then ring Roger and say, 'Get me out of it.'

Eric never did anything for himself. He didn't even take his own driving test: he got someone who looked vaguely like him to sit it for him. He never had to fill his cars with petrol, tax or insure them. Someone else did it. He never paid any bills: they all went into a drawer and someone from the office would collect them. One day I found a cheque for five thousand pounds in a drawer and said, 'I'm going up to London. Shall I take the cheque up to the office so they can bank it for you?'

'No! Don't touch it,' Eric said. I asked why not, and he told me, 'I've got the cheque. That's good enough.'

On another occasion someone sent Roger a large cheque, and when it didn't arrive, he discovered it had been dispatched to Hurtwood Edge. He asked Eric if he had seen it. 'I've had it for ages,' he said. 'I put it in the drawer.'

'Why?' asked Roger.

'I'm not giving it to the bloody bank,' said Eric, indignantly. He had no idea about money or banking or anything – not even royalties. He just wasn't interested.

Every week Roger's book-keeper, Gladys, would give Eric his allowance of two hundred pounds. Eric called it his 'wages', pocket money for cigarettes and drinks. Restaurant bills went straight to the office and we had accounts at various shops, like the wine merchant's and the butcher's. Eric also had a cheque book but Roger wouldn't allow him a joint account. If he wanted to buy anything like cars or jewellery, he had to ask Roger and Roger would fix it. His job was to keep Eric happy, but that didn't extend to me. His loyalty was to Eric.

I had little money of my own. I didn't feel I had the right to ask George for any, and Eric was adamant that I shouldn't take it even if it was offered. He wanted to provide for me and keep me in the manner to which I had become accustomed, but that didn't translate to my bank account. With George I had always had a Harrods account. The first Christmas after I left him I went to Harrods, as usual, picked out lots of presents for my family and friends, then went to pay and discovered that the account had been closed. And I didn't have enough money in my bank to pay for it all. I rang George, told him what had happened and how embarrassed I had been, and he sent me a cheque for five thousand pounds.

Eric told me to tear it up – an instruction I ignored. It was a matter of pride to him – and I guess he must have felt a bit guilty for having taken me from George who had always been such a good friend. He always said that George put up no fight, and he was right. With hindsight I think George might have behaved as he did because it was his friend, someone he respected and loved, who was in love with his wife. He was such a selfless, generous person that he let it happen. In the end, when the divorce was negotiated in 1977 on the grounds that we had lived apart for more than two years, my lawyers insisted I must have some sort of settlement and I was persuaded to take £120,000. Apart from that I kept the red Mercedes George had given me, but Eric hated me having it so I sold it and he bought me a black AMG Mercedes, which I had for years.

Alcohol was an everyday feature of our lives. When Eric had been drinking so much on tour I had put it down to the pressure. When he was passing out every night at Goldeneye, I put it down to the bad influence of the gardener. At home I ran out of excuses. The

Ewhurst village pub, the Windmill, was at the end of the drive, about three minutes' walk away, and they were brilliant about protecting Eric. If anyone asked where he lived they would direct them miles away.

Eric loved the pub. When he was at home we would go there most lunchtimes. I had never gone to pubs or drunk beer until I met Eric, but I went to keep him company and then he would invite all these people who happened to be there back to the house afterwards and carry on drinking all afternoon. At first I thought it was quite fun – but after a while, the novelty wore off.

In April 1975 Eric was advised to leave the country for a year for tax reasons, so we went to the house of my friend Sam Clapp, on Paradise Island in the Bahamas. It was where I had taken Paula to wean her off heroin, but this time we stayed in the big house, which overlooked the beach, where the sand was as soft as snow. It was everything the island's name implied. We took with us a nineteen-year-old called Simon Holland, whose parents ran the Windmill, to act as a kind of gofer. He would drive the boat to the mainland, Nassau, to collect visitors, help me with the shopping and do odd jobs.

We had a lot of visitors, including Ronnie and Krissie Wood, and Mick Jagger. Krissie was just pregnant, and one day Eric and Ronnie went to Miami to record leaving the three of us at the house. When I came down in the morning to make tea, Krissie said 'Ssssh.' I crept into the kitchen and there was Mick, up to his elbows in soapsuds, washing the dishes from the night before. He was incredibly fit and said we must go for a jog along the beach. So we set off and as we ran, we heard a chorus of 'Oh, look, that's Mick Jagger!' as we sped past the sunbathers, trying to catch up with him.

One morning I woke with a searing pain in my tummy. I could barely stand up so Simon took me across to Nassau in the boat, dropped me off and arranged to meet me later. As it was Saturday, most doctors' surgeries were closed and I was shunted around for hours before I finally saw someone at St Margaret's Hospital. By that time I was doubled up in agony but I had also been ravenously hungry and bought myself a slice of pizza. The doctor diagnosed acute appendicitis. He wanted to operate immediately because, he was afraid my appendix might burst: had I had anything to eat? I had to own up to the pizza so the procedure had to wait, but eventually I had it done, and all was well. The next day Eric came to see me with Jerzy Kozinski, the Polish author of *The Painted Bird* and *Being There* – he was also one of the many locals with whom we had made friends.

Another local and neighbour was the Irish screenwriter, Kevin McClory. He invited Eric to appear in a show he was producing in County Kildare about a circus, starring John Huston and Shirley MacLaine. Eric played the part of a clown and John Huston the ring master. We were put up in Baberstown Castle Hotel where we slept in a room in the tower that was supposedly haunted. In the middle of the night I awoke to the sound of water running of its own accord in the basin – and the same night Roger Forrester's battery-operated watch inexplicably stopped.

A few years later Eric and Roger bought the hotel and we often visited with friends, and inevitably settled down to some serious drinking. During evenings in the bar, silence would be called and whoever could sing or play an instrument would be invited to perform. It was quite wonderful to be in a silent bar, crowded with drinkers listening to a farmer's wife singing 'Danny Boy' or 'If I Were a Blackbird'. Marianne Faithfull sang one night when she popped in for the evening.

Life on the island was idyllic – every day was another perfect day in paradise, and at night we would walk on the beach, our feet kicking up tiny phosphorescent fish that sparkled in the moonlight. I could have stayed for ever, but Eric hadn't wanted to go in the first place and, with his creative personality, developed island fever. He was drinking heavily and wrote a song during that time called 'Black

Summer Rain'. I couldn't understand how he had come up with such a dark title in such an idyllic place.

A tour of New Zealand, Australia and Japan came as a welcome diversion for him. While he flew to New York to pick up the band, then on to New Zealand, via Anchorage, I flew London, Anchorage, New Zealand. By coincidence both flights landed in Anchorage at the same time. I spotted Eric in the transit lounge, crept up behind him, put my hands over his eyes and said, 'Guess who?' We wanted to fly the rest of the way together, but the airlines wouldn't let us. However, worse was to come. When my plane touched down in New Zealand the air stewardess told me I wouldn't be allowed to get off it: the cannabis conviction had followed me to the other end of the earth. Eric was furious when he discovered they weren't letting me into the country; he ranted and raved at the authorities, but there was nothing anyone could do. I had no choice but to fly on to Australia, where I didn't know a soul, and wait for him and the band to arrive three days later.

Roger took care of everything, as managers do so brilliantly. He knew some disc jockeys at a radio station in Sydney with whom Eric was to do an interview and rang to ask them to meet me at the airport and look after me. They took me to the Sebel House Hotel on the waterfront – deeply luxurious – and we went to a wonderful Japanese restaurant. They were such fun and brought lots of friends with them. The next day they invited me to join them on their weekly Saturday pub crawl, but I declined and instead spent the day at the zoo, with koala bears and wallabies.

I loved Sydney. It seemed ahead of the game. Eric and I met a group of arty people there who were doing wonderful things photographically, film-wise and with clothes. There were dozens of designers I had never heard of who were big in Australia, producing all sorts of exciting things that weren't available in England or America. But the other Australian cities seemed still to be set in another era and none awoke in me any affection.

In Japan we were taken care of by a promoter called Mr Udo. He took us to wonderful Japanese restaurants, where the food was amazing. To me, Japan smelt of soy sauce, and I loved sashimi and sushi, and seeing the doll-like girls and women who came into the hotel for tea. They were beautifully made up, with white-powdered faces, immaculate hair and kimonos, as if they were in the Kabuki theatre, and they walked with little shuffling footsteps. In those days you saw few women in jeans, and they were treated as second-class citizens: they would follow their men, faces expressionless, several paces behind.

Back at Hurtwood Edge, with the tour over and the tax year complete, we settled down to normal life – although it was far from normal. Eric only came alive when he was in front of an audience, feeding off the energy and excitement of the crowd. That was where and how he communicated. He once said to me that he saved all his emotion for the stage. When he was at home he was restless and uneasy.

In some respects he was like George. The guitar was never far from his side and he would pick it up to play chords and riffs, which I loved hearing while I was cooking or reading, often in front of the television, which was constantly turned on. He had none of George's anxiety about the radio and other people's music, so the house was full of it; we even had a jukebox.

The house seemed made for parties – it had been the setting for great ones in the 1930s – and when there were just the two of us I always felt it had a melancholy air. In the early days Eric and I threw some fantastic parties at Hurtwood Edge, but he wasn't good with people in the way that George had been. He was only comfortable with friends at the pub, and musicians, who mostly ended up in the pub, and Ripleyites, the boys he had grown up with, people like Guy Pullen, Sid, Scratcher, Pat and Frank. We didn't go out much further than the Windmill, or the pub in Ripley, and I had to think twice before I invited my family to visit.

My mother didn't like Eric. She hadn't approved of him when he was going out with Paula and wasn't much happier when I was with him. I think she found him too raw. He didn't have George's charm and was lacking in social graces. He didn't do polite small-talk. She had adored George because he had adored her and been so sweet with my brothers and sisters. I usually waited until Eric was away before I saw them. He didn't even like me talking to them or friends on the telephone. He wanted me to himself.

Sometimes – at Christmas, for instance – he had no choice and my family came to see us. He liked Colin because he became a drinking partner. Colin had never found his niche in life – I think he rather envied the rock 'n' roll lifestyle that Jenny and I were living, but Mummy had wanted him to get a proper job so he worked in publishing, at Hamish Hamilton, for a while, then as a photographer. He travelled around Europe for months on end, and ended up, divorced, with a grown-up son and two young daughters, selling locally produced foods in Norfolk. Boo and Eric also got on reasonably well, but David had so loved George that I think he would have found it hard to warm to anyone who replaced him. Jenny was the one by whom Eric probably felt most threatened because I was closer to her than I was to the others. She was quite frightened of him, didn't like the way he played mind games. He reminded her of our step-father but, like me, she didn't know how to handle situations in which she felt uncomfortable.

One night, unusually, Eric and I were going out, but I couldn't decide what to wear. I was taking a very long time to do my makeup and hair, putting on one dress, then another and another, throwing them all into a pile on the floor. Poor Eric had been ready for hours and was waiting patiently. He was so sweet – at least, in the early days. The worst he would say if I annoyed him was 'You're a silly clown'.

While he waited for me he was in the sitting room, fiddling with his guitar. He went through phases in listening to music and at that time he liked a country singer called Don Williams. We talked about how beautifully simple his lyrics were, each song telling a story about everyday happenings. Eric had been thinking of writing something similar and had already worked on some music for it. Suddenly, as I was flinging dresses on and off, inspiration struck. When I finally got downstairs and asked the inevitable question, 'Do I look all right?' he played me what he'd written:

> It's late in the evening; she's wondering what clothes to wear.
> She puts on her makeup and brushes her long blonde hair.
> And then she asks me, 'Do I look all right?'
> And I say, 'Yes, you look wonderful tonight.'

It was such a simple song but so beautiful and for years it tore at me. To have inspired Eric, and George before him, to write such music was so flattering. Yet I came to believe that although something about me might have made them put pen to paper, it was really all about them. And I think the depressions they suffered were to do with the creative process – the need that all creative people have to delve deep inside themselves to bring to the surface whatever they are creating. 'Wonderful Tonight' was the most poignant reminder of all that was good in our relationship, and when things went wrong it was torture to hear it.

I had no idea until I met Eric that I was capable of experiencing such deep feelings for another human being; before, I had always held back. I was frightened of strong emotion and intensity, and in a way, I was right to be. There is always a price to be paid for excess – a *yang* to every *yin*, a negative to every positive. Jenny once asked me whether I would have swapped the passion of my relationship with Eric for a more gentle kind of love. The answer was no. It was like hitching a ride on a shooting star: a fantastic experience that caused immense pain but I'm glad I had it. And I know I will never have those feelings again. That sort of experience doesn't come twice. But because he inspired such passion in me I was willing to be with him and forgive his bad behaviour, which I should not have done.

As the drink took hold, Eric began to live his life in five-hour cycles: his body needed alcohol every five hours, so there was no set pattern to life, or his moods. He could be loving and caring or angry and withdrawn, and if I went out, shopping in Cranleigh or to London perhaps, I was never away for more than five hours, and I would never know what mood I would find him in when I came back into the house. I might expect the worst and find him sweet and sober on my return, which would leave me racked with guilt for having had such nasty thoughts, or I would come home expecting sobriety and find him comatose on the sofa. He ate sporadically. I would make him something delicious, like the Indian food he loved, and take it to him where he was slouched in front of the TV and he would say he wasn't hungry. He came to bed every night with a pint glass of brandy and lemonade, at whatever time he found his way upstairs – sometimes he would undress first, sometimes not. I used to dread the sound of his lurching footsteps on the wooden stairs, not knowing what to expect next. And when he woke in the morning he would finish what was left, then pour himself a fresh glass. He was drinking about two bottles of brandy a day, plus however many pints of beer he had in the pub.

I tried to tell him he was drinking too much, which didn't go down well. Then I began to pour his drinks for him, so I could put in more lemonade. Later I marked the bottle so I could keep a check on how much brandy had gone, but nothing made any difference to Eric. I even tried not drinking myself, thinking he might notice and cut down but he didn't. After a couple of days I would tire of that and get hopelessly drunk with him, which of course he loved. But the next day I'd feel lousy. The real problem was that I didn't know how dangerous alcohol could be or that drinking in the way Eric did was an illness. In those days, well-known people did not stand up, as they do today, to admit they were alcoholics. Nobody spoke about it.

Even the Ripleyites had trouble keeping up. They usually drank at the Ship, which was a hard-core drinking-man's pub in Ripley, and would often come home with Eric on Sunday for lunch when the pub closed. I would cook for however many appeared, usually at four or five in the afternoon. They would appear bearing the most hideous presents bought en route in Shere, under the influence of too many beers. And the drinking would carry on into the night. There was a snooker table on the first floor at Hurtwood Edge to which everyone gravitated. Eric slept badly and never wanted to go to bed but the others all had nine-to-five jobs and had to be *compos mentis* on Monday morning – when Eric would bring them a cup of coffee laced with vodka. I don't know how they ever got to work. If he was bored and had no one to play with in the early morning, he would go into the kitchen, fill a saucepan with spoons and rattle it to wake everyone up. He had to have playmates.

It wasn't until later that I realised how shallow and narrow my life was becoming. On a normal day we would wake in the morning, have breakfast and suddenly it was lunchtime and we'd go to the pub. It was always cosy and welcoming there and, of course, everyone was thrilled to see us – the locals, the publican and his wife had become friends. But there was something sinister about other people who came in. They wanted to get Eric drunk so that they could watch him turn into the village idiot. I hated it, but Eric couldn't or didn't want to see it happening, and although I tried to explain, it didn't penetrate. Explaining anything to someone who has had too much to drink is useless: they can't hear you properly, and I always chose the wrong moments to try.

The problem was that when Eric was at home it was playtime and he wanted playmates. He was a wonderfully entertaining person when he was in the right mood – funny, wild, unpredictable and forever playing practical jokes; exciting to be with. He bought Ferraris, which he drove too fast, racehorses – he gave me one for Christmas – Armani suits, and life was one big party fuelled by vast amounts of alcohol. And because Roger or Alfie was always around to pick up the pieces, he had no responsibilities, and neither did I. All I had to do was try to feed him, make sure he got to the studio on time when he was recording, and pack his suitcase when he went on tour. I tried to be what he wanted me to be, and to make life wonderful for him, but we were like a couple of children playing at being grown-ups.

When Eric was a little boy he had always wanted an animal so he invented an invisible horse or dog that he called Bushbranch, which was what we called the racehorse he bought me. She never did very well but we had a lot of fun watching her run. Eventually she was bought by Lester Piggott, who won two or three races on her. We had others, too, one called Nello, Eric's name for me – Nell or Nello and I called him El – and another called The Ripleyite, but the only one that did well was Via Delta, which won at Ascot. We were there, and so were the lads from Toby Balding's yard in Hampshire, where the horses were in training. The breeder and everyone else came back to Hurtwood Edge for fish and chips. But the horses didn't last: Eric had a fad, then moved on to something else.

There were other times, though, when Eric didn't want to play. He had the most disconcerting ability to switch off, regardless of what was going on around him or who he was with, and withdraw so deeply into himself that he wouldn't communicate, just gave off a dark vibe so that whoever was around would know he didn't want to see them and slink away. That included me.

I hated it when he did it to me, but when he did it to visitors it was infinitely worse. I'd say, 'Don't you realise that your friends have come to see you?'

'Well, they shouldn't have turned up. I don't want to see them. I've got nothing to say.'

I used to excuse him in the same way that I would excuse George when he went into himself or started chanting. Both men were so creative that I think there were times when they had to retreat from the world and listen to what was going on in their heads. The creative process never stopped. Sometimes I would watch Eric when he was asleep and his foot – or both feet – would tap in time to whatever he was hearing. Eventually it dawned on me that when he switched off, whether he was asleep or had just pulled down the shutters, he was listening to music. And that I could understand. But where most people in that situation would think, I can't do anything about this idea now, it will have to wait, I've got people here to entertain, Eric was like a child: his wants and needs were immediate and paramount and he had no understanding that other people's had to be considered.

At times his eccentricities made me laugh – particularly his need to get into the right mood to watch TV. When the Test match was on, he would change into his cricket whites, and if he was planning to watch a film like *The Godfather* he'd insist on pasta for supper.

Having lived with George for ten years, and spent so much time around other musicians, I accepted Eric's behaviour and I suppose I fell into the trap of doing the same as everyone else. I looked after the house, and I packed his suitcases. And if something wasn't exactly as he wanted it, I knew about it. He had at least two hundred shirts and he'd go berserk if I couldn't find the one he wanted that day. He'd describe it in minute detail and I'd find him one that was similar. It wouldn't do. My life revolved around him. I played the part of the little woman.

CHAPTER ELEVEN

Mrs Clapton

I had known little about Eric when I had allowed him to seduce me away from George. I had seen him as a romantic character, impetuous, free-spirited and talented, not just as a musician but as an artist, and I had built him up so much in my imagination that in the flesh he could never have lived up to my idealised, romantic image. I was madly in love with him, but as I negotiated the moods, the depression, the destructiveness that went with the drinking, I began to wonder whether I had made a mistake in leaving George, whether I should have tried a bit harder when things had gone wrong, fought for our marriage and not walked away. After all, I had never stopped loving him. I'd thought he had stopped loving me, but he was so upset when I left that perhaps I'd been wrong.

Not long after our year on Paradise Island, Eric and I were in Jamaica, where he was recording, and to my joy Chris O'Dell, my friend from Apple days, turned up. She had been touring with the

Rolling Stones and was staying in the same hotel, the Terra Nova, in Kingston. It was so nice to see her and have someone to talk to who knew George and the ghastly situation I had left behind, who had been there and whom I could confide in. Inevitably we spent a lot of time talking about the past and Friar Park, and I began to feel miserable and to miss George. In a rather drunken moment, we decided to telephone him. When we got through, George sounded so pleased to hear my voice that I was going to ask him whether I had made a mistake – or maybe tell him I thought I had – but Eric walked in and I had to hang up.

Eric did such a lot of touring and spent so much time in airports and hotels, and got so sick of them, that Roger decided he would make the next tour of Europe more interesting by hiring the Orient Express. We had three carriages, one for dining, one for sleeping and one for sitting in, which were ours for the tour, but as there was no engine we had to hitch up to other trains, which pulled us from A to B. Every morning a man woke us with a glass of champagne, plus tea or coffee, and it went on from there. It was the best tour but, again, we behaved like mischievous children; Roger was the headmaster, trying to keep everyone under control. A newspaper reporter was on board until and everyone got fed up with him. When the train slowed down in the middle of nowhere, we threw him off without his passport. And then we got hold of the passport that belonged to one of the promoters and embellished the photograph so that he looked like a monkey. He had a terrible time trying to get back into Britain.

Then Eric did a tour with Ronnie Lane and his band – they did the warm-up before Eric came on – and I was persuaded to go on stage with Ronnie's wife, Kate and Roger's wife, Annette – all dressed up with lots of red lipstick and feathers in our hair – to do the cancan. We flew to Nice where we decanted into two rather scruffy-looking tug-boats – one took the two bands, plus wives and girlfriends, the other was for the roadies – and set off for Cannes. In Cannes the captain said the weather was too bad to sail for Ibiza, but Roger insisted we went on because the boys were due to play at the bull-ring there. Of course, we hit a storm. The boat had no stabilisers – a pool table and a piano, but no stabilisers – so it rolled terrifyingly. Charlie, a member of Ronnie Lane's band, was playing the piano as it slid from one side of the cabin to the other, while the rest of us played poker, money and cards falling everywhere. It was so scary I thought we were going to drown. I even put a message in a bottle. Eric, though, was calmly totting up his winnings.

For the most part touring wasn't much fun for wives and girlfriends – it was such a male thing, boys bonding, working hard and giving a lot of themselves through their music, then wanting to play hard. They'd laugh, drink too much and pick up girls. Often a musician will choose a pretty girl in the audience and sing to her, then the roadies will invite her with a few other pretty girls to come back after the gig for a drink. Musicians have so much energy when they are on stage but afterwards they are exhausted. When they get back to the hotel, though, they've found a second wind – and all those girls are throwing themselves at them, not considering for one moment that there may be a wife or girlfriend in the picture. If I was with him, Eric would tell me to go upstairs and warm the bed to get me out of the way. And I'd be so irritated, but I thought I had to accept that this was what happened on tour. Often I would fly home and leave him to get on with it, but I knew what was happening in my absence.

Then Eric decreed that wives and girlfriends were banned from touring. We used private planes most of the time, and Jamie, the drummer's wife, got on one day and started knitting. Eric flipped. Knitting didn't go with rock 'n' roll and he told Roger to get rid of us all.

Although I had found touring difficult, Eric's ban meant I didn't see him for weeks on end. I sometimes felt that out of sight was out of mind. He didn't phone or write as George had done when he was away. While I was still with George, Eric had written passionate and compelling letters that arrived almost daily, but now that I was installed in his home and his life, he didn't bother. It was as though the excitement had been in the chase, and once the quarry had fallen, he no longer valued it. I had to sit at home for up to six weeks at a time, imagining what he was getting up to. It wasn't easy.

During one of his long absences I became friendly with a set of twins, who were models, Jenny and Susie McLean. We saw quite a bit of each other, and once when Eric was at home Jenny came for the day and I invited her to stay the night. The next morning, when I got up, she and Eric had gone shopping together and then to the pub, so I went to see my sister Jenny, who was living nearby.

When I got home after lunch, Eric and twin Jenny were sitting close to one another on the sofa, and there was a horrible atmosphere as I came into the sitting room. I said nothing and left them alone. An hour or so later I went back and they hadn't moved. I started to say something to Jenny, but Eric butted in: 'Can't you see we're having a really intense and intimate conversation here?' He was very drunk.

I said, 'Why?'

'Because I'm in love with this girl. Go away and leave us alone. Just fuck off.'

I was so shocked that what he had said took a moment or two to sink in. This was exactly what had happened with George and my French friend after Cilla Black's New Year's Eve party all those years ago. I ran upstairs and sat on the bed, shaking. I didn't know what to do. After all we had been through, all the letters, the passion, the pain and the hurt, how could he reject me and move on to someone he had known for five minutes? I sat upstairs, tears streaming down my face, feeling a complete and utter fool. I had given up George for this.

Eventually I rang my sister Jenny, who said I should spend the night with her. She came to collect me in her car. It was dark, pouring with rain, and I met her in the drive, soaking wet and distraught, my umbrella blown inside out. I must have looked like something out of a black-and-white forties movie. All I could think was, Thank God I've got Jenny. I was so wounded.

Jenny and her two little girls, Amy and Lucy, were living in a house called Willow Cottage, which – the way we drove – was about ten minutes from Hurtwood Edge. Her marriage to Mick Fleetwood was finally over. It had fallen apart in 1974 after they had moved to Los Angeles, which was when Fleetwood Mac became successful and Mick was constantly away touring. Jenny had found it very difficult and leant increasingly on drink and drugs. When they divorced, she came to live in England, but after a few months she moved back to Los Angeles and they remarried. It didn't last. She and the girls returned to England again, moved into Willow Cottage, then she and Mick divorced a second time. They still loved each other but they couldn't live together. However, it was wonderful for me to have her so close.

After a day or two I knew I had to get away from Eric. I phoned the house and I told him what I was planning.

'Good,' he said. 'We really need a bit of a break.' The twin, Jenny, he admitted, was still there.

I phoned some friends in Los Angeles, Rob and Myel Fraboni and took the next plane out. I felt as though my heart would break and cried so much on the flight that the stewardess asked me to move to the back of the first-class cabin so I wouldn't upset the other passengers.

I stayed with Rob and Myel, a music producer and his wife whom I had met through Eric, for several weeks, wondering what to do with my life. I had no intention of going back to England and no plans to see Eric again. Then one morning, after a party on the beach in Malibu, I was woken by an agitated Rob. He walked me out on to the balcony. 'Doesn't that ocean look beautiful today?' he began.

'No, Rob,' I said. 'Nothing looks beautiful with the kind of hangover I've got.'

Undaunted, he told me he had had a call from Eric in the middle of the night. 'He said he wants to marry you, and he asked me to ask you on his behalf. He wants me to be best man and says that if you don't want to marry him then, "On your bike!"'

I was so hung-over that his words just wafted through my befuddled head. Then he handed me the message, as he had recorded it, on the back of an envelope. Eric wanted me to marry him on Tuesday in Tucson, Arizona, just before the start of his next American tour. It was now Friday morning. I said, 'What a strange message.'

'He wants an answer very soon,' said Rob.

'Oh, my God, Rob, I don't know. Let me think about it.'

I had a shower, got dressed and the three of us sat down to talk about it. Myel thought I should definitely marry him – because we could have such a nice wedding and a lovely party and everything; it would be fun. Rob liked the idea of being best man, so we decided the answer was 'Yes'. I rang Eric and, having ascertained that Jenny McLean was no longer in the picture, said I would marry him.

I was thrilled. How could I not be? The drink was a problem, but other than that he was wonderful: the most exciting, creative, talented, interesting person – and I was in love with him. But in the bottom of my heart I knew this wasn't right.

On reflection I see that being in love with him was like a kind of addiction. If he was happy and pleased with me, I was happy too, but I was deeply affected every time he went into one of his dark moods. My mood reflected his, which wasn't healthy.

What I didn't know until Roger Forrester confessed a few days after the wedding was how the whole thing had come about. He and Eric had been playing an endless drunken game of pool at Roger's house in Frimley Green and they had had a bet. Roger had bet Eric that he could get his photograph in the newspapers the following morning. Eric bet him ten thousand pounds that he couldn't. So Roger went straight to the telephone and told Nigel Dempster, then gossip-columnist on the *Daily Mail*, that Eric Clapton would be marrying Pattie Boyd on 27 March in Tucson, Arizona. By the time they woke up the next morning the story, plus photograph, was emblazoned across the *Daily Mail* and the two went into a total panic. What to do? A few million people now knew about the wedding; the only person who didn't was the bride. Hence the hasty phone call – and the desperation for an immediate answer.

I had three days to find a dress, to have a blood test to make sure I didn't have rubella – which you have to do when you marry in America – to gather together some friends and family and get to Tucson. The first person I rang was Jenny. I told her to jump on a plane straight away and come to be my maid of honour. She had been out the night before and had such a terrible hangover that she was in bed when I phoned. She said she couldn't possibly get there, she had no money. I rang the Windmill and arranged for her to collect some from the landlord. She made it to Tucson about an hour before the ceremony. Chris O'Dell was there, too, and Myel and Rob, then Eric and Roger arrived with the band, and we all stayed at the Sheraton Pueblo, a glorified motel.

Roger had organised everything – the hotel, the church, the limos, the reception – and because of Eric's needle phobia, he had even persuaded a member of the band who looked a bit like Eric to have the rubella test for him. To confuse the press he had booked the ceremony in every church in Arizona. We ended up in the Apostolic Assembly of Faith in Christ Jesus, a funny little building with a Mexican priest.

I wasn't allowed to see Eric on the night before so the next morning Jenny, Chris, Myel and I went to the church together and into a little room at the back where we changed, chatted and drank champagne. They were having a lovely time and I had to shut them up to ask, 'What about *me*? Do I look all right?'

I wore a cream silk-satin dress with a lace jacket. Roger gave me away, Rob was Eric's best man, as promised, and Alfie and Nigel Carroll were ushers. Nigel had been going out with Paula, which was how we'd met him, and he made Eric laugh so much that Eric had asked him to come and work for him. The road crew and the band had hired the most unbelievable black and powder-blue tuxedos with string ties but they had forgotten to order shoes so they were wearing filthy trainers.

The service was lovely and Eric looked wonderful. At the end the minister said, 'I would like to give you Mr and Mrs Clapton,' and clapped, so everyone else did too.

The reception was in the hotel – if you could call it a reception. Eric and I had no sooner cut the cake than we were in the midst of a cake fight. I think Eric probably threw the first slice. He had been behaving really well, then suddenly went berserk – perhaps because he had realised he was with his playmates. So the beautiful tuxedos were soon covered with cream and icing. Everyone was drunk and the whole thing turned into chaos. Not the traditional wedding but perfect rock 'n' roll.

I couldn't have been happier, but there was no question of a honeymoon. The next day Eric's tour began and he insisted on bringing me on stage and proudly introducing me as his wife, then singing 'Wonderful Tonight' to me. It was touching and so joyous. The audience went wild.

After Tucson they played Albuquerque, El Paso and Dallas, and at each gig I stood in the wings, watched him and felt so proud, happy and in love. Then it all changed. The next stop was New Orleans, which I was really looking forward to, but Eric told me he wanted me to fly to Los Angeles, collect my luggage and go home.

I couldn't understand it. We were having such a lovely time, why did he want to get rid of me? And then one of the roadies told me that Jenny McLean had checked into the hotel in New Orleans. Eric and I hadn't even been married a week. When the band realised what was going on, the roadies practically mutinied and Roger ejected her.

It would have been a joy to marry someone who was faithful to me, but I had grown up with strange values. I knew my father and step-father had had affairs, and in my subconscious I probably accepted that this was what men did. It had seemed so obvious to me as a child that Bobbie was having an affair with Ingrid, and I couldn't understand why Mummy didn't notice. Perhaps she knew what was going on but decided to ignore it, afraid to confront him, maybe, for fear of losing him. And history was repeating itself. I had let George be unfaithful to me – just as my mother had with Bobbie – and now I was letting Eric be unfaithful too. It hurt like hell but I found excuses.

Being a musician on the road, I thought, was a bit like being a soldier away from home. They got lonely and they felt that what they did on tour didn't count. How could I expect him to resist all those girls fawning over him, telling him how great he was and taking their clothes off for him? Besides, his idea of fidelity, like most men's, was totally different from mine or most women's. In his eyes a one-night stand wasn't love, it was sex; it didn't mean anything. So either I could be forgiving and understanding because Eric couldn't help himself, or I could think, I would never do it, so why should he? Stupidly perhaps, not wanting to lose him, I chose to be forgiving.

In May, when Eric was home briefly between tours, Roger organised the most extravagant wedding party for us at Hurtwood Edge. Three hundred people came – Eric's family, my family, the Ripleyites, the local farmers and tradespeople, and lots of great musicians, who jammed together. We had Jeff Beck, Ronnie Wood,

Bill Wyman, Donovan, Robert Plant, Robert Palmer and Jack Bruce. George, Paul and Ringo came – for some reason John wasn't invited, but he said he would have come if he'd been asked, which was sad because if he had, it would have been the first and last time the Beatles played together since the break-up – the next year he was dead.

Lonnie Donegan turned up, uninvited, and said, 'Where are they all?'

I took him up to the smallest room in the house where they were smoking joints and said, as I opened the door, 'Guess who's here?'

They all jumped up and tried to hide the evidence, then George said, 'I remember when I was a little boy and I knocked on the door of your house and asked for your autograph,' and Donegan said, 'That's why I'm here. I want it back!'

Mick Jagger came with Jerry Hall, who had been engaged to Bryan Ferry but had left him for Mick. Moments later Bryan Ferry arrived and asked who was there. When I told him that Mick and Jerry had just arrived he turned on his heel, jumped into his car and zoomed off, taking half the drive with him.

The party started at three or four in the afternoon and went on with people coming and going until morning. We had two marquees, a small one for the children, which was full of toys and games, and another with a dance-floor, a stage for the musicians and loads of guitars. Roger had asked his friends from the East End to come as security, and as Eric was walking down the drive in the middle of it all, out jumped a guy from the bushes with a sawn-off shotgun and aimed it at his head. 'I live here,' said Eric, indignantly.

Fireworks began at about midnight. Roger had asked Paines, the manufacturers, to design the display and it was the most amazing firework show I have ever seen. Half the village could see them and the noise was loud enough to wake everyone in Surrey. The village policeman was with us (wise move) and when Roger said, 'Oh, God, I'm going to get complaints about these fireworks,' he replied,

'Fireworks? What fireworks?' He was great. He used to come in for a drink in the early hours of the morning and we'd give him a brandy or two and send him on his way. We never had any trouble.

By the time Eric and I went upstairs to bed it was daylight. We were ready to drop – but Mick and Jerry were tucked up and fast asleep in our bed, with little Jade, his daughter with Bianca, sleeping sweetly beside them. Trust Mick to have found the best bed in the house.

Eric visiting George and me at Friar Park in about 1973. I was feeling very awkward because I knew exactly why Eric was there.

Eric in the garden at Friar Park. I was taking lots of photos at that time because I had just made myself a dark room in the house.

George and Eric in the little TV room at Hurtwood Edge. George had phoned to say he was in the area and wanted to see us.

Waiting at a station. Roger Forrester tried to make a European tour more interesting for Eric one year by hiring the Orient Express.

Yvonne Elliman, who sang with Eric's band, and Roger carrying my bag. He was like the headmaster on tour trying to keep everyone under control.

Our wedding reception in Tucson, Arizona. Within minutes of cutting into the bottom tier, a fight had broken out and cake was everywhere.

Jerry Hall, Jim Capaldi and me at my wedding party at Hurtwood Edge. When Eric and I finally called it a day we found Jerry and Mick Jagger fast asleep in our bed.

Terry Doran, George and Olivia at the party. It lasted all day and all night.

Eric, me and a local from the pub playing with bows and arrows on the terrace at Hurtwood Edge. The brandy bottle was never far away.

The back garden, originally designed by Gertrude Jekyll.

Me in high spirits one Christmas Day at Hurtwood Edge in the early eighties, posing for my brother Colin.

Ronnie and Eric at Hurtwood Edge – Ronnie is right-handed so they were clearly just mucking about.

Eric and the band on tour on a private jet. He and Terry Doran – a perennial court jester – are touching feet. After the knitting incident, women were banned.

On holiday on the island of Nevis in the early eighties. Eric was relaxed and in good shape and we spent a happy time swimming, reading and snorkelling.

Eric and me in Bahia, Brazil. Robert Stigwood had given us first class tickets for Concorde's inaugural flight to Rio.

Eric had planned concerts in Jerusalem after Cairo but the authorities wouldn't allow the equipment in, so he and I went to visit the pyramids on horseback instead.

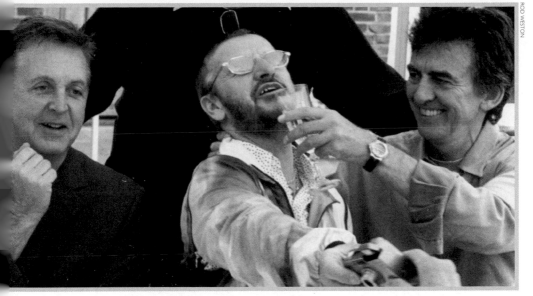

Paul, Ringo and George at a party to celebrate Ringo's birthday at his house in Sussex. George being a minx, trying to get Ringo to drink alcohol after twenty years.

Seventieth birthday celebrations for my mother *(on the right)* at her flat in Devon and her twin brother, John *(extreme left)*. *From left* Colin, Paula, Jenny, Boo, David and me.

Rod and me at Ronnie Wood's fiftieth birthday party in a marquee
at his house in Richmond. The dress was Saloon Bar.

At Ol Jogi Estate when Rod and I went to stay with Donna Hurt in Kenya.
I was told I could stroke the cheetah but on no account to run.

CHAPTER TWELVE

Spiralling Out of Control

One snowy winter's afternoon when Rob and Myel Fraboni were staying, the doorbell rang. That's odd, I thought. It was practically dark and the snow was deep on the ground. We were getting stuck into Bloody Marys. The day before Rob and Myel had arrived from France, laden with cheese, wine and chocolates. I had cooked some pheasants and we'd stayed up far too late, drinking and laughing. The next day we were rather hung-over and, after tea and toast, it had seemed to be getting dark again so we moved on to Bloody Marys.

I opened the door to find a bedraggled Spanish girl standing in the cold. She had fallen over in the snow and torn her jeans. I waited expectantly for her to speak. She explained, in broken English, that she had come to see Eric. 'Have you?' I said. This was going to be theatre!

I invited her into the kitchen and called Eric. 'There's a girl here,' I said, 'and you must know her because I certainly don't.'

215

Eric was squirming with embarrassment. He had obviously met her on the road and given her his address, then forgotten about her. Her name was Conchita, Little Shell. Rob and Myel looked interested.

Eric asked if I could lend her something to wear because of the tear in her jeans. I said I was too tall; nothing of mine would fit. So he turned to Myel and she said, 'No,' equally firmly. So, still in her torn jeans, this curious little girl began to follow Eric and Rob into the study. 'What on earth's going on?' asked Myel, and called after Conchita in French. She was in love with Eric, she said, and he had told her she could come to England and stay with him.

It was ghastly but hysterical. There was no way we could kick her out; it was snowing, she had no money and Ewhurst is miles from anywhere. She stayed for two days, after which we sent her back to Spain. She continued to write to Eric, telephone and send Christmas cards, saying she hoped they would see each other in the coming year. In the end I came to feel rather sorry for her.

If I had expected there to be a change in Eric after our marriage, that he might suddenly, having made vows in church, become faithful, I was to be disappointed. Jenny McLean had been sent packing but I was under no illusion: she would be replaced in the next town or on the next tour. When they were one-night stands, they didn't threaten our marriage and I could cope.

What was far more worrying was Eric's drinking, which got worse and worse. I, too, was drinking far more than was good for me – as Eric cruelly pointed out in the song he wrote called 'The Shape You're In'. But I always felt I was in control and at least I was eating and sleeping normally. Eric wasn't.

I felt isolated by his drinking. Alcoholism was taboo in the seventies and eighties and, to begin with, I hadn't wanted to admit there was a problem, but I knew I couldn't go on pretending. Anthony Hopkins, who is a recovering alcoholic, kept leaving messages for Eric and asking to meet him. This was what he did,

I discovered; he encouraged people he knew were having trouble to come and meet him, but Eric didn't know Anthony Hopkins so he took no notice. I spoke to a few doctors about it but no one in the medical profession seemed prepared to acknowledge there was a problem. And most people who knew Eric thought it was funny and laughed at the crazy things he did. But it wasn't funny for me when he climbed on to the roof of the house, or when I had to drive back from Ripley with him sitting on top of me, trying to drive too.

Guy Pullen, Nigel Carroll and his wife Jackie came to Spain on holiday with us once. In the mornings I cooked everyone fried eggs for breakfast. One day I didn't have enough eggs so Eric went to get some and came back saying it had cost him sixty pounds. I said I'd only wanted eggs, but he had found a bottle of vintage port so we had to drink it for breakfast. That same holiday Nigel and Guy went golfing and left Eric passed out in the house, but during their game he woke up and went to look for them – stark naked. At this even Guy recognised that Eric was in trouble. He sat him down one day and told him so. 'When the first thing you have in the morning is a packet of cigarettes with a large brandy and lemonade, you have a problem,' said Guy. 'Have you never heard of Shredded Wheat?'

Another year we went on a sailing holiday around the Greek islands with Roger and Annette Forrester and their children. One day we arrived at a little port and spotted Robert Stigwood's boat *Jezebel* across the harbour. It was beautiful, built in the 1920s, about 160 feet long with a magnificent clipper bow. We thought we should go and say hello, and Robert invited Eric and me to dinner. The *Jezebel* had wood panelling in the drawing room and library, and wood fireplaces in both.

At the end of the evening, instead of allowing Robert's driver to take us back to our boat, Eric insisted on borrowing the *Jezebel*'s Riva, another lovely boat that was used as a tender, and going back across the harbour. We got in and Eric insisted on driving, but he was so drunk that it was careering all over the place. When I tried to take the controls, he wouldn't let me and there was a bit of a fight. Eventually we made it – goodness knows how – and by some miracle Eric managed to stop without damaging either boat.

The next bit didn't go so well. He tried to step from one boat to the other, and when he had a leg in each, the tender pulled away and he fell into the water. The headline flashed before me: 'Rock Star Dies'. Eric couldn't swim under normal circumstances, but he was so drunk that he didn't even try. He sank like a stone with his arms by his sides. Then his head came up and I yelled, 'Give me your arm!' He raised it and I hung on for dear life, but he was heavy, slipping away from me and making no effort to help himself. He went under again, then bobbed up, and I shouted for help as I tried to keep his head above water. Finally someone on our boat heard me and came to the rescue.

Clearly Eric had nine lives. I can't remember how many times he crashed his cars and miraculously came out of the wreckage alive. In 1980 he cheated death again, in America. He had just started a forty-five-concert tour and for months beforehand had been complaining about a pain in his back. Other than taking mega-quantities of painkillers, washed down with brandy and lemonade, he had done nothing about it. After the first couple of gigs he was doubled up, and the only thing that kept him going was huge doses of Veganin. His condition went downhill so quickly that when they arrived in Minneapolis Roger took him straight to hospital. When they X-rayed him, they discovered he had five enormous ulcers, one of which was on the point of exploding into his pancreas. The doctors reckoned he was forty-five minutes from death.

I was at a children's birthday party when I had a call from Roger: 'Come immediately. Eric's in hospital.'

For the next few weeks while he was in treatment, Roger and I were stuck in a hotel in Minneapolis with ten feet of snow outside.

Minneapolis in winter is not the most exciting place. The lake is frozen and the locals' idea of fun is to drive a car into the middle and place bets on when it will sink.

Eric never did anything by halves. If he took up a hobby it became an obsession. Now it was fly-fishing, which he had got into with Gary Brooker, who owned the Parrot at Ockley, a neighbouring village pub. Gary was a singer, songwriter and keyboard player with Procol Harum – his big hit had been 'A Whiter Shade Of Pale', and he and Eric had known each other in the sixties. They had found each other again by chance when we wandered into the Parrot for a drink one evening and Gary was behind the bar. From then on Eric and various friends used to play in the pub sometimes and Gary was a regular visitor to Hurtwood Edge, as was Phil Collins, another local musician.

So, when Eric was allowed forays from the Minneapolis hospital during his lengthy stay, he found a fishing shop, bought about twenty-five rods and practised casting in the hospital corridors. He also went to visit a fishing friend in Seattle – at which point I went home. While he was there he was involved in yet another accident. The car he was being driven in ran a red light and was hit by a taxi. Eric bruised some ribs, but after a few days the pain was getting worse, so he saw a doctor for painkillers and was told he had pleurisy. He was flown straight back to hospital in Minneapolis, and immediately wrote asking me to join him: 'I know it's hard for you to drop everything and jostle your way through the airports, but that's what I am asking you to do, you are the only one I can truly rely on for strength and cheer, and you can spend as much money as you like while you wait for me to mend . . .'

The day before he was due to go home Roger and I decided to have a word with Eric's doctor about his drinking. We pleaded with him to tell Eric he mustn't drink, explained the situation, told him how much he habitually drank and how worried we were. The doctor told Eric it was fine to have the odd drink, but he wasn't to drink a whole bottle of brandy. Eric saw this as the green light. He mustn't drink a whole bottle of brandy . . . so he switched to whisky.

There were some frightening moments. We once went to stay with some people in Rutland. One of Eric's roadies had married into a very grand family and we had been invited to their house for the weekend. We were going to a well-known restaurant for dinner and Eric had tried not to drink all day; he was quite nervous about meeting these people.

When we arrived at the house, Eric refused a drink and we went to the restaurant – the guy was called Womble and his wife, Mia, was a duke's daughter. Her brother and other relatives were joining us for dinner. Eric was sitting on my right, and suddenly, not far into the pre-dinner cocktails, he was shaking and convulsing. I thought he was having a heart-attack and about to die. Someone said he was having a fit, so while an ambulance was called, I rang Roger.

When we arrived at the hospital, the doctor said Eric had had an epileptic fit caused by lack of alcohol. He spent the night in hospital and in the morning Nigel Carroll went to collect him. He never had another epileptic fit but, then, he never went without alcohol in quite that way again.

Meanwhile, he was straight back to two bottles a day and touring. Roger was so worried about his health that he would bug Eric's hotel room. He would hide a baby alarm in the bedroom, then he and Alfie would take turns to sit up and listen to make sure he was still breathing. Roger wasn't a drinker: he was responsible – he had to be, among the huge mob of children that constituted the band. They thought he behaved like a schoolmaster and did terrible things to him, like throwing him fully clothed, briefcase in hand, into a swimming-pool, or stealing his new shoes and using them for target practice with their airguns.

But touring was big money. The ulcer episode had wiped out most of the American tour and cost them forty-two sell-out concerts. Roger had to keep them on the road. It was like a military manoeuvre, organising the cars, the planes and the trucks, but in all the years they were together, they only ever missed one show, apart from the ulcer disaster, and that was because of a tornado. Roger hated everyone drinking too much on tour and taking drugs but he was on his own: if the boss partied, the crew partied. Roger's drug was Valium, which he took on prescription in huge doses – I think it was the only way he could cope with Eric – and thirty cups of coffee a day. So Roger was my ally.

The crunch came shortly before Christmas in 1981. Eric and I went to a Genesis concert in London. Eric was jumping up and down, applauding, until suddenly he said he wanted to get out, he had to get out, he had to get a drink, and became frantic, desperate. He fought his way out, climbing over people in their seats.

That evening, I think, he realised he needed help. I told Roger what had happened. 'Don't worry,' he said. 'I've got him into a treatment centre on the seventh of January but I'm not going to tell him until after Christmas.'

It was a huge relief: along with the drinking, Eric had been going into deep depressions and saying he didn't want to live any more, he couldn't see the point in anything – and that had been a whole new worry.

I could see Christmas would be tricky, and it was. The house was full, as it always was at that time of year, with a mixture of family, friends, members of the band or road crew and anyone else who was at a loose end. Nigel and Jackie were with us one year and the turkey was so enormous it wouldn't fit into the fridge so I put it in the garage. When Jackie went to get it for me on Christmas morning, Willow, the Weimaraner, had dragged it on to the floor and was chewing it. We washed it, stuffed it and put it into the Aga without saying a word to anyone.

Usually I loved Christmas, everything about it. On Christmas Day we'd get up late and open the stockings in front of the fire with a bottle of champagne. We'd maybe go for a walk, watch the Queen on television, there would always be guitars playing and good music, snooker, board games, dice, and we'd open presents. We'd sit down to lunch at about six, a great feast, pull crackers and wear paper hats. Each year I'd experiment with a different stuffing for the turkey, find new recipes for puddings and mince pies, and track down the right wines to go with it all.

It had been such a pleasure, in moving to live with Eric, to reclaim my role in the kitchen, but because he had so little interest in food it was an empty one. However, my brother Boo had become a chef and we would ring each other and talk about food. After he qualified he went to work for a hotel group and was abroad for twenty-six years, so most of our foodie conversations had to be over the phone, but at Christmas we would spend hours comparing notes about what we were doing, whose recipe we were following and what wines we were having with each course. It was always lovely when he came home on holiday, or Eric and I went to see him in America, Egypt or wherever he was, and we could cook together.

That Christmas of 1981 lunch was nearly ready when I realised that Eric was missing. No one had seen him for hours. I looked all over the house and there was no sign of him, so I went out into the garden. It was dark and snowing heavily, and I had visions of Eric, having passed out, lying somewhere freezing in the snow. He had had his usual liquid breakfast and been drinking steadily throughout the morning. I ran all over the garden, searching, getting more and more frightened. Finally I went up to Arthur's house at the top of the drive, my face streaked with mascara. He said Eric had been there for a Christmas drink or six but had left some time ago. 'Oh, Arthur,' I said, in despair, 'where is he now?'

And Arthur said, 'He's probably in the basement.'

I went back to the house and tried the one place I hadn't looked, and there was Eric, slumped over a pile of logs, comatose. I tried to rouse him but I couldn't, so I had no choice but to leave him.

On 7 January Roger and Eric flew to America and Eric checked into Hazelden, an addiction treatment centre in Minnesota. After Christmas Roger had said to him, 'You're not a drunk, Eric, you're an alcoholic' – and for once Eric hadn't argued. He was incredibly nervous, but he wanted help.

I was happy to see them go, glad that the insanity we'd been living with was about to end – until I started to worry that it might change him and therefore our relationship. I was used to dealing with a drunk: how would I cope with a sober Eric? I might not even know him when he came back.

Roger stayed with Eric the entire six weeks, living in a hotel in Minnesota and visiting him every day. I went out for a week, on Hazelden's instructions, to join the Al Anon group, the offshoot of Alcoholics Anonymous for relatives. I found myself in a group of people who were married to or living with addicts – and they were normal people, not severely damaged or strange. They made me feel so welcome, and talked about their own alcoholic or drug addict with such incredible honesty. I had never dared tell anybody, or probably even admit to myself, that I was living with an alcoholic, and my life had become so difficult. I hadn't felt I could confide in friends because I didn't want to be disloyal but I felt safe with those people, and with them I could talk about all the things I had been keeping so painfully to myself. Their experiences, feelings, dreads and fears were exactly like mine – they might have been describing my life. We had all been keeping the same secret, living the same life, and we had thought we were the only ones.

We did an interesting role-play. We had to make ourselves into a human sculpture with the alcoholic on his hands and knees in the middle. Everyone else leant against him, symbolising all the people in his life who looked after him – wife, children, mother, father, brothers, sisters, nieces, aunts and so on. When the alcoholic gets better, he is removed from the sculpture and everyone else collapses. All the ills in a family with an alcoholic member are blamed on him and his affliction until, subconsciously, their whole way of life revolves around him. Once he is better, he is no longer the same person, and everyone else has to learn to stand up straight too.

I found Al Anon wonderfully helpful. I became stronger every day and, slowly, the damage began to heal. At the end of the week I didn't want to leave. It was a nice, safe, cosy environment, and it was structured: I knew what was going to happen every day, which I hadn't in my normal life for a long time.

When Eric came home he was introverted and quiet; all he wanted to do was go fishing, so I became a trout widow. He was also a football fanatic, driving all over the country with Roger to watch West Bromwich Albion. And whenever we booked into hotels it was always as Mr and Mrs Albion. But the fishing was the worst. He would leave the house at about seven thirty and wouldn't be back until late afternoon – with five or six fish that he wanted cleaned and frozen. I learnt how to gut them very quickly in my Marigolds. Sometimes I would go with him and spend the day photographing wild flowers, but mostly he went alone and that was the way he preferred it. He wasn't easy to be with. I felt he was angry – angry that he couldn't do the one thing he enjoyed in life, which was have a drink. He couldn't understand why it was denied him. Even after six weeks at Hazelden, I don't think he really understood that he was ill.

When he wasn't fishing he was touring, and I was alone again for long stretches. I didn't even have the pleasure of gutting his fish. He had invited Gary Brooker, who played keyboard, to join the band, so he had a fishing companion on tour and the rods went everywhere. At every stop they fished and he insisted Roger book them into hotels with fishing facilities. Another obsession was buying clothes. This was nothing new but he went into overdrive. He would go to Armani and find a nice suit, then want it in every colour.

He was on tour when a new Ferrari was delivered. At that time one of my friends was Linda Spinetti, who lived nearby. Her husband, Henry, played drums with Eric's band and we spent a lot of time together while they were away. We used to go swimming and ice-skating and generally hung out together. I told Eric on the phone that the new car had arrived and asked whether I could bring it to the airport to meet him. 'Yes, yes, yes,' he said. 'That would be lovely.' So, I put on a pretty dress, went to collect Linda and off we set. The interior was cream leather, the sky was blue and it was a beautiful spring morning. It was delicious and we were so happy as we zipped along the lanes and around the M25.

I stayed in the car when we arrived at the airport, and Linda went into the terminal building to find Eric. Inside, she saw Roger and told him I was waiting. 'What car is she in?' he said urgently.

'The new Ferrari,' she said.

He looked worried – he knew what was about to happen.

Eric was furious with me. He said, 'Someone has driven it before me. I can't drive it now. I'll have to sell it.'

Life was very different with the sober Eric – *he* was very different. He had never been good at expressing himself verbally, but now he didn't want to talk at all. He'd lost his sense of fun. The practical jokes, mad antics and laughter had gone. It was as though he had lost his personality. Worse, I detected in him an underlying sense of injustice. I was still drinking and so was everyone around him – no one had told me I should stop, which, in retrospect, might have helped him. We both went to our respective meetings, AA for him, Al Anon for me, once or twice a week, and he was on the Twelve Steps to recovery, but he said the only thing he wanted to do was drink and he was angry that he couldn't.

He stayed on the wagon for about six months. Then he went on tour and, in Copenhagen, dipped secretly into the mini-bar in his hotel suite, thinking no one would know – forgetting, or perhaps unaware, that everything he had taken would show up on the bill. Then he started smoking dope with some of the roadies, and once he'd done that and felt he'd handled it, he convinced himself that the odd drink wouldn't hurt. When he came home he pretended he wasn't drinking – I heard all of this from one of the roadies – but I soon discovered he had some coke too and I couldn't believe that that was a good idea. I didn't know who I could turn to for help.

Eric was cunning about his drinking and, initially, he tried to hide it from me, but eventually it was out in the open and worse than ever, escalating out of all proportion. I couldn't bear to be around him. He was getting very angry – the lovely, gentle man who had never until now called me anything more than 'a silly clown'. Now he would shout at me for no reason; if I left him at all, even if it was just to go into Cranleigh for some shopping, he would rant and rave when I got back, so unless Roger was coming down, I couldn't go anywhere or see anyone. And I felt that he was always watching me. He was drinking a terrifying amount and wanted me to drink with him. When he poured himself a drink, he poured me one too; when he ordered a drink in the pub, he ordered one for me. So I drank but not because I wanted to. I drank because that was what Eric wanted me to do and my life was all about Eric, his wants and needs. I knew it was no way to live. At night I went to bed before him, hoping I would be asleep before he came up, and cried. I'd pray he would pass out when he came to bed and not try to touch me. There were times when he was more like an animal than the loving, passionate husband I'd known, and reeked of brandy. At other times he'd come to bed, put his arms round me as I sobbed and say, 'It's all right, it's going to be all right.' I so wished I could believe him but I was frightened. I thought he'd end up killing one of us.

One day I decided my long hair had to go. I couldn't explain why at the time but I know now that that's a classic response to emotional collapse and self-loathing. So, being a coward above everything else, I rang Jenny and said, 'Let's go to Vidal Sassoon and have our hair cut off.'

'Yes,' she said.

So off we went. We both had the same cut, to a length of about four inches all over, and as the hairdresser was snipping away, chatting to the stylist next to him, I thought, God, what a dreadful mistake, but it was too late. It made me look as ghastly as I felt.

What clinched it was the day I saw a photograph Jenny had taken of me. I didn't recognise myself. My face was puffy, I had put on weight and my hair was limp and bedraggled. What really scared me, though, was I knew I had lost more than my looks: I had lost the 'me' in me, my sense of identity. I didn't know who I was any more.

One afternoon in September 1984, when Eric had passed out on the sofa in the sitting room, I packed a suitcase and left. I took the coward's way out and wrote him a note. I didn't dare do it any other way, and I couldn't have done it when he was awake. I went to stay with my mother, who was then living in Haslemere, in Surrey, so she could be close to Paula, and every single day for the four weeks that I was there Eric sent me a dozen red roses.

Then, one day, there was a knock at the door. I opened it and there was Eric, looking so thin, shaky and nervous I scarcely recognised him. Evidently he had had nothing to eat since I'd left. I invited him in and he pleaded with me to come back. He said how sorry he was that he had behaved so badly, he loved me, he needed me, it would never happen again. I wanted to believe him and I wanted nothing more than to go back to Hurtwood Edge and for life to be happy and normal and for him to be the funny, sexy, fabulous Eric he had once been. Instead I steeled myself. 'No. You're still drinking. You shouldn't be drinking. I can't do it.'

The most upsetting part was that I was in the midst of IVF treatment. Eric and I had been trying to have a baby since we'd first started living together, but it hadn't happened. If ever my period was late I would think, This is it. I'm pregnant! I would be so excited and plan which room would be the baby's and how I would decorate it, then think about which schools he or she would go to, maybe even look at one or two. Then, ten days later, my period would arrive.

At that time I was doing some work with the National Children's Homes and I asked about adoption. They told me that at thirty-six I was too old. I couldn't believe it so I spoke to my doctor, who confirmed it was true. I could only adopt, he said, from a third-world country. I would have been happy to have a child from any country – I didn't care what colour, shape or size it was – but I was frightened that Eric in a drunken moment, might say something offensive and horrible and I didn't feel that I could expose an adopted child to that risk. And so, reluctantly, I decided against it.

Eventually my GP, sent me to see Professor Ian Craft who had just opened a fertility clinic in London. The in-vitro fertilisation procedure had been pioneered by Patrick Steptoe and Robert Edwards, and Louise Brown, the first 'test-tube baby', was born in 1978, so in 1984 IVF was still in its infancy. I wasn't sure how keen Eric was on the idea, but Professor Craft understood his reluctance. It was a common problem, he said, and he would be happy to talk it through with Eric. Eric wouldn't do that, but he did go along with the IVF, and it indignities. However, he wouldn't alter his lifestyle to improve the outcome: he didn't cut down the drinking or the smoking, both of which can affect sperm count – which was never investigated. I had all the tests, and I was the one at whom the finger of inadequacy was pointed.

Eric didn't welcome the process because it was unnatural, and I couldn't argue with that, but I thought that if science had progressed so far we should take advantage of it. And I did so want a child. I had watched my sisters and my friends have their babies; it seemed so unfair that I couldn't. Each time I got as far as having an embryo implanted, I was full of excitement and optimism, convinced that a new life was growing inside me. Then I had to face up to the fact that it had failed.

After a month with my mother I moved to a little house in Devonshire Close Mews in the West End, which Roger paid for, and started to make contact with my friends, most of whom I hadn't seen in years. When I tried to ring Belinda, there was no reply, so I went round to her flat and discovered she had moved. And then Marie-Lise was killed in a horse-riding accident, which knocked me for six. She had been living with the actor John Hurt since 1967 and they were both old friends from my days with George. Before John became famous he had acted in small fringe theatres; George and I went to see everything he did. When John was cast as Bob Champion, the jockey who had cancer and went on to win the Grand National, he had to learn to ride, so Marie-Lise taught him. They were out together one day, without hard hats, when a gust of wind spooked the horses. Marie-Lise was thrown over a hedge and on to a road. She died instantly.

It had been Marie-Lise who told me I needed to wear glasses. All my life I had been short-sighted but never known it. It might explain why I was so cripplingly shy – I couldn't see people properly. One day I was looking out of the window in her flat and put on a pair of glasses she had left lying around. Suddenly I could see the road sign outside. Marie-Lise sent me straight to an optician.

Chris O'Dell was in London, now married to a lovely man called Anthony Russell. I saw a lot of them. His parents owned Leeds Castle in Kent and we had some wonderful weekends there. Over the last two years I had also become friendly with Carolyn Waters, married to Roger Waters, the bass guitarist and singer with Pink Floyd. She and I had known each other vaguely in the sixties when she'd worked in the Apple shop with Jenny, but we hadn't spoken until she telephoned one day out of the blue when Roger wanted Eric to guest on his first solo album *The Pros and Cons of Hitch-Hiking*. He didn't know Eric, so he had asked Carolyn to ring me. We arranged to meet and became friends. They would come down to Hurtwood Edge with their children, and Carolyn's birthday was around Christmas so we went to them for great parties.

The next year Roger and Eric appeared in a series of concerts in aid of ARMS – Action Research Into Multiple Sclerosis. Our old friend Ronnie Lane was suffering from the disease and Eric helped to organise a series of concerts in London, New York, Los Angeles and San Francisco, which Glynn Johns agreed to produce. He got Jeff Beck, Jimmy Page, Charlie Watts, Bill Wyman, Kenny Jones and Steve Winwood among others; Carolyn and I went to the one at the Royal Albert Hall in London, and afterwards we all went to the Hard Rock Café in Green Park. We were sitting in a booth, chatting away, when the dreaded twin, Jenny McLean, appeared and said hello to Eric. I freaked, and although Carolyn had no idea who she was, she got rid of her instantly.

She and Roger lived in a beautiful house in East Sheen, on the outskirts of London, and quite often her brother, Will Christie, was at the house. He was a lovely man, very good-looking, kind and gentle. He was a photographer so we immediately had something in common and he gave me a lot of help with and advice on cameras. He got me using my Hasselblad, which had confused me: it had two shutters, one on the body, the other on the lens. I didn't know how or when to use them until he showed me. He and I had first met at a mutual friend's wedding, and when Eric was on tour we met again at a party at the Natural History Museum. The paparazzo Richard Young was there and the next day there was a photograph of us in Nigel Dempster's column in the *Daily Mail* with a story about how we had become good friends and Will was helping me with my photography. I don't know who spoke to Richard Young, but when Eric saw it he was furious. He and I were still together but things were bad between us. He wanted to know what was going on. 'Oh, God, El, he's just a friend. Nothing's going on.' I don't think he believed me.

After I left Eric, Will and I went out together. He was so easy to be with – there was no unpleasantness, no pressure, no black moods, just fun, and I felt safe with him – cherished for the first time in years. He helped me find a way out of the horrible murky world in which I'd been living, and encouraged me to see a therapist, which I might never have done without him.

My sister Jenny had been in therapy for years and had tried to persuade me to see her therapist. She had had her own share of problems. The failure of her two marriages to Mick Fleetwood had been very painful. During that period she had been dependent on drink and cocaine and eventually she had hit rock bottom. Therapy had helped, so when she and the girls had been living at Willow Cottage and she had seen what was happening to me, she had decided I needed the same sort of help. I knew I did too, but I was too frightened to do anything about it – I was afraid that if I saw this psychotherapist I would be opening up Pandora's Box: the sadness might come out in such a torrent that I wouldn't be able to stem the flow. I saw myself in that Edvard Munch painting *The Scream*.

By the time I left Eric, Jenny had given up drink and cocaine for good and had met Ian Wallace, a drummer who had played with King Crimson, Snake and Bob Dylan. They went to live in Los Angeles and were married in 1984.

I took Will's advice and went to see Karen, who was a dream analyst and astrologer as well as a psychotherapist. Lying on a sofa in her basement consulting room in Shepherd's Bush was everything I had feared it would be. All I wanted to do when I got into that room was lie on the floor and scream, 'Help me!' So I tried not to go. After one or two sessions I'd had enough, but she would always say firmly, 'See you next week.' And over many years she did help me, but the other person who helped me was Will. He was so sweet and so amusing, but he knew how unhappy I was and didn't force anything. He was a strong, protective shoulder to cry on, and I fell in love with him.

Eric knew I was seeing Will and bombarded me with letters and phone calls, pleading with me to go back. His letters were always poetic and passionate, and had I been on my own, without Will and Karen, my resolve might have collapsed but I stuck to my guns. In

December he came back from a tour of Australia and Hong Kong with the most beautiful present for me: a little ruby heart framed with diamonds on a chain. I remembered how much I loved him, but I didn't crack. I had to salvage some part of myself, and going back to Eric and the life we had shared was not the way to do it.

Immediately after Christmas I went on holiday to Sri Lanka, with a girl I scarcely knew called Sara Levinson. I had met her once or twice, then bumped into her again in a coffee bar. She was a university lecturer, so had long holidays, and couldn't decide whether to go to South America or Sri Lanka. I thought Sri Lanka sounded nice and she said, 'Come with me!' So I did.

Sri Lanka is the most beautiful island with fabulous beaches and mountains and huge statues of Buddha everywhere. I fell in love with it. The one person we both knew on the island was the publisher Anthony Blond, who had a house in Galle, the capital of the southern province, and he invited us to spend New Year's Eve with him. We stayed in a Dutch colonial hotel called the New Oriental. One evening we were sitting in the bar, which was pretty deserted, wondering how we'd find Anthony's house, when a jolly-looking group of people walked in and started talking about Anthony Blond. How extraordinary. We pointed out the coincidence and started to chat.

Among the group there was a property developer called Rod Weston, who had bought some land in Sri Lanka and knew the island well, his girlfriend Francesca Findlater, a dentist called Roman Franks (who became my dentist) and Eric Fellner, a film-maker who went on to make *Notting Hill* and *Bridget Jones*. They had been in Galle for Christmas and were also going to Anthony and Laura's for New Year. The next day we met up again at lunch, then again at the Blonds' for the party. Afterwards Sara and I went off to explore.

We had a guide to show us the island and one of the places he said we had to see was Sigaria. It's a plateau more than two thousand metres high, with the ruins of a fortress on the top. Twelve hundred steps lead to the summit, which I climbed. I have never been so frightened in all my life. He said we had to set off at five thirty a.m. and after about an hour we reached a little platform where you can look at the wonderful views and buy Coca-Cola. We stopped for a drink and then the guide said it was time to get going again. Sara said she didn't want to go any further but I thought we shouldn't let the guide down so I followed him up alone.

From this point the steps were hewn out of the rock and were very shallow. I take a size-six shoe and only half of my foot could fit on to each step and the only thing to stop me falling thousands of feet to my death was a thin rope loosely strung between metal stays drilled into the rock. At one point I made the mistake of looking down and Sara was a tiny speck miles below. We were still only half-way up and I thought, I can't move, I can't breathe, I can't go up, I can't go down, I want a helicopter to get me out of here.

I burst into tears and called up to the guide, 'I can't move!'

'Yes, you can. You can do it slowly.'

'No, I can't!' I felt paralysed. Then I remembered that there were no rescue helicopters: this was Sri Lanka. I had to get my head round it.

With tears rolling down my cheeks, I went on up and, about fifteen minutes later reached the top. It was the most incredible relief – and also the most incredible sight. How on earth had men carried the materials to build an entire fortress up that mountain? But you could see why they had and why it was considered so holy. We were almost in the sky, and could see for miles. Fortunately there was another route down, which was much easier, or I might still be there today.

After three glorious weeks I came back to London to find a letter from Eric. This one wasn't passionate but it was just as potent as any of the poetic letters of the past. He had been snowed in at Hurtwood Edge and talked about the birds he found frozen to death each morning in the garden, even though he was putting out an extra bird tray. I immediately saw in my mind's eye the glorious terraced garden with the huge views. Not much fun for Zulu the cat, he said. And he told me how much Trouper, whom I missed, loved catching snowballs that exploded on her nose – 'and then she wonders where they've gone . . . silly dog'. There was news of Rose and Pat, and then he finished with the clincher: 'I miss you and need you so much my love, and I ask you, please, please don't take up with Will again the moment you get back, I think it would be the end of me . . . Please come home, where you belong. I promise I won't let you down again. – I love you – El xxx'

Despite my holiday I was still feeling wobbly and confused about what I wanted and where I was going. There had been so many letters, phone calls and red roses that I couldn't just turn my back on him when he clearly loved and needed me so much. I was so mixed up and tearful that I didn't know what to think.

Then he rang and asked me to go to Israel with him. I agreed, and we flew to Eilat. The next day we took the car and drove for miles along the coast, with the beautiful pink hills of Jordan just visible across the Dead Sea. Eric stopped the car at one point and explained that he had been given a couple of tablets he wanted us to take. They were called Ecstasy and had been created, he said, for therapists to give to couples who needed help in resurrecting their lost intimacy. I found it difficult to believe that a pill could turn my head and heart round but he was convinced they would help us – and me in particular. So we each swallowed our pill and Eric carried on driving until the Ecstasy kicked in and he couldn't go any further. He asked if I could take over.

A feeling of deliciousness came over me. I could do anything! After a while we stopped and went into the Dead Sea. It was so weird. The water was body temperature and deliciously viscous, the mineral content so high that it lifted our legs and spirits. We lay in the water and talked.

Telling Will was almost the hardest bit. I know I hurt him very badly and I felt very torn about doing what I did. He had been a true friend and helped me through some nightmarish times and I will never forget how kind and gentle he was to me during those months. I don't know how, or if, I would have survived without him. But my bond with Eric was too strong for me to resist.

CHAPTER THIRTEEN

Things Fall Apart

A rriving back at Hurtwood Edge was emotional. Trouper was so thrilled to see me, bounding about and wagging her tail so much that her whole woolly body did a little dance. It was wonderful to see the animals again, the house and the garden, Arthur and his wife Iris. Eric showered me with presents and lots of Giorgio Armani clothes, but I didn't know whether I had made the right decision: the drive for reconciliation was coming from him, but I had made the decision and had to live with it. I prayed that he wouldn't go back to drinking too much and that our lives could be relatively normal. But that is what every wife, husband, child or parent who lives with an alcoholic tells themselves. They are all living in Cloud Cuckoo Land, and so was I. I went back to living with and for Eric.

Still, too, I had no one to talk to, apart from Karen, my therapist. I longed for an older woman, whose judgement I respected, to confide in. I needed her to let me talk through what was happening to me and how I was feeling, not to tell me I *had* to do this or that. I needed to be able to work it out for myself. But my mother wasn't that person. To her, everything was black or white: I had to leave him immediately or stay and get on with it. No discussion, no weighing up the pros and cons. In my experience, life wasn't like that.

The honeymoon period was soon over. Two weeks after our return from Israel Eric went off on a UK and European tour, and I was alone again. The loneliness always set in several days before he left the house when he would start to detach himself from me emotionally. It was a kind of subconscious letting go, essential for him, I am sure, but quite difficult for me – and difficult again when he returned. It always took him at least ten days to readjust to the normal routine. On tour he was used to having everything done for him: if he took a cigarette, someone was there to light it; if his glass was nearly empty, someone would fill it. I wasn't prepared to do that. I was the harridan telling him to light his own cigarette, so he would be moody for a while, frustrated and at a loss to know what to do. On tour he had lots of mates around him. If he wanted to be on his own he would say so or he would retreat to his hotel room, but if he wanted to play he had his playmates. At home in the country there was just me and I was a poor substitute. Curiously, he would never pick up the phone and invite friends to come over. If someone phoned him or turned up at the house, that was fine, but he would never do the asking.

While he was in Europe I had organised a party for his fortieth birthday in March. We hadn't had many parties, mostly because Eric was so anti-social, but that night surrounded by his friends and family – about seventy in all – he seemed happy. And the house came alive again. I found a marvellous magician and illusionist, called Simon Drake, who dressed as a guest and surprised everyone by suddenly going into his act.

At about two in the morning the phone rang and it was Ringo and

Barbara, his second wife, whom he had married after he and Maureen were divorced in 1981. They had crashed their car on the Robin Hood roundabout and been taken to hospital.

Jeff Beck left the party for his house in Kent at about three a.m. Half an hour later there was a phone call from someone in Rowhook: 'We've got one our of your guests in our garden!' Jeff had missed a sharp bend in one of his hot-rods. I said I'd go and pick him up, and arrived to find an old lady and her husband, both in dressing-gowns and slippers, and Jeff, looking so rock 'n' roll in his leather jacket with blood pouring from his face. 'Thank you for coming to save me. Celia [Hammond, his girlfriend] is going to be so cross with me for crashing the car.' He was much more worried about her wrath than the gash on his nose and the gushing blood that the elderly couple were trying in vain to staunch. His nose bears the scar to this day.

Almost immediately afterwards Eric started a fifteen-week tour of America and Canada. He broke off in July, in the middle it, to play in the Live Aid concert in the JFK Stadium in Philadelphia, organised by Bob Geldof in aid of the starving in Africa. I flew across and joined him, and I can't remember a more electrifying day. There were ninety thousand people in the stadium and the energy levels, both on and off stage, were beyond belief. The show ran simultaneously at Wembley Stadium in London and absolutely everyone was playing at one or the other location. We sat in the hotel in Philadelphia, with Mick Jagger and others popping in and out, and watched the Wembley concert on television. We saw Phil Collins play in London, then left for the show. By the time we arrived backstage, Phil was in Philadelphia ready to drum for Eric: he had taken Concorde so he could play in both concerts. Eric played three songs – 'White Room', 'She's Waiting' and 'Layla'. He had been nervous but I'd never seen him play so brilliantly and never felt so proud to be his wife. It was the world's biggest ever rock festival. More than a billion and a half people watched it on TV and it raised £30 million – three times what Bob had expected.

After our reconciliation Eric had lifted his ban on wives and girlfriends, but life on the road was pretty hard-core and my memories of touring before I walked out on him were not good. He would shout at me in restaurants and across hotel lobbies. Perhaps he thought he was being funny but no one else did: the roadies and the rest of the band would think, Poor Pattie. I never shouted back, which chipped another notch in my self-esteem. If a tour was particularly long Eric would get bored and ask me to join him. He would be all over me when I arrived but gradually he would want to hang out with the band, see what girls were around, and tell me to go home so he could slide back into his old habits. I went to the odd concert – and wouldn't have missed Live Aid for the world – but I didn't want to trail around, watching women throw themselves at him.

So in October I didn't go with him to Milan where he met an actress called Lori del Santo. Her name was unknown to me until one evening Eric suggested we go out for dinner. I thought, How romantic, and phoned the Italian restaurant in Cranleigh to make a reservation. We almost never went out to eat, so this was a real treat. Our first course had just arrived when Eric said he had something to tell me. I froze. I knew instinctively, in the way one does, that what he had to say was not good.

He'd met a girl called Lori when he was in Italy. They had slept together a couple of times. He still loved me but he thought he was in love with her too.

I don't know how I got through the rest of dinner. This was what I had dreaded. I could put up with infidelity, if it was purely physical. Girls like Conchita were no threat – they were not predatory – and girls plucked out of an audience after a gig were out of the door by morning. Sex was no threat to our marriage. Emotion was a different matter.

But, as usual, I put it out of my mind, pretended it wasn't

happening. I didn't know what else to do. How could I have allowed Eric to destroy the shred of self-esteem I was still clinging to?

Life went on. Christmas approached, and I began my usual preparations. One day I was in the kitchen putting flowers into a vase when he came in and told me that he had had a phone call from Lori. She was pregnant. I felt panic, fear, uncertainty, terror of what might happen next. What would I do? How would I cope? 'Can't she get rid of it?' I asked.

'No, she's Catholic. And she doesn't want to.'

I felt sick. I couldn't breathe properly and my heart was pounding so hard that I couldn't think. The stalks of the flowers I was arranging got shorter and shorter as I kept to my task. I heard myself, as if disembodied, saying it would be all right, we would still be together, but my brain was shutting down. I was in shock. I needed space to digest what I had heard. I had been trying to have a baby for twenty-one years, and this woman had slept with my husband once or twice and was carrying his child. I thought my heart was about to disintegrate.

Eric was clearly infatuated with Lori. He told me how beautiful she was and what wonderful photographs she took – another stab to the heart – and now she was expecting a baby too. I really think, in a funny way, he expected me to be pleased. When they met, he told me, she had professed not to know who he was. He was impressed by that – the oldest trick in the book, and he had fallen for it. They were introduced by his Italian promoter in a Milan nightclub, and Roger Forrester, who was there at the time, thought it was a set-up. She was a friend of Adnan Khashoggi, the powerful, Saudi-born arms dealer and businessman. It was the final nail in the coffin of my marriage.

Christmas was full of false jollity for family and friends, anger between us and far too much alcohol. I told Eric I didn't want to share a bed with him any more – I didn't sleep with him again – so he moved into the bedroom above the kitchen, which he didn't like.

He was angry that I wouldn't sleep with him, but I think that that was mostly to do with fear. He was afraid he was going to lose me. I continued to see Karen – she and our sessions were all I had to hold on to.

From the start Eric had seen therapy as a threat, and in some ways he was right to. Karen encouraged me to open my eyes and see what was happening: that my life was all about Eric. And while that can be nice, and lots of couples do live for each other, he had the winning hand. He had his creativity – his work, his recording, his travelling – and I had nothing. I was taking photographs but I had little else. My identity, my sense of self, was dependent on him, and because he made me think he valued it so little, my self-esteem could not have been lower.

The baby was born in London in August 1986. I was in the South of France, staying with the Genesis guitarist Mike Rutherford and his wife Angie. Angie's sister and brother-in-law, another Mike, were also there. Angie had asked me to join them so I didn't have to be around at the time of the birth. She was pregnant and so was Chris O'Dell. Everyone seemed to be pregnant except me. I was thrilled for them, of course, but I found it hard. I was forty-two and my marriage was on its last legs so I had to face the unpalatable fact that I might never have a child.

One evening we were sitting on the garden wall when the phone rang. It was Eric, wanting me to know that he was the proud father of a son, Conor. He was so excited. He had watched the baby being born, and went on and on about how moving, how marvellous, how miraculous it had been. His enthusiasm was unbridled. I might have been his sister or a friend, not his jilted wife. He had no thought that this might be news I didn't want to hear.

I went back into the garden and told Angie and both Mikes of Conor's arrival, and as I did so, I realised that Eric had genuinely thought I would be happy for him. I am normally so good at holding things in, but that night as I started to speak I was overwhelmed with grief and pain. For the first time I let go and cried uncontrollably.

Angie and Mike were marvellous – and then Bill Wyman appeared. He had a house a quarter of a mile down the road, which was under siege from the paparazzi. He was in trouble because his girlfriend, Mandy Smith, was under age – they had started going out when he was forty-seven and she fourteen. He asked if he could come and stay to escape and was with us for about ten days while the press kept vigil outside his empty house. Angie's pregnancy was making her feel horribly ill, I was in meltdown and Bill was in danger of being thrown into jail, but he made us die laughing. He is the most fantastic raconteur and each night we would sit at the Rutherfords' long dining-table and laugh.

I went back to England feeling much stronger but still uncertain of the future. Lori and Conor had gone back to Italy, and Eric had this idea that we could stay together and carry on being husband and wife, the baby could live with us every so often and everything would be fine. I thought the mother might have rather different ideas. Then he thought that perhaps if Lori wouldn't let the child come to us by himself, he could go to Italy every few weeks. He didn't really love her, he said, and promised he wouldn't sleep with her, just go to see Conor. I didn't understand how it could possibly work: how could he go to Milan and play happy families, then come back to me in an empty house with no baby? The dog was no substitute. Perhaps I might have come to terms with it if I had had children, but I had nothing to concentrate on except Eric, and it was just too intense.

However, as I was going through a second bout of IVF treatment I agreed to try, and started 1987 with renewed energy, determined that our life would sort itself out. I fondly imagined that Eric's love for me and his baby would, in time, bring us together and that I would have a share in Conor's upbringing. A baby of my own would complete the picture. However, Lori, it seemed, wasn't happy with the idea of us having Conor so Eric announced that he would be going to see him in Milan once a month, starting on 24 January.

While he was away I was having ultrasound scans to discover whether the implanted embryo had taken, but I couldn't forget about what was going on in Milan.

Four days later Eric was back, full of news about what Conor could do, lit up by his funny little ways, bubbling with excitement. The pain was so deep I had to avoid looking at it. I had to keep myself constantly on the move and think about other things. I went to lunches galore, to charity meetings, to weekends away, anything and everything to escape. I was like a fish skimming the surface, flitting from one glittering distraction to the next, afraid to look into the sinister depths below, knowing that they were seething with monsters waiting to devour me. It was the only way I could survive.

Meanwhile Eric embraced the brandy again. He lurched from a state of drunkenness to oblivion in four-hourly intervals now, and only woke, it seemed, to drink more and shout abuse at or criticise me. He accused me of using the house like a hotel. I could feel his pain and longed to make it better but I couldn't help him. He was caught between the ecstasy that Conor's birth had brought him and the agony of losing me, which he could see would be the other consequence of his child's arrival. He wanted everything, and he couldn't have it. It was an intolerable situation and got worse with every week that passed. I thought he was going to go mad with the drink or kill himself, and eventually I knew I had to get out for his sake as well as mine.

I told him I couldn't do it any longer. We had to divorce. He still thought we could work it out, but I was too sad, too defeated. Angie Rutherford's brother, John Downing, was a lawyer and he helped me find someone to represent me. I went to see several people. One asked what my husband's hobby was and when I said, 'Fishing', he said, 'Then he can't be that bad a bloke.' He was out. And another, whose name was Raymond Tooth, frightened me so much I thought he was going to have Eric assassinated! He was also out. I paid him fifty pounds for the consultation, and every time his name appears in the newspapers because he's handling a high-profile divorce, the article always says that he got millions for Pattie Boyd. Nonsense. I phoned him recently and said, 'You owe me a lot of money for all that free advertising. It's time you put the record straight.'

The one I settled on was much more gentlemanly – maybe too gentlemanly, given how much money he got me. He told me that on no account should I leave the marital home, so I stayed at Hurtwood Edge and Roger found a flat in London for Eric.

Eric hated the flat. He said he couldn't work there, he needed the house. Roger told me he wanted me out. I said, 'My lawyer has said I mustn't leave the house.'

'I think you girls should have a nice holiday,' Roger said, and somehow persuaded me to go skiing in Courchevel in France. I took Nicole Winwood with me – she had recently separated from Steve. I had never ski'd before and loved it. Then one lunchtime our instructor, Jean Louis, said he couldn't take us out in the afternoon because there was a white-out and it was too dangerous. I couldn't bear not to be busy so I asked if there was something we could do instead. We could skate, he suggested. Well, I'd done that with Linda Spinetti when Eric and her husband Henry were on tour – and sometimes we'd roller-skated on the black and white marble floor at Hurtwood Edge. Nicole didn't want to skate, so Jean Louis took me on my own. For a second I lost concentration, and because I was in boots that didn't quite fit, I went flying and broke my left wrist. I spent the rest of the holiday with my arm in a cast.

I went back to Hurtwood Edge, where Eric was living again but in a separate bedroom. It was not a happy arrangement. He was angry and things were tense between us. One morning – it was my forty-third birthday – he burst into my bedroom at six o'clock in a drunken rage and told me to get out. He was screaming and shouting obscenities at me, and so worked up that I thought he might burst a blood vessel in his neck. He accused me of not being a proper wife because I wouldn't sleep with him, then hurled my things out of the window, still yelling at me. This was not a time to argue. I got dressed, picked up my things from the drive, got into my car and drove to London.

I drove around for hours in a state of abject misery. I felt numb, as if I was invisible. I had been due to meet a few girlfriends for lunch at San Lorenzo, so at about one o'clock I drove to Beauchamp Place. I must have looked ghastly, my face puffy and tear-stained, and Mara Berni, the motherly owner, asked what had happened. I told her and she gave me a little Madonna to bring me comfort – her kindness brought on more tears.

I spent that first night at Blakes, Anouska Hempel's hotel in Roland Gardens, then Alan Rogan, Eric's guitar technician and a friend who had often spent Christmas with us, said I could stay at his place in Twickenham for a few weeks while he was on tour.

From there I went to Nicole Winwood, who was living in a flat in Chiswick. She insisted we have a good time so I didn't have a chance to wallow in misery. All the while I was telephoning Roger, asking him for money and somewhere I could live more permanently. Eventually he came up with two flats for me to look at. I chose a little two-bedroom affair in Queensgate Place and moved into it in July.

I had left Hurtwood Edge with little more than the clothes I had dressed in on the morning that Eric had thrown me out and needed to retrieve more. I asked Chris O'Dell if she would come with me, and she agreed, but on the day she was busy with marital problems of her own and couldn't come. Such was my emotional fragility that I felt disproportionately let down and miserable. At that time everything made me burst into tears; I had no confidence, I was confused and lost, and the smallest slight, even from a stranger, could reduce me to a quivering heap. In the end my mother helped. She was the last person I wanted to see – she was so emotional – and she tipped me over the edge. I left most of my stuff behind, including all my music and some Beatles' white labels – worth thousands now. I walked from room to room, not wanting to be there, not knowing what to take. I came away with my photographs, my passport and little else. I had to leave my lovely Trouper, but I couldn't keep her in my rented flat in London and I knew Arthur would take care of her.

Eric bombarded me with letters and phone calls, which were occasionally abusive but mostly beautiful, poetic and apologetic. 'You were cut open from head to toe,' he wrote from Antigua, 'and I held the scalpel. I still have it in my hand, and I will probably use it again. May God forgive me if I do – Will you help me please Nell, stop me hurting people, and forgive me?' In another he wrote:

To the Adorable Butterfly – I can picture you in my minds eye (eyes?) flitting from one green and fertile bush to another giving the lesser insects a brief glimpse of what a truly pure and beautiful creature can look like, think of how much pleasure you give them, how much light you cast upon their starved souls.

But you need light too, or your wings will become brittle and dry, and your flying days will be over. Take some time and spread your wings in the sun, allow someone (me, is the healer I have in mind) to shine on you, so that your heart becomes young and vibrant again, and your wings grow supple and strong, and then fly, and I'll meet you somewhere above all the nonsense and we will learn to live again as we are meant to – Majnun, El, Slowhand, Rick, all of ME! xxx

It was agony. I knew I had done the right thing in leaving him but I was terribly unhappy. It would have been so much easier to cave in and go back to him, to believe all his silken words and romantic images, and my self-esteem was so low at that point that I might just have done it. But in my heart of hearts I knew it would never work.

Even if he managed to stop drinking, he would still have the baby. And I didn't have the strength to cope with that. I didn't have the strength for anything. I lurched from day to day, drinking far more than was good for me; I saw people, did things, put on makeup and held my head high, but I was only going through the motions.

Inside I was a wreck. The Sunday tabloids produced girl after girl who was supposedly pregnant with Eric's baby. And every day, alongside Eric's poetry, there were upsetting letters from lawyers. The only thing holding me together was Karen. I had been seeing her for two years now and she knew almost everything there was to know about me and my life. Then one weekend Eric appeared on a television chat show and was charming, articulate and didn't appear to be the slightest bit drunk.

When I saw Karen on the Monday, I said, 'I suppose you now think I've been making up all the things I've told you about Eric, that everything I've been telling you is a lie.'

'That's not the point. What matters is how *you* see it and what *you* feel about the situation. It's nothing to do with him or how anyone else sees it.'

And then I got it. I saw that life is about how situations affect each one of us and how much each of us can tolerate. I had reached my limit. And, even though I was seeing Karen, I was still the one who had to live it.

Time passed, but I still burst into tears at the slightest thing. One day a policeman stopped me in Cranleigh for erratic or careless driving. I was already upset: I couldn't bear going anywhere near the house or along any of the familiar roads we used to take to get there from London, but on that day I had had to go there for some reason, and when the policeman pulled me over I pleaded with him not to fine or arrest me or anything. 'I'm too upset,' I said, sobbing helplessly. 'I can't cope with life.' He was so kind. He told me to park the car and calm down before I drove any further.

Soon afterwards I was stopped by the police again. I had been at a charity lunch in Barnes, which had gone on for most of the afternoon, and I'd had a lot of wine. John Downing, Angie's lawyer brother, was in the car ahead of me. We were planning to go and have dinner somewhere so I was following him. He was travelling quite fast and I was trying to keep up. As I whizzed over Hammersmith Bridge the police stopped me. John kept going – I don't think he saw what had happened, so I was alone and frightened.

I had a terrible fear of authority, and for the first time in nearly twenty-five years there was no one to call, no one to help me. No Brian Epstein, no Peter Brown, no Roger Forrester. I was on my own and in deep trouble. The policemen made me blow into a breathalyser and, of course, I was over the limit. Once again the floodgates opened. I pleaded with them to let me go. I promised I wouldn't do it again – the usual old story – but they took me to the police station in the back of the patrol car. I was charged with drink-driving and had to appear at Richmond magistrates court. Fortunately it was the day before Margaret Thatcher won her third general election so the newspapers were full of her and my conviction went unreported. I was fined and banned from driving for a year.

It was a wake-up call. I should never have been driving and I shudder to think that I might have injured or, worse, killed someone. I was far safer on public transport, but it had been twenty-five years since I'd sat on a bus or found my way on to the Underground. I had to ask my friend Belinda, whom I had tracked down after a few phone calls, to show me how it worked: stations and ticket-buying had changed since the sixties and I was frightened to go alone, afraid I'd be mugged or recognised, and that people would wonder why I was travelling on the tube. Once upon a time I had been so brave, so fearless – I was the girl from Africa who was game for anything – but now I was afraid of everything. I felt vulnerable among so many strangers and the roar of the trains coming in and out of the tunnels made my heart pound. My confidence was shot.

However, the Underground was clearly the fastest way to travel around London, and once I got over the initial fear, I became quite expert. But every journey was a trial. At every station enormous posters of Eric would be staring at me from the walls, up and down the escalators and along the tunnels.

It wasn't just the Underground. I would go into shops and they would be playing Eric's music and the tears would start to flow. It was like one of those horror stories – I couldn't get away from him, he was haunting me – everywhere I turned he was there. I felt as though I was falling apart, losing my sanity. I was walking around but I didn't feel part of the world everyone else was walking around in.

I met friends for lunch and felt as though I was in a bubble, watching us eating and chatting: I had nothing in common with their world of husbands and children. I could hardly speak, and if anyone spoke to me I was lost for words and the tears would come. It was scary but I didn't have the energy to do anything about it. I thought alcohol might dull the pain, and cocaine ease the depression, but all they did was make matters worse. I just wanted to go to bed and sleep.

I was having a breakdown. I was grieving – not just over the loss of my marriage to Eric, but finally, after all these years, the loss of my marriage to George. I had gone straight from George to Eric without taking breath, and I had always wondered, in my heart of hearts, whether I had done the right thing. When things had been bad between George and me, when he was ignoring me, I had taken the easy option and let Eric seduce me. I knew I should have fought for my marriage to George.

I remember bumping into him in the late seventies at a party Jim Capaldi gave in Maidenhead. Jim was a founder member of Traffic and drummed with both Eric and George. I had had no idea that George and Olivia would be there, but it was so nice to see George and there was something about him that night, something I can't put my finger on, that made me realise nothing had fundamentally changed, that we still loved each other. It was warming and lovely to know that the feeling was still there. Eric and I were playmates, but George and I were soulmates, and I had let something special go without analysing what was happening between us.

Now, though, I had all the time in the world to think about what I had lost. And I wasn't just grieving the loss of my marriages and husbands: I was grieving the loss of any potential pregnancy. I was forty-three, about to divorce for the second time: the likelihood of my ever having a baby was almost non-existent, and that was the hardest pill of all to swallow.

CHAPTER FOURTEEN

Fighting Back

S hortly after I left him, Eric went into rehab for the second time. As I'd hoped, the shock of my leaving had pushed him to the edge of the precipice. In AA terminology, it was 'tough love': giving up on someone you love so that they have to face what they are: while you're with them, however bad the relationship, a little part of them says they must be okay because you're still there, still with them. You enable them to carry on with their destructive lifestyle. By detaching yourself – with love – they have no crutch to lean on and must either collapse and die or learn to stand on their own two feet. It was the people sculpture we'd done at my Al Anon classes at Hazelden. Eric, I knew, was on the point of collapsing and dying. And I know it was as painful for him as it was for me, but I like to think I may have saved his life a second time – the first when he nearly drowned in the Greek islands.

It was hard to go from being a rock star's wife, with someone to take care of everything, to being an ex with nothing. Going down is so much harder than going up. Leaving Hurtwood Edge for a tiny rented flat in Queensgate Place with practically no furniture was a comedown and my friends were horrified that Eric's manager had thought such a very small place adequate for me. But my self-esteem was so low I didn't question it. I was busy adjusting to my new life. I had been an alcoholic's carer for so long that I had forgotten how to live for myself. In losing Eric I had lost my role, and if I wasn't Mrs Clapton any more, who was I?

One day I picked up the phone and rang an old friend from modelling days, Amanda Lear. She was Salvador Dalí's muse and was living in the South of France. 'Amanda, hello,' I said. 'It's Pattie. I used to be Pattie Boyd.'

'You still are!'

'Oh – am I? I suppose I am.'

Gradually I began to pick up the pieces with old friends. I saw Edina Ronay and Dick Polak. Like most people they hadn't been to Hurtwood in years. Edina always remembers Eric coming home from the pub pissed one lunchtime and insulting my cooking, as he often did, and their small daughter Shebah saying, 'You can't talk to Pattie like that,' and Eric being lost for words. And I saw Jose Fonseca and Dick Kries. They came to the flat one evening and I was complaining about the size of the dining room, which wasn't large enough to swing a cat, and Dick, who owned the Casserole in the King's Road, said, 'But people can still come. They don't need to sit down at a table for dinner. As long as everyone's having fun and you make a nice meal, it will be fantastic.' And I thought how clever he was. He had expanded my mind on a social level. Buoyed up by that, I gave a big dinner party, to which Zandra Rhodes came, and Dick, Jose, Belinda and others, and we sat on rugs and cushions on the roof and it was just so nice to see friends.

I caught up with Mary Bee again, and Chris and Anthony, and Ringo and Barbara, who were living in Ascot but had an office off

Walton Street, and I began to see quite a lot of Rod and Francesca, too, the couple I had met in Sri Lanka.

I also saw a lot of Jill Wetton, now Briggs, whom I had met with Angie Rutherford a few years before. She reminded me of my sister Jenny, and it turned out they had been born on the same day. At that time she was married to John Wetton, a musician with King Crimson, who was an alcoholic. We discovered we were living similarly secretive lives and became very good mutually supportive friends. She was very much on a downward spiral when we first got to know each other and I sent her to see Karen.

While I was distracted by friends I could be relatively cheerful, but when the music stopped I was still on my own, the flat and my life hauntingly empty. To make matters worse I had to go into hospital. I had been suffering from severe abdominal pain and ended up having an operation for fibroids. The doctor advised a hyster-ectomy at the same time, and because I was so low and so depressed by the failure of two attempts at IVF, I agreed. One evening I was feeling very miserable – I'd had far too much to drink – and suddenly longed to talk to Alfie O'Leary, the kind, gentle giant who looked after Eric. They were on tour in America and when I finally got through to his hotel room and heard his friendly Cockney voice, I was so overcome with grief I couldn't speak. I sat holding the phone to my face sobbing helplessly, unable to say a word. Eventually I had to put the phone down. Years later he said to me, 'Did you phone me while I was on that tour?'

I was so embarrassed that I said, 'No, no, it wasn't me.'

One day my mother came to see me in the flat. I had just bought myself a white sofa – everything in the flat was white – and I said, joking, 'All I need now is a white kitten.' The next week she turned up on my doorstep with Polo. He was white, Turkish, had one green and one blue eye and was quite the most adorable, intelligent cat I've ever had. He was the one glimmer of sunshine in a very dark phase.

One night in October, Belinda came to supper. I gave her gravadlax as a starter, we chatted away and she admired Polo. When she was leaving I went out into the hallway to say a final farewell and a gust of wind slammed the door behind me. What to do? I had left candles burning and the kitten inside, but no locksmith was going to come out at that time of night. There was no alternative but to relax, spend the night at Belinda's and sort it out in the morning.

The next morning we looked out of the window at a scene of total devastation. It was the night of the 1987 hurricane. There were cars squashed under fallen trees, chimney pots, roof tiles and bits of masonry in the streets and no one could go anywhere. When I finally got back into the flat, having found a locksmith to let me in, the candles had burnt out and Polo was full of gravadlax.

The process of building myself up again, reconstructing a degree of self-esteem, was slow. John Downing took me to parties where people didn't want to talk to anyone unless they were going somewhere fast. It was the eighties and the idea of someone like me saying to them with a big smile, 'No, I don't do anything,' was not what they wanted to hear. At first I thought it was funny, that they were being silly, and then I grasped that I was the one who was wrong, not them. I wasn't working. I amounted to nothing. I felt empty, useless. I felt as though I had been in a dream all these years and had achieved nothing. I was looking at my life from their perspective and all I could see was someone who was sad, crushed and low. Every thought was negative.

What was more, I was so ignorant about the practical everyday things that everyone else took for granted. I didn't know I had to buy a tax disc for my car, or a television licence. I didn't know about water bills or rates, and I'd never paid an electricity or telephone bill.

Eric was giving me a limited amount of money to live on, but I knew that once the divorce was finalised it would stop and I would need a job. My education hadn't been the best, and I knew I was probably unemployable but I had to try.

I rang David Mlinaric, the interior designer, to see if I could be his assistant but he already had one. I rang Charles Settrington, now the Earl of March, who was a brilliant still-life photographer and asked if I could work as his assistant. He laughed and said, 'But you're Pattie!' No one would help me, or believe I needed help.

Then I met a friend of Jenny who had done a nutrition course at St Bartholomew's Hospital. It sounded interesting and, loving food and cooking as I did, I decided to enrol. I went to all-day lectures once a month for a year. It was based on the idea of healing people through diet and minerals, the premise being that if you eat the right food your body and mind will be well. I had immense difficulty keeping up with the note-taking. It had been a long time since I was at school and my brain wasn't in that mode any more so my notebook was full of half-finished sentences. But I did a lot of homework, studying and reading round the subject. I ate copious amounts of brown rice, no bread, no dairy products, and my friends laughed at me. But apart from making me bossy about what everyone ate I knew that in order to properly diagnose and treat people, I would need medical training, so after a year that was the end of my career in nutrition.

Roger Forrester swears to me that I was not hard done-by in my divorce from Eric, but I feel sure he ran rings round my lawyer. Eric came to see me and looked so fragile I felt sorry for him – but he was always a good actor. I agreed, maybe foolishly, to settle out of court, so all I got was a modest flat and a similarly modest lump sum to invest and live on. Talk of 'millions' that I had reportedly been given were unfortunately wrong. In theory I was entitled to 50 per cent of his earnings during the time we were together and those, it seemed to me, were conveniently low; the biggest income he ever had was from *Unplugged*, the album he released just after we separated. According to Roger, who is only too happy to point it out now, my mistake was that I didn't insist on sharing in future royalties on the songs Eric wrote while we were together. If I had, the last eighteen years might have been very different. I am always overdrawn at the bank.

I found a two-bedroom flat overlooking the river at Thames Reach in Hammersmith. It was built by Richard Rogers, whose architectural practice and, more importantly, his wife's restaurant, the River Café, was next door. As I was trudging round potential flats I discovered how strongly I had been influenced by my Kenyan childhood: I needed a vista – I couldn't bear to look out on to other flats or roads. Although the flat was small, the views were spectacular towards the old Harrods Depository, a lovely Victorian building, rather Turkish in a way, a wildfowl sanctuary and a long stretch of the Thames. At night the sun would set behind the dome of the Depository, throwing the most beautiful light.

Every year I used to give a lunch party on the Saturday of the Oxford and Cambridge Boat Race. Belinda would do a huge flower arrangement and I would make an enormous risotto and lots of different salads, and friends would come and we'd sit on the balcony and be so busy talking, drinking and smoking that often the boats would pass and we'd miss them. I had lovely parties at Christmas and dinner parties too. The only problem was that the people I'd bought the place from had put down lovely Provençal tiles on the floor and I had metal chairs – excruciating for those in the flat below – so guests moved them on pain of death. I tried to make friends with the occupants beneath me, a German couple, but unsurprisingly they soon moved out.

The divorce, on the grounds of infidelity and unreasonable behaviour, was finalised in 1989. It seemed to have dragged on for a ridiculously long time, which again I attributed to Roger. When I discovered that he and Eric had sworn affidavits, I realised that although he had been my ally when I was trying to get Eric off the booze, he had switched sides and I had been divorcing them both.

The day the decree absolute came through, Carolyn Waters, Nicole Winwood and a few other friends insisted on taking me out to celebrate. We went for dinner at a French restaurant off Soho Square. There was champagne, excitement and toasts to 'Being Free!', and I was smiling, laughing and keeping up the banter, but I felt as though I was wearing a mask. Inside I was so sad. I didn't feel there was anything to celebrate. All I felt was a sense of over-whelming loss. Interestingly, I now realise that when George and I were breaking up he founded the record label called Dark Horse (which he said described him), and after I left Eric, Eric wrote a song called 'Behind The Mask'. Both seemed to say the same thing.

The antidote was to keep busy and try to find a way to earn a living. Since photography was the one thing I knew and had done for years, albeit as an amateur, I decided that that was the way to go. With Simon Kirke, a musician (who had drummed with Free and Bad Company and toured with Ringo's All Star Band), I signed up for a three-month course in photography and printing. It was run by a husband-and-wife team – he was Latvian, she French – and two or three times a week we went to their house just outside Wandsworth. On some days they had models for us to photograph in the studio, and on others we did location work. We printed in a darkroom where they had about six enlargers. At the end of three months I had the confidence to start taking photos professionally.

To begin with I turned my sitting room into a studio and practised on nieces and nephews, other family, friends and their children. I took shots for anyone who needed photographs. Then someone started a modelling agency for older models and asked if I would join them. I didn't want to model again but I said I'd take the photos and that was what I did. However, the agency was ahead of its time and that little burst of activity came to nothing, but it was good practice.

In the midst of all of this a girlfriend said that a friend of hers was having a designer clothes sale at her house near Guildford and I must go. The friend turned out to be a photographer by the name of Lesley Deaves (now Aggar) and she and I became friends. It was fun to have someone to compare notes with, and since she was living in a large house in Shamley Green with a darkroom and I had no space in my flat to do any printing, I installed my enlarger in her darkroom and we had a wonderful time processing our film together and criticising one another's work, which was very helpful. She was in the process of breaking up with her husband so we had other things in common and plenty of spare time on our hands.

We joined the Royal Photographic Society, went to lectures, took exams and had to present our work before a panel of judges in a little theatre in Bath, which was a bit of an ordeal but we came away feeling very proud of ourselves with LRPS after our names. We went on some lovely photographic trips led by people with even more letters after their names. Once we went to Spain to learn darkroom techniques. It was a bit odd, I suppose, to go to sunny Spain to shut yourself up in a darkroom but we visited an amazing place in the hills behind Málaga with the most extraordinary rock formation. We photographed a Jurassic Park – a square mile of giant rocks with a few little rock plants here and there but otherwise nothing.

The best trip was one we saw advertised in the RPS magazine to Venezuela. We flew across Angel Falls, the highest free-falling waterfall in the world, and in the Canaima National Park we walked behind a waterfall that must have been about a quarter of a mile wide. We wrapped our cameras in polythene bags and edged our way slowly along a slippery wet ledge with nothing to hold on to, shouting to each other above the thunderous roar of the water, mesmerised by the swirling white mist. One slip and we would have been dead. Our tour leader was called Ed Paine. He had worked for the Vestey family and loved South America with a passion. We also had a teacher, the top man from Jessops, the chain of photographic shops. With Ed in charge we never knew what to expect, just that we would be laughing.

One day he took us hang-gliding in Merida, a charming

university town sandwiched between two mountain ranges and two rivers. We drove to the top of a mountain, walked to the edge of the cliff and looked down at the riverbed miles below. I thought, There's no way I'm going to do this, it's much too scary. Then I thought about my life: It's been really interesting, really nice, I've got lovely friends, we're all going to die at some point and, quite frankly, I'd rather die jumping over this cliff in Merida than in Bond Street or at home. This is far more glamorous, so I'll do it!

By this time one or two people in our party had had a go and were raving about it. You didn't do it alone: there were young kids, who turned out to be medical students, all rather gorgeous, who jumped with you in a double harness and pulled the strings. So I said, 'Yes,' strapped myself into my harness, clutched my camera tightly, ran towards the edge, closed my eyes and jumped. When I opened my eyes I was floating. The day before we had been to a condor conservation area and seen the young birds learning to fly. They were huge and would try to lift off, fail, run along the ground, flap their wings some more – and finally they soared into the air. I felt like a condor.

We came down on a jutting piece of land, and I did as I was told and ran as we landed, then more frantic running and we took off again. I had wanted to go back to where the group was but my co-pilot said, no, there weren't enough thermals to lift us, so we floated down and down, and then more running as we touched the ground.

At that moment I saw why we'd been so short of thermals: six fabulous American fifties cars were parked with their roofs down and several gorgeous girls – lots of red lipstick, dark hair, radios cranked up – were leaning against them, waiting for the boys. Two or three others came down and landed in the same place. Then the boys, the girls and the music disappeared into the night, leaving us stranded, not speaking a word of Spanish and not knowing the name of the place where we were staying. We sat by a tree in the pitch dark, and eventually Ed Paine rescued us.

After that, we stayed in a place miles from anywhere, where we were given soup for breakfast, lunch and supper. Bit odd, but I love it when things are different from what you're expecting. After two weeks of hard work, Lesley and I, with a couple of other girls, decided to take a week off and went up to the north coast of Venezuela opposite Margarita Island and the Los Roques Archipelago. We stayed in a private guesthouse – with a million mosquitoes – and after breakfast our host would pack a delicious lunch for us in a basket, and a boatman would take us to a different desert island with the softest, whitest sand. There, he would put down the picnic basket, string up a hammock for each of us and leave us for the morning. We would play in the sea, snorkel, wander through the mangrove swamps and waterways, and in the afternoon he would pick us up and take us round the other islands to see the birds. I saw my first scarlet ibis: they roost at the tops of trees, and what I'd taken for hibiscus blooms turned out to be hundreds of sleeping scarlet ibis.

Encouraged by my teacher, I began to approach newspapers and magazines with ideas for spreads. *OK!* magazine commissioned a collection of photographs of Richard O'Brien, who had written *The Rocky Horror Show* and was appearing in a television programme. He was a friend so I did the shoot in his house, then a writer interviewed him. I did a Christmas feature for the *Sunday Express* and borrowed beautiful china and table settings from Thomas Goode, and got Lyn Hall of La Petite Cuisine to make the food and write the recipes. Unfortunately many of the publications I contacted wanted to turn me into the feature and would send along a photographer to take photos of me taking photos. Or they would want me to model for them, which wasn't what I wanted at all. It became easier to do travel photography, which gave me a wonderful excuse to go to exotic places. I have never been brave enough to travel on my own (or go to the cinema by myself) but I am pretty fearless when it comes to destinations. I love experiencing new things – that's what life is all about – and I'll try everything that's on offer.

I saw a lot of Rod and Francesca, and often she and I had lunch together. Fran and Rod had been together for ten years and were going to get married in the South of France but their plans went awry. They had so many arguments about where they would hold the ceremony that eventually their relationship petered out. Curiously, Rod had bought her an engagement ring in Sri Lanka on the holiday when they'd met me, and had intended to give it to her as a surprise at Christmas. He had wrapped it up and put it under the tree in their flat. On Christmas Eve, they were burgled and all the presents, including the ring, were stolen.

After they broke up Rod had a series of disastrous affairs, and would chat through each one with me. When Phil Collins invited me to the première of *Buster*, his first big movie, I didn't want to go on my own so I invited Rod. I enjoyed his company – he was entertaining and comfortable to be with – and he was very good-looking. I thought he would be a perfect walker, and he was. He came with me to many other parties, and afterwards I would go back to my flat. Occasionally he came too, and I'd go to bed and he'd be asleep on the sofa in the morning. Then one night, after about a year of this, when we got back to my flat I said, 'Come on, come to bed.' Almost the next day he started to move his clothes in; first his jeans, then the jackets and cowboy boots. I should have said something – I wasn't expecting him to move in at quite the speed he did – but I didn't because it was nice to have him around. And it was healing. With Rod in my life I felt better about myself. He's younger than I am, and when he was growing up, Julie Christie and I had been his idols. He was so loving, supportive and encouraging. I felt as though I was slowly crawling out of a dark hole where I had been for a very long time, and although it took time for my eyes to adjust to the light it was wonderful to feel the warming rays of the sun on my back.

Rod was quite different from either George or Eric. His

background and education were much closer to mine. His father was a lawyer, he had been born in Wimbledon and had gone to King's College, Wimbledon, then to art school in Kingston, where he had studied graphics – the same course Eric had taken some years before. Because of that I thought he and Eric might have something in common but they couldn't stand each other. Then Rod had fallen into modelling in much the same way as I had. He had been going out with a photographer's assistant who had suggested he should see an agent. Modelling had taken him all over the world – he became the Brutus boy and the Wrangler boy – and he had made a lot of money. Then he had bought and sold property.

What I loved most about him was his innate sense of fun. He wasn't obsessive about chanting, fishing or anything else – in fact, he didn't seem to take anything very seriously. He loved life, parties and people as much as I did. Socially he engaged with all sorts of people and was charming to everyone. He made me happy, and he encouraged me to keep up with friends and family – unlike Eric. Rod was good for me: he helped me rediscover my self-esteem.

But curiously, for about three or four years after he and I started seeing each other, I dreamt about going back to Eric. The main problem was always how I would tell Rod. It was bizarre to have the same dream in such detail like that over so many years – I would have loved to know what it meant, but I wasn't seeing Karen any more. She had helped me over the worst and I was on an even keel now that Rod and I were together.

For the first couple of months that we were together we kept it quiet, and then we went to Kenya for Christmas, ostensibly as just good friends. I had been back just once since my childhood, with Jenny in the early seventies. We had stayed in the Norfolk Hotel in Nairobi where we had met up with Ronnie Wood and gone down to Mombasa, where I had swum in the sea for the first time – my grandmother had taken me there on holiday. The sand was so soft it made the same crunchy noise that virgin snow makes when you walk in it, a kind of silky squeak. On that first trip, the plan had been to find the places where we'd lived as children, but we had such a wonderful time on the beach and driving through game reserves that we never did.

On this trip Rod and I stayed with John Hurt's first wife Donna, who has a lovely ranch near Nanyuki that she and John built in the foothills of Mount Kenya. John had gone to Kenya to make the movie *White Mischief*. He had fallen in love with the country and bought a piece of land. It has the most stunning views of the mountain, which is almost always snow-capped. Donna is a bit of a wild girl and there's nothing quite like going on safari with her: she always seems to know exactly where the animals are and has no fear. I was driving with her once when she said, quietly but firmly, 'Don't get out just yet. Look to your left.' Above me, camouflaged by leaves, a leopard was snoozing on a branch. If he'd felt peckish, it would have been the end of me.

One day we went to Ol Jogi estate to visit a friend of Donna's who trained animals for their owners. Everyone was sitting on the veranda drinking beer and I was standing in the garden by the steps that led up to the house when the swing door flew open and out came a cheetah, which padded down the steps on her way to the garden. Someone said I could touch her but must on no account run. I stroked her, and her purr was a hundred times louder than Polo's.

Francesca was fine about Rod and me being together, and she and I continue to be the best of friends. The only difference was that before when we'd had lunch together she had moaned about Rod's shortcomings; now I did the moaning. One year she and I went off to South Africa for a week. We wanted to see Robben Island, off Cape Town, where Nelson Mandela had been incarcerated for so many years. He's one of my heroes. At home I have a copy of his inaugural speech as the first black president of South Africa. We were taken round the prison by an ex-con, who had been locked up with him and vividly described their life there. In the dining room there was an old board with three columns: blacks, coloureds, whites. Each column specified the amount of rice a category of prisoner would have each day. The whites got most, and the blacks least. The coloureds, I discovered, included anyone with Indian or mixed blood. It was a bleak island, with strong, bad vibrations and an odour I can only describe as being one of suffering. I found it depressing. Just twelve kilometres across the water, which was a dense, dark emerald green, Cape Town twinkled in the sunshine, guarded by Table Mountain, its flat top swathed in cloud.

One day we took a tourist bus to a black township where the poverty was staggering but I took some great photographs. Our guide told us we were invited for a beer in one of the houses. We followed him into a dark room where, in the far right-hand corner, a woman was stirring a huge pot of something that was bubbling and foaming. Men sat round the edges in a neat line. We were told to sit too. Then she poured some of the noxious-looking liquid into a metal bucket about ten inches in diameter. It was passed from man to man and each took a sip. I thought Fran and I were going to be ill but we couldn't refuse because we were guests. I have seldom put anything more disgusting into my mouth. We said thank you and fled before the bucket came round again. From there, we went into a one-bedroom hut in which four people lived; they had practically nothing, but what they did have was polished, loved and looked after, and they showed us round with pride.

Then we saw the other extreme of Africa. We had read about a wonderful-sounding hotel some way out of Cape Town and booked ourselves in for a night. We drove for three hours and the suburbs gave way to scrub and the Tarmac to gravel, dust and wilderness. Suddenly, just as we were thinking we must have gone in the wrong direction, we came to some gates, drove through them and found ourselves in another world: perfectly tarmacked drive, lush flowers, immaculate lawns, and a host of smartly dressed boys in khaki uniforms – shorts, jackets and hats – who leapt forward to greet us. They told us to leave our bags and jump into the Land Rover they had waiting. They were going on safari and had thought we'd like to join them.

In we climbed, and drove around looking for game. We saw Cape buffalo, zebra, bush pigs, guinea fowl and several different types of antelope, then looked at some ancient cave paintings. After about an hour the Land Rover came to a halt, we got out and the driver produced a perfectly stocked cocktail cabinet. There we were, in the middle of the African bush, binoculars in one hand, vodka and tonic in the other, while the setting sun turned the skyline crimson. It felt surreal, colonial, almost as if we were in a movie.

Eric and I had seen each other a few times since the divorce. He had stopped the emotional pressure, although he still wrote the odd letter. Once when he had tried to get in touch and failed, he said that hope was the only thing that kept him going 'but sometimes it's enough just to know that you are somewhere in the world, smiling'. And in a letter from New York, where he was working on an album with my 'other ex-hubby', as he called George, he said he had written another song about me. 'I think it will be the best one on the album,' he said. 'It's called "Old Love", don't be offended, it's not about you being old, it's about love getting old, and it's great, well, you'll see when you hear it.'

I felt flattered, but every week the newspapers published photographs of him with some beautiful young girl on his arm and I knew that even if I'd wanted him back it was probably too late.

Sometimes he would come and collect me from the flat and take me out for lunch. I was amazed at the difference in him. He was sober and he would say, 'I'll pick you up at twelve thirty,' and be there on the dot. In the old days, time had been of no consequence. Now, everything about him was precise and organised. He was a different person from the one I had lived with, and I felt great love for him but no desire. I think he felt the same about me. He enjoyed having lunch with me and he still loved me, but he wasn't trying to pursue me. On the way back once I said, jokingly, how sad I was to be living in my little two-bedroom flat in Hammersmith, and he said, 'It's your fault for divorcing me at the wrong time.'

Once I went to Hurtwood Edge. Eric had Conor staying and rang me to say he wanted me to meet his son. He was the most adorable little boy, and Eric was besotted, but it was difficult for me to see them playing so happily together in the house that, but for Conor, I might still have been calling my home. Eric didn't have him to stay as much as he would have liked. Once he wrote to me saying that Conor appeared to be suffering from traumatic asthma and it was frightening when he had an attack. Apparently it was triggered by emotional stress or even a change of environment and Eric said that he would have to leave him in Italy for a while, maybe visit him there where he felt secure. 'It's so sad,' he said, 'but I must go by what is best for him.'

Two years later, in March 1991, I was about to go out to a dinner party at Mike and Angie Rutherford's when Alan Rogan phoned with devastating news. There had been a terrible accident and Conor was dead. He didn't have the details, but it transpired later that the little boy had been running along the floor in his mother's fifty-third-floor apartment in New York and fallen to his death through a window that a cleaner had left open. The idea that an architect could design something like that defies belief.

Eric was in New York at the time, as were Roger Forrester and Alan Rogan and the rest of the crew. They were in a hotel a few blocks away when it had happened. Eric had spent the previous evening with Conor at the circus and had been planning to take him and Lori to lunch that day, followed by a trip to the zoo. Instead he had a call from Lori, in hysterics, telling him his son was dead. He ran the ten blocks to find paramedics, ambulances and police cars. Roger identified the body and asked the morgue to change the lightbulbs so the room was less brightly lit before he let Eric see the little boy. I couldn't begin to imagine the pain Eric would be going through. This was the worst thing that could possibly have happened to him.

I had no idea how to get in touch with Eric so I wrote to him at the house. When he came home he rang me. He was very fragile – not tearful, just so numb he could hardly speak. He asked me if I would come to the funeral in Ripley. Little Conor was to be buried alongside Rose, Eric's grandmother, in the churchyard of St Mary Magdalene. Roger had organised everything and done his best to keep the press at bay, but the road was jammed with photographers. We met at Eric's mother Pat's house, next door to the church. That day Eric reminded me of the figure who had stood on my mother's doorstep when I'd left him in 1984: haunted. I was terrified he would start drinking again. Lori was there and I spoke to her but she didn't want to talk; she was completely grief-stricken and just wanted to be close to Eric. I think she wondered why I was there – forgetting perhaps that I had been married to Eric when she had this baby.

Lori and Eric sat at the front of the church. About a hundred people were there, including George – all the Ripleyites, all our friends. I sat between Nick and Adie Cook and was engulfed by sadness. Any child's funeral is horrendous and Eric had been so happy to be a father. He had never known his own father, and fatherhood was so important to him. He was cool and contained, and didn't give in to what must have been a strong temptation to douse the pain with alcohol. As ever, he turned to music to express his feelings and wrote beautiful songs about Conor. 'Tears In Heaven' chokes me every time I hear it.

Soon after Conor's funeral, the phone rang in the flat and it was Eric. He wanted to come over and see me in half an hour. 'I just wanted to warn you,' he said. 'The press are on to me. They know about my daughter.'

'Daughter?' I said. 'What daughter? Christ, Eric, how many more children do you have?'

It was another twist of the knife and I didn't know whether to laugh or cry.

The next morning the newspapers were full of the story in all its salacious detail. Luckily Rod was there to pick up my pieces. The daughter, Ruth, was the result of an affair Eric had had when he was recording *Behind The Sun*, in Montserrat in 1984, and she had been born the following January. Her mother, Yvonne Kelly, lived on the island with her husband. She had worked as the studio manager. What cut deepest was that Eric had known about the child all along. While he had been declaring undying love to me and pleading with me to go back to him, he had been paying Yvonne maintenance for the last six years.

CHAPTER FIFTEEN

A New Life

When I was first with Eric he persuaded me to try to find my father. He was so obsessed by his own missing father that he felt it was important, and so I asked Mummy to get in touch with him for me and, my heart in my mouth, took the train to Exeter where he was living with his second wife, Angela. What would we talk about? I worried. I didn't know what he liked or whether he would be interested in me. Then I remembered he had worked at the Jockey Club so I thought I could tell him that Eric had bought me a beautiful racehorse, but I was so nervous I couldn't think of any of the race meetings where Bushbranch had run.

He met me at the station. I hadn't seen him since I was nine but I recognised his cornflower blue eyes. At first he seemed pleased to see me, but behind his smile he was awkward. He said we couldn't walk in the main streets of Exeter in case one of his wife's friends saw us. I was aware that she didn't want anything to do with his first family, but not that no one in his new life knew of our existence. We had a cup of tea in some horrid back-street café and that was it. I caught the train home. I had imagined my father as a sort of David Niven figure and hoped he would want to know all about what had happened in the last twenty-odd years, perhaps be a bit proud of me and tell me he'd missed me. But he asked me nothing and volunteered nothing. I got back on the train with an aching sense of loss.

Much later I discovered that Colin had also been to see Jock. When he was seventeen he had phoned the house and Angela had answered. Colin had asked if he might speak to his father. 'He's not here,' said Angela, 'and he doesn't want to talk to you.'

'I'm sorry,' retorted Colin, 'but I want to talk to him.'

Eventually she gave him the number where Jock was working in Exeter, and Colin arranged to see him. They met in the street and my father, for some reason, had brought a friend who hovered on the other side of the road as if for protection. Goodness knows what he thought Colin, aged seventeen, was going to do to him. Having been beaten by his step-father, Colin had a fanciful vision of his real father, and longed to hear him say, 'You're my son,' and all the other things that boys without daddies imagine.

Colin shook Jock's hand and said, 'I just wanted to say hello,' and Jock said, 'Have five shillings,' then tried to press money into his hand.

Colin was mortified. He refused the money, said again that he had only wanted to make contact, shook hands again and fled.

Jenny was next to seek him out, and her meeting was every bit as awkward as mine, but she did say as they parted that it would be lovely for Colin, her and me to see him together. One day when I was living in the flat on the river she drove to Devon and brought him to London. We went to the Waldorf Hotel for tea. By this time he and Angela had parted so he felt less constrained about meeting us. What we didn't know was that he had two daughters with her, our half-sisters. It was only when Jenny published her book,

Musicians In Tune, about the nature of creativity for her psychology thesis, that one got in touch. She came to visit me in Hammersmith, and the moment I saw her blue eyes, I didn't doubt she was my half-sister. She said she and her sister had been brought up ignorant of their father's previous family until one day when her mother was driving her to school. They had been listening to the radio when an item on the news reported that Eric Clapton and Pattie Boyd had married. Her mother had lost control of the car and ended up on the pavement, sparking my half-sister's suspicion.

I was happy in my flat on the river, but after a while I yearned for the countryside. I rang Eric and asked if I could come to see him. He still had Hurtwood Edge but he had also bought a beautiful house in Chelsea, and that was where I went. I was nervous about going to him cap in hand, but over tea I asked if he would consider buying me a cottage in the country. He said no. It would cost a million pounds and another million to furnish. I said, 'Nonsense' – and thought, That's what he spent on his house in London! All I wanted was a humble weekend cottage, I said it wouldn't cost anything like that, so he agreed to talk to Roger.

A few days later, Roger rang to tell me I could buy something up to the value of £300,000, so I started looking. When Tony Smith, who manages Genesis, discovered what I was up to, he suggested I rent a cottage on his beautiful estate at Chiddingfold. It was in a glorious setting, overlooking a lake with huge rhododendron bushes to either side. His wife hated being on her own in the country, he said, so I'd be doing him a favour in keeping her company. I was there for a year and he must have grasped that I didn't have much money because he seldom cashed my rent cheques.

After about a year I found a little place in West Sussex. The estate agent sent me the details and urged me to look at it. I said no, I didn't want a house on a road, which this one was, but she insisted it was only a lane and I really should see it, so I did. She was right: the position and the views were perfect, and although the outside didn't strike me as particularly special, the cottage had a nice feel. Rod was very enthusiastic – we could make it fabulous, he said, and he's good at that sort of thing. But it was £345,000, so I had to persuade Roger to let me have it even though it was over budget. Eventually he agreed. The house was bought in Eric's name for me to live in rent free. I moved in on 1 April 1995 and the only furniture I had was a pretty little rattan sofa, painted yellow, which I took out of the flat, and a rug. Thanks to Dick Kries and his advice all those years ago, lack of furniture didn't stop me inviting people for lunch. We had picnics on the lawn, and inside, we took it in turns to sit on the sofa.

Eventually I realised that the only way I could furnish the cottage without eating into my investments, which I needed for the income, was to sell my flat on the river. It was Rod's idea: he said I should move into his flat in Kensington, then use some of the money I made from selling my flat in decorating and furnishing the cottage, then redesigning the garden. I could put the rest of the money into a couple of flats Rod would buy to do up. So, I put my flat on the market and sold it quite well. I also sold a 1960 Gibson Les Paul standard guitar that I had bought as an investment from Alan Rogan. Within three years it was worth 50 per cent more than I had paid for it. I should have hung on – according to Alan, it's now worth ten times the original sum.

I'd had two amazing gardens – at Friar Park and Hurtwood Edge – and now I was desperate to do interesting things at the cottage, but before I set to work I decided I should learn a bit about how to do it. My friend Jill Wetton, another keen gardener, and I enrolled on an eighteen-month horticultural course at Brinsbury Agricultural College in Billingshurst. We thought we would learn about planting in a rather ladylike fashion, but it was infinitely more comprehensive. It was all about why and where you grow things, the importance of soil type and that sort of thing. On day one we had to dig beds in the freezing cold, which came as quite a shock but we loved it.

Because we were both mad about cooking we spurned the canteen and took it in turns to make lunch. We would vie with each other to cook ever more wonderful soups, and in summer we had lovely salads on the lawn. Two years later Jill and John divorced. She had also been unable to have children and, strangely, he had a child by another woman he'd been seeing.

Rod and I spent weekdays in London and weekends at the cottage. He designed the interior and came up with some very clever plans, and I did the garden, which was two or three acres with a swimming-pool and a triangular piece of lawn at the front. I turned that into a rectangle, then built a barn beside the pool, where I set up a darkroom, and made a wall to enclose the pool area. I dug a large pond with an island and planted yellow iris around the edge with black bamboo. Then I put in a pergola with a dining-table beneath it. One day my father came to lunch. Paula was with us too, Rod and maybe Jenny. Paula was supposedly dry, but throughout lunch she kept leaping to her feet and saying, 'Would you like some more?' then grabbing our plates while our knives and forks were in mid-air and whizzing back to the kitchen to replenish them. This happened so many times that I became suspicious, as did Rod. Eventually I followed her and heard the freezer door close. 'Paula, what's going on?' I challenged.

'Oh, I'm so happy to see Daddy! Can you believe it? Isn't it wonderful? Look at him out there,' she said. 'It just makes me want to cry.'

'Pull yourself together! We didn't see him for all of our childhood. How can you be so emotional now? This is ludicrous.'

And, of course, she was drunk. Every time she'd taken a plate into the kitchen she had had a slug out of the vodka bottle in the freezer.

Paula had been a real worry. Since our Bahamas trip I had tried several times to clean her up. Once, when she was married to David Philpot, her second husband, I had kidnapped her from her flat in South Kensington, with the help of Alfie O'Leary and Roger, and taken her to Brighton. They knew the problem only too well. She had been drinking heavily while she was living in Los Angeles with Andy, and every time Eric had been in town, she had phoned Roger to ask if she could borrow money. She'd asked me, too, and everyone I knew, and could never pay it back. Every time I saw her she'd say, 'You couldn't lend me a tenner, could you?' which, over the years, mounted up to an awful lot of money. Finally, I said, 'Paula, no more. The money I give you is going on drink and drugs and I'm not going to finance it any longer.' After that I gave her clothes, because she never had money to buy them, but I expect she sold what I gave her to service her habits.

I'm not sure what I thought I was going to do with her in Brighton, or even why we chose Brighton, but David was a heroin addict, too, and they were in such a mess that I just had to get her away from him. But he found out where we were and telephoned: 'Pattie, you can't do this. Unless you bring her back right now I'm going to tell the newspapers that you take drugs and you've kidnapped my wife.'

'I haven't kidnapped her, David. She's here for a little holiday.'

'I've got friends in that area. Paula is coming back to me. She's my wife.' He sounded so menacing I took her straight back. I didn't like him, but I suppose you can't really kidnap someone, however much you want to help them – and you can't help someone unless they're willing to be helped. And Paula wasn't.

At the time she only had her son William – this was before Emma and Cassie were born – and he came to stay with Eric and me at Hurtwood Edge almost every weekend. I remember sitting in the garden at the Windmill one day and asking him what he wanted to drink. 'I'd like a hair of the dog, please,' he said. He had his own room in the house with a big box of toys at the end of the bed. It was his second home and he adored Uncle Eric – they went fishing together and Eric helped him play the guitar. We loved him, and he could never understand why he had to go back to Paula on Sunday night. I considered fostering him – and I helped pay his school fees – but even as a little boy he was protective of his mother and I don't think he would truly have wanted to leave her.

And Paula wouldn't have wanted me to have him permanently. Like every child of an alcoholic, no matter what age, Will had become the parent. I remember Paula coming to stay with us once, when he was about seven, and I couldn't find her so I went upstairs. Her bedroom door was ajar. She had collapsed on the floor and Will was shaking her, trying desperately to wake her up, saying, 'Mummy, Mummy, please get up, please get up.' But when he saw me he quickly stood back from her and said, 'I think Mummy's fallen asleep.' If I had taken him away from Paula, he would have worried about her.

One of the greatest sadnesses about my divorce from Eric was that Will suffered. He had assumed, not unreasonably, that Uncle Eric would always be there for him and when Eric wouldn't return his calls or lend him money for another guitar or any of the things Will had taken for granted as a child, he was hurt. Through no fault of his own he had lost someone he loved.

We all tried to help Paula. Mummy took her to Scotland to try to clean her up, which worked for a while, but nothing lasted. She couldn't come to any family get-togethers because they triggered the desire to drink, as did giving birth. She cured post-natal depression with smack and when she managed to kick that she was back to alcohol.

When Emma was two Paula realised they would all die if they stayed in London – she was drinking alcohol and cough mixture – so they went to live in Cork, in Ireland, for a while where she went to AA meetings and was dry for months. Then she went to a fair with some Irish girls, had a beer and couldn't remember anything until she woke up in a psychiatric institution. That terrified her: she was lining up with all these mad women for her food, ranting and raving, and no one knew what to do with her. When she and David split up, she came back to England with three children and had nowhere to live so the council put her into bed and breakfast accommodation until they found her a house in Haslemere.

Then she met Graham, an ex-roadie, and the drinking continued. Emma had terrible rows with her mother and moved out when she was seventeen. She found a room in a pub where she worked at night, having attended college during the day. Cassie didn't speak until she was twelve – at least, not to me. I think she held too many secrets, not realising that I knew what was going on at home. Just before Cassie's seventeenth birthday, Paula went to live with Graham in a narrow boat on the Worcestershire canals, leaving Cassie alone. I took her some food and presents on her birthday so she could have a party, but I was a poor substitute for her mother.

About five years ago, as a last resort, we tried intervention – the polite way of saying we captured Paula and took her into treatment against her will. Jenny was working for a well-respected addiction clinic in Arizona, called Cottonwood, and managed to get Paula a place. The whole family was in on it but I was elected to tell her. I arrived at her house – she was still in Haslemere – and said, 'Paula, it's booked. You're going to Arizona.' She burst into tears. 'I'm staying the night with you and we're leaving tomorrow to go and talk to the others in London.'

She was terribly upset, but after a while she said, 'Thank you. I do need to go.'

I felt awful controlling her in this way but she was slowly killing herself and we couldn't bear to stand back and watch it happen without trying everything. Eric had given her a car when she had been sober – she had rung him and asked for one – but she'd fallen off the wagon and sold it to buy drink. He vowed that was the last time he helped. My mother then bought her a car and again she sold it and drank the proceeds.

Part of the treatment at Cottonwood involves the alcoholic in confronting family members about issues they feel may have contributed to their addiction; in return, the family confronts the alcoholic about their destructive behaviour. This is vital because often the alcoholic is so drunk they don't know what they've done. The clinic insisted that Mummy was there. During those sessions Paula talked about her childhood, claiming that she had suffered abuse at the hands of our step-father – my mother accused her of telling lies. She came away saying it was a dreadful place that had twisted Paula's mind and made her say the most horrible things. And when I asked her whether she had described what Paula did when she was drunk, she said she hadn't wanted to talk about it in front of other people. She was being loyal – and doing what she had done all her life. She failed to grasp that Paula couldn't be helped unless she was faced with the truth, but she couldn't do it.

Meanwhile I had quite a lot of work on. Ronnie Wood was commissioned by Andrew Lloyd-Webber to paint a triptych to hang at the Theatre Royal, Drury Lane. It was an epic piece of art. He wanted to capture a crowd of celebrities dining at the Ivy restaurant, which he saw as a seminal element of London life. He asked me to help. Andrew selected about sixty celebrities – including Lulu, Cilla Black, Joan Collins, A.A. Gill, Melvyn Bragg, Naomi Campbell, Salman Rushdie, Kate Moss, Jerry Hall, Mick Jagger and Tom Stoppard – and each one came to Ronnie's studio in Richmond for a sitting. He would sketch them while I took the photographs he wanted as a guide when it came to putting the paintings together. They were big canvases – each one five feet by six.

Ronnie's favourite wine at that time was Lynch-Bages and Andrew gave him several cases. I'd arrive at lunchtime, we'd open a bottle and whoever came that afternoon joined in. It was very jolly, but it ended when Mick said that unless Ronnie stopped drinking he couldn't tour with the Stones. The paintings were finally hung in 2004, with some of my photographs alongside them.

Living with Rod was like living in a cocktail party. With most people, socialising is the icing on the cake. With Rod, it was icing all the way. I had more than met my match. He liked to drink, which rang alarm bells, but his capacity didn't come anywhere near Eric's. It was social drinking – and Rod was social every day of the week, usually at lunchtime and in the evenings. He had a huge number of friends and between us we had more invitations than we could possibly accept but Rod wanted to go to everything. At first it was fun. I loved dressing up, going out, meeting people, drinking champagne and eating wonderful food, but when we had done that every night of the week in London, I began to feel I'd like a rest at weekends when we were at the cottage. Not Rod. He wanted big lunch and supper parties. I've never bought convenience food or anything ready-made and never will, so it meant shopping expeditions and menu planning. Much as I adore cooking and entertaining, by the time we went back to London I was worn out.

We also had some wonderful holidays and weekends with friends, including Lynne Franks, the PR guru, immortalised by Jennifer Saunders as Edina in the BBC's *Absolutely Fabulous*. I had met her through the ladies' committee of the Nordoff-Robbins music-therapy charity, which Jill Wetton had asked me to join. Lynne was another member and was often so busy at work that we had to go to her office for our meetings, and she was so funny; Jennifer Saunders had her to a T. She always had masses of food there and would bring in more for us.

Lynne Franks became my new best friend, and she invited Rod and me to stay with her at her house in Majorca for a bank-holiday weekend. Dick Polak and Edina Ronay were also invited and I had discussed with Dick the sort of car we should hire. I'd said, 'Let's not get the cheapest'. Unfortunately he did. We arrived quite late at night, had a few drinks and went to bed. The next morning Lynne suggested a long walk with a local friend to Michael Douglas's beautiful house. Off we went but it started to pour with rain so we ran back to the cars. Dick and I got into the rented car, which Rod drove, and Lynne, her friend Juliet and Edina climbed into Lynne's. They followed us. It wasn't far to the house so none of us had bothered with our seat-belts. We were driving down a steep hill with a cliff on one side and a sheer drop on the other and came round a corner quite fast, to meet a coach driving up the hill. This was the first rain for months so the roads were greasy. Rod braked, but there was nowhere to go and the minute I saw the coach I thought, If this isn't a dream it's going to hurt. I wasn't wrong. My leg was injured, my ribs were bruised and I had held on to the door handle so tightly when I realised what was about to happen that my wrist had snapped and a bone was protruding through the skin. Rod's ribs were broken on one side and had punctured a lung. Dick, who had been in the back, walked away without a scratch.

Dick was terrified that Lynne would come round the corner and go straight into the back of us, so he helped me out and sat me down on the side of the road. Then he tried to get Rod out too, but he was trapped, slumped over the wheel.

Then the others arrived – managing to stop in time. Lynne, who is a Buddhist, started to chant while Juliet phoned for help. After a very long time, an ambulance arrived. Rod and I were dragged into it and taken off to intensive care in a private clinic in Palma.

All I remember about the journey was Edina trying and failing to undo my Cartier watch – a fortieth birthday present from Eric – and a little love bracelet I was wearing. Eventually the doctor hacked them off with a knife as I shouted at him to stop. He didn't: I got both pieces back in bits.

After two days in the clinic, I asked if Rod could move into the spare bed in my room. A funny old man arrived in a wheelchair, and I wondered who on earth he was. When I realised it was Rod we both had hysterics, which, with our ribs, was torture.

Back in London I went into the Wellington and it took four operations and a bone graft from my hip to sort out my wrist.

Everyone was very kind and George and Olivia sent me a huge bunch of flowers.

Rod and I went back to Sri Lanka several times. I bought a little beach there, and I pay a man to look after it for me, but since all the coconut trees growing on it are owned by different individuals it's a bit complicated to build a house. We also went to Barbados, St Lucia, France, Spain, India and Bali.

Bali was interesting. We drove through the beautiful countryside where people lived the simplest lives, and then we'd come to a village with one television set that everyone was glued to.

We stayed with friends in Denpasar, the capital, had another car crash and I broke my other wrist. Again, Rod was driving, and I was in the back when he hit a motorbike that had appeared from nowhere. My wrist was painful but I pretended it wasn't broken because I had heard that the brother of a friend had died after an accident in Bali because medical equipment had been in short supply. I had it rebroken and set when I got back to England.

At the same time the doctor carried out a bone-density test and discovered I had osteoporosis. He put me on Fosamax, which was very strong and I wasn't allowed to eat, drink or walk for half an hour after each dose. Then, by coincidence, I heard a lecture by two American doctors and Leslie Kenton, the nutritionist, about what the drug companies are doing to women – with the pill, hormone medications and diuretics – and how we get into a vicious circle and end up with osteoporosis, needing yet more pills. 'Don't take this stuff' was the message.

Then I heard of a brilliant nutritionist on the Isle of Wight. She agreed to meet me at Gatwick and suggested I take Osteocare, which is an alternative calcium and multivitamin supplement, and do weight-bearing exercise. I went to *t'ai chi* classes and Pilates, which I love and still do twice a week, and after two years – my doctor couldn't believe it – there was no sign of osteoporosis.

Another year Rod and I went back to Kenya for a friend's fiftieth birthday party on Lamu, an island off the northern coast that had originally been an Arab trading post. Lots of friends came from England and more from Kenya. After four days of partying we went to stay at the Muthuga Club in Nairobi, then to Donna Hurt's.

Another time we went to stay with Ringo and Barbara, who were living in Monaco, and later to the house they had in Cap d'Antibes. We visited Ronnie Wood and Jo, his second wife, who took a house near Aix-en-Provence, and at Christmas one year we went to my brother in Salt Lake City. We drove there from Los Angeles via Las Vegas, and came back through Monument Valley, Sedona and the Grand Canyon to stay with Chris O'Dell in Arizona.

I spent my own fiftieth birthday skiing in Courchevel with friends including Christian and Christine Roberts. Rod and I had met them with Amanda Wakeley, the fashion designer, who invited us to spend a weekend on her fabulous yacht. It was then that Christian and I discovered we had been born on the same day of the same year at the same time. He was an actor and had inherited a lot of money and used it to fulfil his dream of living in Barbados. He and Christine had built the most beautiful house, then bought the next-door property, which had been a famous garage called the Lone Star, and turned it into a boutique hotel, bar and restaurant, still called the Lone Star. Rod and I went to stay with them several times and Christian and I celebrated many happy birthdays together. On our fiftieth we woke up everyone in the chalet at four a.m. – the time at which we were born – opened a bottle of champagne and stood on the balcony in the freezing cold in our dressing-gowns wishing each other a happy birthday.

Rod's fiftieth birthday came several years later. He is nine years younger than I am but I told him that once he had reached fifty he would no longer be a toyboy. He wasn't very pleased to hear this, but I sent him into the adult world in an excellent way. I gave him three parties: a cocktail party in the flat in Kensington for about a hundred and fifty people, mostly London friends, and two lunch parties in the country for local friends and family. We had a Raj tent and caterers, and I found some Indian musicians to sit on the lawn and play tablas. The cake was covered with icing-sugar wine bottles.

George and I didn't speak on the phone much, but we saw each other from time to time at parties. He had become almost an older brother to me, someone with whom I felt entirely comfortable and to whom I could say anything. Every now and again he would send a little present – a tree for the garden or an ornament – and he invited Rod and me to Dhani's eighteenth birthday dinner, saying we *had* to be there: we were family. I hadn't seen much of Dhani while he was growing up but he was uncannily like George when I'd first known him.

One Christmas, we were all together at a big lunch party given by Ringo and Barbara at their country house. Everyone was there, including George and Olivia, and Eric with a new girlfriend, Melia McEnery, a young, pretty American he'd met in Los Angeles. Eric was being unfriendly but I don't think he ever liked Rod – and Rod found him unapproachable and boring. We were at a table with Roger Taylor of Queen, and the Rutherfords.

At one point I went and sat next to George and said, 'God, George, Eric's being so weird, he can hardly say hello to me.' We had a good laugh, and when Eric and Melia were leaving, George said, 'Eric, 'bye, man. Aren't you going to say goodbye to Pattie?'

It was really awkward. It was as if in giving up drugs and alcohol, Eric had become a different person. Maybe he had always been shy and quiet, the alcohol a prop. He wasn't the vivacious man I'd known.

After they had gone George told me about a nightmare he was having with a business partner in whom he had lost faith. George thought he was failing to manage the finances. He was so stressed about it and so angry – it was all he could talk about. A few months later I heard he had cancer of the throat. I can't help thinking the two things were connected.

Then he was stabbed at his home by an intruder. I heard it on the news and immediately rang Harry, George's older brother, who lived three or four miles from Friar Park. George had been with Harry and his wife, Irene, at their house that evening, and had said how happy he was at Friar Park and how safe he felt there. When he got home and pressed the clicker to open the electric gates, some madman who was hiding in the bushes must have slipped in behind him.

George and Olivia had gone to bed and in the middle of the night George had heard glass breaking. He woke Olivia and told her he was going to investigate. She tried to stop him but he insisted. The man had smashed a window and come up the stairs with a knife in his hand. George met him in the minstrel's gallery and there was a fight. Then Olivia appeared, picked up a lamp and hit the man over the head. George had been stabbed in the chest. Eventually the police arrived and grabbed the intruder. He was a schizophrenic in his thirties with a thing about the Beatles. It was horribly reminiscent of what had happened to John Lennon.

I had heard about John's death from Eric. He and I had been arguing and had spent the night in separate rooms. The next morning – 8 December 1980 – he came to wake me with the news that John had been shot dead in New York. I was appalled. I left Eric in Ewhurst and went to London, to the Beatles' office, and hung out with everybody there. I had no idea how to get in touch with Yoko, or where she was, but the offices in Savile Row were the heart and soul of what had been the Beatles' kingdom. That day it was where I wanted to be.

George's wounds were not life-threatening. His lung was punctured but he was only in hospital for a few days. He wasn't noticeably changed, but I think the trauma had a much more lasting effect and weakened his body's ability to fight the cancer. Having had it in his throat he went on to develop it in his lungs. He died on 30 November 2001, a little less than two years after the attack.

I heard about his death from Alan Rogan who rang me early in the morning at Rod's flat. I burst into tears; I felt completely bereft. I couldn't bear the thought of a world without George. When I left him for Eric, he had said that if things didn't work out, ever, I could always come to him and he would look after me. It was such a selfless, loving, generous thing to say and it had always been tucked away at the back of my mind. Now that sense of security had gone. I was devastated. I'd known that his death was inevitable, but I'd kept hoping that, with all his money, they would find a cure for him. At the end I hadn't grasped how ill he was as I hadn't seen him for a few months. The last time had been at my cottage: he had phoned to say he was coming to Sussex to visit Ringo and Barbara and wanted to see me – I think he was curious to know where I was living. I was so glad we'd had that last meeting.

Danae Brook, a *Daily Mail* journalist, whom I had known slightly, on and off, for some years, was due to come to the flat at ten o'clock on the morning George died. She wanted a photograph I had of somebody she was writing about. I was walking about like a zombie when, suddenly, she was there and wanting to interview me. I didn't say anything to her but when her piece appeared it was all about how we had modelled together and been chums, and she had been with me soon after I received the news that George had died. I felt exploited.

His funeral was in Los Angeles. I didn't go, but I was invited to the memorial concert, which took place a year later in the Royal Albert Hall, organised by Eric. I couldn't go: I had booked a spiritual holiday in Peru. Instead, I watched it on video. On the day, I took myself away from the rest of the group and spent the day high in the mountains, thinking of George, the tears trickling down my face. I was happy to mourn him alone and in my own way.

You never know with grief how long it will last, but I think I'll miss him for the rest of my life. We shared so much and grew up spiritually together and there are so many things that no one else knows about that we did together; and for many years there were so many questions I wanted to ask him and so many things I needed to speak to him about. And then there were the dreams. I would dream he was alive and I would say to him, 'Oh George, it's so wonderful that you are alive after all, this is so fabulous; I knew they had all made a mistake.' Some dreams can be incredibly vivid and so very real and then I would wake up and within the first couple of seconds I would think he was alive, and then that wave of reality would wash over me as I became more conscious.

I'd gone to Peru with a collection of friends, including Pat Booth. She had been living in Miami since our modelling days. She'd married, had two children and become a massively successful writer with fifteen novels to her credit. Our spiritual holiday was led by a healer who lives near me. In preparation for an ayahuasca (jungle vine) experience, a traditional religious and magical ritual still practised in the jungle, we were told to eat no dairy products and drink no alcohol for a week before our departure.

We flew to Lima, then took another plane and a boat, and finally arrived at a jungle lodge. That evening, after dinner and a talk from the shaman, we were taken into a room with twelve mattresses on the floor, one for each of us in the group. Incense was burning on a table in the centre. First we were given a small cup of the jungle juice, then told to lie down. I shut my eyes and waited for the 'great medicine, the visionary vine' to take effect while the shaman and his aide chanted. Ayahuasca is an hallucinogen but not in the same way as the manufactured LSD. It had the most extraordinary effect on everyone. My visions were constantly moving geometrical patterns of great clarity and colour. I could hear the jungle breathing as the people at either side of me were being sick. It was all part of the cleansing detox process, which lasted for about six hours.

We went on to walk the Inca trail, then took a boat on Lake

Titicaca, the highest commercially navigable lake in the world, as high and as cold as Mont Blanc in Switzerland. We stopped at the Uros, a group of forty-three artificial islands made entirely of reeds. Amazingly a whole community lives on them.

Peru was fabulous, but of all the places I have travelled to, Bhutan was the most beautiful and spiritual. It is tragic that this little kingdom in the Himalayas, which borders India and Tibet, has fallen prey to the influences of the Western world: television had arrived three years before I did. The Bhutanese are Tibetan Buddhists, and foreign influences have always been tightly controlled to protect their culture, which had scarcely changed since the Middle Ages. We went trekking with Mike and Angie Rutherford, Penny Smith, the TV presenter, and her actor boyfriend Vince Leigh. We booked through a normal travel agent and then I ran into Lenny, an old friend from the sixties and the king of Bhutan's nephew. He was always terribly exotic, dressed in the finest Bhutanese leather riding boots, beautifully cut jodhpurs, and jackets with Nehru collars and brocade. He said, 'Don't bother with travel agents. My daughter will arrange everything for you in Bhutan and take you to special temples and places where tourists don't go.'

So we were taken around by Lenny's daughter, who introduced us to her husband and some princes and princesses. They had a dinner party for us at one of their houses, which was very casual and relaxed. They told us that the king was considering relinquishing the job and giving the kingdom back to the people: the country was self-sufficient, in good working order, and he felt the Royal Family had done as much as they could. At one point I noticed that Angie was very pale and Mike was guiding her to the loo. Someone said, 'She's had one of those betel nuts.'

They aren't actually nuts: they are the seed of the betel plant, wrapped with a piece of lime in a lime leaf. When you chew them, they turn your mouth, lips and teeth red. The man next to me, whose head was shaved and who was wearing Bhutanese clothes but spoke as though he was straight out of Yale University, told me that Bhutan betel nuts were special. I decided that if I was going to have a betel-nut experience this was the place to have it. I took one and started to chew, and after a while I asked, 'How long does one have to chew for?'

'Enjoy, enjoy.'

A little later I realised I couldn't move. I could just about speak but that was it, and I thought what an odd addiction it was – in the East millions of people chew betel and all that happens is that they can't move.

Our trekking guide, Karma, always carried an ice-blue umbrella and, since it wasn't raining, I couldn't work out why. He told me it was to protect him from the snow, wind and sun. Whenever I thought I'd lost him, I looked for the blue umbrella.

I had brought with me some homeopathic pills to help prevent altitude sickness, and fed them to everyone each morning. We carried plenty of water in our rucksacks as we had been told it was essential to keep drinking – we should sip three pints a day or the altitude might affect our brains. As a start we did a day's trek to acclimatise, and then it was the real thing with Sherpas and ponies packed with sleeping-bags, tents, saucepans and everything you can imagine. The lead pony had a bell round his neck, which we could hear tinkling as we climbed higher. When we stopped for lunch, we would find it laid out by the Sherpas, who had gone ahead. We would sit by a stream in the mountains, eating sandwiches and hard-boiled eggs, then off we'd go again. About three hours later, we'd arrive in a clearing and there would be our tents, all set up for the night. There was a dining tent, sleeping tents and a tent for the loo, which was a hole dug in the ground. We'd have supper when the sun went down, then play dice and card games. It was hot during the day, but the temperature dropped steeply at night, and if it snowed, was cold in daylight too. We wore layers of clothing, and I had trousers that I could unzip above the knee to turn into shorts.

I took lots of photographs of particularly beautiful scenes or prayer flags. They are made of fabric with prayers written on them in Sanskrit. Buddhists stick them into the ground for the wind to carry their prayers across the world. There were so many in the mountains, some in such precipitous places that I wondered how someone had managed to put them there.

One day we stopped for lunch in a little woodland clearing and suddenly the temperature dropped by about ten degrees. It was unbelievably cold and I had to find the bottom bits of my trousers and zip them on to the shorts. My hands were so cold that I couldn't make the zip work, then realised I was trying to attach the wrong leg so swapped them round. Meanwhile Angie was freezing so she, Mike and Penny went on with our guide to find where the Sherpas would be setting up camp for the night, leaving Rod, Vince and me with our other Sherpa.

I was still struggling with the trouser legs, and by the time I had them sorted out it was snowing heavily and a thick fog had come down. We set off behind the Sherpa, walking, walking, walking. I kept wondering why we hadn't met the others – and then the Sherpa turned round. He was lost.

It was so cold: I only had a tiny jumper on and no hat. Rod had a whistle and started to blow it and Vince shouted, but there were waterfalls everywhere so no one would hear them. Oh, my God, I thought, we're lost and we're going to die. Then I luckily remembered that if a bear suddenly appears you have to run in a straight line because they can only run in zig-zags.

The Sherpa kept saying that Timpu, which is the capital of Bhutan, was about four hours' walk. It was now two o'clock and the sun would go down in about three hours. Not a hope. Then he ran off.

Rod was furious. 'How dare he leave us alone?' Vince gave me a hug; then began to dance as if he was in a musical. So, we had Vince dancing around in the high Himalayas, a Sherpa running around in the fog, Rod angry and me thinking I was about to meet a bear.

Then the Sherpa came back, and after about twenty minutes the blue umbrella appeared and I thought, We're saved. How marvellous. Karma took off his jacket and gave it to me, then held the blue umbrella over me. It was still snowing but we walked higher and higher. Just as I was on the verge of freaking out, we came to a clearing where there was a beautiful monastery and young monks. There were the tents, and the others were waiting for us beside a roaring fire.

Just over a month after George had died, Eric married Melia at the church in Ripley. Their friends had thought they were going to the baby's christening but when that had taken place they found themselves witnessing a marriage ceremony. I was pleased for Eric, but became very aware of my vulnerability with the cottage, which he owned. If anything happened to him, his new wife would inherit his estate, and my home, on which I had already spent a great deal of money, would be in her hands.

It coincided with my desire to build an extension. I had never liked the flat roof over the kitchen because of the potential for leaks, and Rod had a brilliant plan to build an extra bedroom and bathroom above it, which would give me three bedrooms and two bathrooms instead of two and one. He had drawn up the plans so I wrote to Eric enclosing them with my bank details, and asked whether he might see his way to lending me £40,000, which I would pay back at so much a year. He replied, saying he hadn't realised he was my landlord and wouldn't lend me any money, but he would put the cottage in my name. After that I slept a lot more easily, knowing the roof over my head belonged to me. Over time I scraped together the money for the alterations, which made a big difference.

However, my relationship with Rod had run its course. He was getting angry with me over the slightest thing and was drinking far too much. I had been telling him for years that he should cut down

– but in the past he had never been an angry drunk. Now he was. I once said to him, 'I hate the way you get drunk. I hate to see you drunk. I have lived with a drunk. I have lived with an alcoholic. You're just like Eric.' Rod just smiled. He thought I was complimenting him.

If I phoned him in the afternoon I could tell from his first word whether he'd had lunch – there were certain friends with whom he would share four bottles of wine, two each. I would ask the friends not to drink so much with him, and they would laugh. It was the Eric syndrome all over again, and I couldn't bear it. I thought maybe Rod had some problem I didn't know about, something that was making him unhappy and, if so, it was silly not to acknowledge it and do something about it. Also, I was sure the drinking was affecting his work.

I wondered whether I was holding him back in some way. I had so many invitations – some from friends inviting us to dinner parties but also to numerous events to which Rod always wanted to go and I didn't.

I had grown up at last. That was not the quality of life I wanted any more. It was a vacuous existence, and I wanted more. One minute Rod seemed to understand what I was saying, the next he didn't. We argued for weeks until finally I said, 'That's it. I don't want you to come to the cottage any more. We're no longer going out together.' I was upset – and his friends told me that he was too – but I felt good because I had *done* something. I had made a decision and carried it out. I had been unhappy for the last two years and I'm sure he must have been feeling the same, or he wouldn't have become such a grumpy drunk.

I didn't want to cut him out of my life, just change the nature of our relationship. And it worked. We're still the best of friends. My cottage is still full of his jeans and cowboy boots; his flat is still full of my furniture and various other bits and pieces.

I've made it sound as though it was easy. It wasn't. I found it unsettling and frightening to be on my own for the first time in my life. I sought out Karen again and saw her once a week. I wasn't convinced I could be alone: the thought that every time I went out for a day, a weekend or a holiday I would go home to no one but my cats, Polo and Molly, was scary. It was fine for today and tomorrow, but the possibility that it might be for the rest of my life was terrifying.

However, I was suddenly free to go on girly expeditions, and soon after Rod and I broke up I went with Pat Booth and Cilla Black to spend a weekend in America with Lynda La Plante, to celebrate the fourth of July. Lynda, who wrote *Prime Suspect* and several other very successful TV series, is a friend of Pat. We flew to New York, hired a car and drove to her fabulous house in East Hampton, where we spent a lot of time lying around the pool, gossiping and telling funny stories. One morning Paul O'Grady, the comedian, turned up and we lost track of time. We were due at Peter Brown's for lunch the day before the big party. Suddenly a limo pulled up, which Lynda had ordered to take us there, so we changed, climbed into the back and set off. We drove through the countryside, still chattering, all dressed up in our dark glasses, frocks, high heels and lip gloss. The journey seemed to be taking for ever, so I asked the driver, 'Are we nearly there?'

'I don't know,' he said. 'I don't know where we're going.'

'What? We don't know where we're going either!'

We all looked at Lynda, who said, 'Well, he's your friend!'

Peter has a little cottage in the sand dunes at East Hampton with a very big deck facing the ocean and every year on the fourth of July he throws a party for about two hundred people to watch the firework display that the village stages on the beach. He had invited us to join him. As usual, I was up for a party but Lynda didn't want to go and Pat was dying to get into her jimjams so she wouldn't budge. It was only when Cilla and I were in the car that she told me Jude Law and Nicole Kidman might be there. They were making

Cold Mountain and Peter had told Cilla not to tell the rest of us in case they didn't turn up. Well, Jude Law! I couldn't wait to get there. And the best bit was going home and telling Lynda and Pat that we'd been lying on the beach next to him.

One of the friends to whom Rod introduced me was a photographic agent, Raj Prem, who saw my work and wanted to take me on. I hadn't known, until his interest prompted me to look through my old boxes, quite how many photographs I had going back to the sixties. There were hundreds that, by some miracle, I had hung on to over the years and through all the moves. It was exciting to find them but also emotional.

There was the most beautiful photograph of George, for instance, lying on a bed in southern India, and it told such a story. We had just done our two months' meditation in Rishikesh and come south because George hadn't wanted to go straight back to England and the business the Beatles were starting up. It was almost as if he had known that this would be the last peaceful time in his life for years to come. And it was. Life had changed dramatically for him after that week in southern India – it had changed for both of us. Seeing the photograph took me right back – and so did several others. There were pictures of Mick and Marianne, Ronnie and Krissie, my chocolate-point Siamese Joss Stick, lots of the Beatles at Rishikesh, Eric, Jeff Beck . . . and everyone looked so young.

Raj thought the collection was big enough and important enough to mount a solo exhibition. I gave him about eighty photographs and they went on show in America at Theron Kabrich's San Francisco Art Exchange. Shared Memories opened on 14 February 2005. I hadn't been in San Francisco for nearly thirty years. I was there with Eric when he performed with Dylan and The Band, plus others, for *The Last Waltz* music movie, released in 1978, and before that George and I had had our scary experience with the hippies at Haight-Ashbury.

It was exciting to walk into a gallery and know every photograph.

It blew me away. But it was also nerve-racking to put myself on the line like that, offering my work for public scrutiny and judgement. I was also nervous about the publicity I had to do – I had never been able to shake off Brian Epstein's injunction about not talking to the press – but I got through it. The gallery sold thirty or forty of my photographs, which I'm told was unprecedented.

It was a fantastic boost to my confidence, both as a photographer and as a person. And subsequent exhibitions – last year's was called Through the Eye of a Muse – at the SFAE again and in London – have reinforced my new-found belief in myself. For years I had been the wife of the famous man: it hadn't been me for whom doors were opened and the red carpet laid down. I was the one who walked two paces behind, while everyone bowed and scraped to George and Eric. No one was interested in talking to me except as a means of getting closer to my husbands. It was an amazingly good feeling to be valued for myself as a professional and to have my work taken so seriously.

Epilogue

In October 2006 Bill Wyman was seventy. He was quite a bit older than most of us, but we're all heading there – even if we're fighting it every inch of the way. He had a huge party at Ronnie Scott's with fabulous music, dancing, champagne and canapés. He had taken over the entire club and it was full of faces from the sixties. All were friends, all looked as fabulous as they had fifty years ago.

Our generation really did lead a revolution: as teenagers we refused to conform and we're still refusing to do what's expected of us, still breaking the mould, still enjoying everything that life has to offer and doing everything it takes to keep age at bay. One day we might have to give in to sensible shoes – but don't hold your breath.

Sadly, several friends didn't make it. Nicole Winwood is no longer alive, and neither is Jim Capaldi, nor Elvis. Alfie O'Leary died of cancer; Julian Ormsby-Gore shot himself; Alice died of an overdose; David Harlech was killed in a car crash; Mal Evans was shot dead by police in America; Ossie Clark was stabbed to death in a frenzied attack by a gay lover; Derek Taylor and Ian Wallace died of cancer. Drink, drugs and depression claimed many others, who died too young: victims, you might say, of the excesses of our time.

I was lucky. I survived. I didn't have the addictive gene or I might have gone down with Eric. We might have drunk ourselves to death. But given my life over again, I wouldn't change anything. I love music. I loved everything that went with rock 'n' roll. I loved being at the heart of such creativity and being young in such a stimulating and exciting era. I have known some amazing people and had some unforgettable experiences.

I regret allowing myself to be seduced by Eric and wish I had been stronger. I believed that marriage is for ever, and when things were going wrong between George and me I should have gritted my teeth and resolved that we could come out smiling in the end. And I wish I'd known I didn't have to be a doormat and allow both husbands to be so flagrantly faithless.

But if I had resisted Eric, I would never have known that incredible passion – and such intensity is rare. I would never have been the inspiration for those beautiful songs. I accept that I paid a high price, but it was in proportion to the depth of the love he and I shared. I loved George very deeply, too, but we were younger and it was a softer, gentler love.

And I don't regret leaving Eric. All I regret is that I had to. It was painful beyond belief, but I am certain that if I had stayed, Eric might indeed have drunk himself to death. And I would probably never have discovered who I am.

I now know that I don't fall over if there is no one there to lean on. If the perfect man came along I would snap him up tomorrow but I *can* live alone, and in many ways I am happier with my life today than I have ever been. I have lots of very good friends – both men and women, some new, some who go back to the sixties – whom I speak to on the phone and see regularly. We have lunches and dinners together, go to the cinema and the theatre, to galleries, concerts and parties, and we have weekends away and holidays, and they're all people I love to be with. I speak to Jenny frequently, and to Boo, who now lives in England, Mummy and other members of my family. There are no emotional strings, no expectations, some disappointments. And if I feel like spending the day potting tomato seedlings in the greenhouse or a nostalgic evening in front of the fire, with a cat on my lap, listening to Ravi Shankar, George or Eric, I can do that and feel comfortable about it. Through self-knowledge I have learnt self-acceptance.

Being the muse of two such extraordinarily creative musicians and having beautiful, powerful love songs written about me was enormously flattering but it put the most tremendous pressure on me to be the amazing person they must have thought I was – and secretly I knew I wasn't. I felt I had to be flawless, serene, someone who understood every situation, who made no demands but was there to fulfil every fantasy; and that's someone with not much of a voice. It's not realistic: no one can live up to that kind of perfection. Now I feel I can be myself – but it took me quite a while to discover that and even longer to work out who I was exactly because the 'me' in me had been hidden for so long. For most of my life I'd been what others expected me to be – the eight-year-old who could cope with boarding-school, the protective, all-knowing older sister whom all her siblings looked up to, the sixties icon, the glamorous model.

Do you have any idea what having your face on the front cover of *Vogue* does for the ego? It seriously undermines it. I knew – as all models know – that I didn't really look like the image on the magazine cover because, like all good models, I knew how to manipulate my body to its best advantage. It's an illusion – the public never see the real person. They see the fantasy, and it's the fantasy they admire and fall in love with: the photograph, the image someone has spent hours getting together. You know that in the flesh you can never live up to it. You play the game and do the things, but when you walk out of that studio you've left the image behind.

Then you have to do the hair and put on the full makeup every day so that people don't see behind the illusion. The more successful you are as a model, the more insecure you may become, preoccupied with your imperfections. When you look at other models all you see is their perfection so you are constantly with people who, you think, are far more attractive than you.

But I have stopped thinking like that and I have stopped worrying. I still have a weakness for shoes and I will always love buying clothes, and if I'm going out I still take a great deal of trouble about how I look, but I have come to realise that what's inside is much more important. Nowadays I'm perfectly happy to go to the local shops in a tracksuit without a trace of makeup and if, as occasionally happens, someone stops me and says, 'Aren't you Pattie Boyd?' I give them a big smile and say, 'Yes! I'm Pattie Boyd!'

Index

Note: 'PB' denotes Pattie Boyd. Subheadings are in chronological order.